W9-AEJ-835

A TEACHING SUBJECT

Composition Since 1966

NEW EDITION

JOSEPH HARRIS

UTAH STATE UNIVERSITY PRESS
Logan, Utah
2012

EDUC

PE
1404
.H364
2012

Utah State University Press
Logan, Utah 84322-7800
www.usupress.org

© 2012 Utah State University Press
All rights reserved
A previous edition of this book was published by Prentice Hall, Inc.

Manufactured in the United States of America
Cover design by Kristin Heal

ISBN: 978-0-87421-866-4 (paper)
ISBN: 978-0-87421-867-1 (e-book)

Library of Congress Cataloging-in-Publication Data

Harris, Joseph (Joseph D.)
  A teaching subject : composition since 1966 / Joseph Harris. — New ed.
    p. cm.
  Includes index.
  Summary: "Reviewing the last 50 years of the development of writing studies as a discipline through
five key ideas, Harris unfolds a set of issues and tensions that continue to shape the teaching of writ-
ing today"— Provided by publisher.
  ISBN 978-0-87421-866-4 (pbk.) — ISBN 978-0-87421-867-1 (e-book)
  1. English language—Composition and exercises—Study and teaching. 2. English language—
Rhetoric—Study and teaching. 3. Report writing—Study and teaching. I. Title.
  PE1404.H364 2012
  808'.042071—dc23
                            2011029926

A TEACHING SUBJECT

EDUCATION LIBRARY
UNIVERSITY OF KENTUCKY

FROM REVIEWS OF THE FIRST EDITION OF *A TEACHING SUBJECT*

Harris offers one of the most interesting of recent approaches to the post-Dartmouth attempt at defining English as a subject. He clearly identifies the teaching of writing as central to defining English. In the pages of this well-written monograph, Harris explores ways in which five key words—growth, voice, process, error, *and* community—*have figured in discussions of the teaching of writing. He is not only adamant on the importance of the study of writing in defining the role of English departments, but equally adamant that the teaching of writing is why we explore writing.*

—Sidney I. Dobrin, *College English*

The contribution of Harris's book lies in how he alerts us to the situatedness and contingency of our practices as writing teachers. His always insightful and gracious discussions of the work in composition since 1966 encourage us to the same intellectual work that he encourages in his students: we are led to reflect on our practices in the teaching of writing not simply to defend them but to imagine how we might change them to better respond to the changing contexts of our own and our students' lives.

—Marilyn Cooper, *CCC*

Harris does not simply marshal a critique—pointing out problems and flaws—and then move onto the next target; he routinely offers substantial suggestions or models. . . . The interchapters offer solutions or possibilities in ways that most academic books do not: a written exchange between a student (Heather), writing about Mike Rose's Lives on the Boundary, *and Harris's colleague and coteacher (Rashmi Bhatnagar) offers a superb example of how teachers might respond to a competent but flat, safe, student essay—the type we see every day—in ways that really push students to think and to see again. This exchange between student and teacher serves well to illustrate "what Harris wants" when he insists that our teaching could be more intellectual and more challenging to students. He wants more wrangling: the goal is not to get outside constraints but to strain against them.*

—Nedra Reynolds, *JAC*

For
PATRICIA,
again, and always

CONTENTS

ACKNOWLEDGMENTS

This book was previously published by Pearson Education, Inc., in 1997, as a volume in the Prentice Hall Series in Writing and Culture. I thank Pearson for assigning me the rights to this work. I am grateful to Kami Day for her careful eye as copy-editor, to Judy Martin for a useful and thorough index, and to Kristin Heal for a cover that elegantly alludes to the first edition. Most important, I thank Michael Spooner, director of Utah State University Press, for his interest in this project and his help in thinking through what form a new edition might take.

❖

I'd also like to restate the thanks I offered to those who helped me with the first edition of this book. Here is what I wrote in 1997:

I'd like to thank my editor, Nancy Sommers, for her unflagging support of this project and imperturbable patience with my delays in completing it. She and Patricia Harris read the whole of this study and offered many useful comments toward revision. I am grateful as well for the help of many others who read and talked through various parts of this book with me, especially David Bartholomae, Stephen Carr, Peter Elbow, Tom Fox, Bruce Horner, Min-Zhan Lu, Richard Miller, and Philip Smith. And while this project was conceived and written as a book, I have also had the chance to publish versions of several sections of it as articles. These include "Rethinking the Pedagogy of Problem-Solving," *Journal of Teaching Writing* 7, Fall 1988; "The Idea of Community in the Study of Writing," *CCC* 40, February 1989; "After Dartmouth: Growth and Conflict in English," *College English* 53, October 1991; "Misreading Movies," *Iowa English Bulletin* 39, 1991; "Reading the Right Thing," *Reader* 27, Spring 1992; and "Negotiating the Contact Zone," *Journal of Basic Writing* 14, Spring 1995. I thank the publishers and editors of these journals for allowing me to draw from these pieces here. I wrote this book while teaching in the English department at the University of Pittsburgh; I doubt that I could have written quite the same book anywhere else, and I know I have learned more than I can say from the generous yet critically attentive talk about teaching that goes on there. And always at the center of things there have been Patti, Kate, and Mora—without whom this book would have probably gotten done much sooner, but also without whom there would not have been much reason for doing it at all.

PREFACE
to the New Edition

My aim in writing *A Teaching Subject* was to offer a brief and inexpensive history of our field. I succeeded in making it brief. But over the years, the price of what was, after all, only a slim volume grew higher and higher until the book finally faded out of print. Even still, several colleagues have told me they would like to be able to use *A Teaching Subject* in their work with beginning teachers of writing. I hope this new and more affordable version will make that possible.

In returning to this book, I was struck by how accurately its title—*A Teaching Subject: Composition Since 1966*—describes both its strengths and limits. I have always thought of myself, first and last, as a teacher of writing. And so I wrote *A Teaching Subject* out of a desire to understand how my work with student writers had come to be shaped by a particular set of problems, concepts, and keywords. This is not a book about the emergence of a new field of study, but one that tries to understand why we teach writing in the ways we do. I think that focus on teaching gives the book its coherence and drive. But I am less content with my subtitle: *Composition Since 1966.* For *composition* is a term in an in-house debate in English departments—one side of a seemingly interminable squabble between teachers of writing and professors of literature. In framing my book as being about composition, then, I ended up narrowing my focus to how first-year writing gets taught in English departments.

Or, not exactly. For it's hard not to notice how many of the key figures in this book actually studied or worked outside of English departments: James Britton, Janet Emig, James Moffett, Sondra Perl, Mary Louise Pratt, Mike Rose, Nancy Sommers. None of these people earned a PhD in English. Even the hero of many writing teachers working in English departments, Mina Shaughnessy, spent most of her career as a university administrator—and none of it as a professor of literature. Now it's clear that most first-year writing programs continue to be located in English departments and that much good work in our field is done by scholar-teachers in English. But it takes a kind of willed forgetting to imagine work in writing as simply a subfield of English studies.

But then, at the time I was writing *A Teaching Subject,* I was an assistant professor in an English department. So even though my PhD was in education, I think I must have assumed that since my own teaching was located in English, then so too must be the field of writing. My colleagues did not contradict me. After publishing this book, though, I switched jobs and spent ten years teaching in an independent and multidisciplinary writing program at Duke University. That experience showed me that scholars from a wide range of disciplines can teach academic writing with insight, imagination, and finesse—that teaching writing really can become a university-wide project. I thus now believe that the teaching subject is *writing*. It only becomes *composition* when embroiled in a set of arguments over what sort of intellectual work matters in English departments—lit vs. comp, rhet vs. comp, theory vs. comp, and so on.

I'm willing, when needed, to take my stand (and hits) as a compositionist in those internecine debates. But my main ambitions lie elsewhere. I am less interested in establishing composition as a disciplinary subfield of English than in increasing the role of writing throughout the undergraduate curriculum. In recent years I've worked with faculty from many disciplines who want to use writing more in their teaching. The first thing I usually tell them is that their charge is *not* to teach "composition," but to introduce students to the kinds of writing they themselves do as scholars. This is something they are almost always pleased to hear. Indeed, to the degree that *composition* refers to work that is merely preparatory or formulaic, I don't think it belongs in first-year writing either. We are not teachers of not-literature. We teach writing that is responsive, critical, intellectual, academic. *Writing*. We should claim the term.

And so, if I were to rewrite this book, I'd no longer want to cast it as a history of "a style of doing English" (xvii). What I see now is a series of attempts to use writing to reform undergraduate teaching. Some of this work has gone on in English departments; much of it has not. But, full disclosure: I have *not* rewritten this book. I am proud of what I accomplished in it, and I don't want to replace what I thought in the 1990s with what I happen to think now. For the most part, then, this volume reprints—with a few corrections of some minor errors and infelicities, and some changes in formatting—the original 1997 text of *A Teaching Subject*.

But there are indeed several new elements to this edition. I've added postscripts to each of the five main chapters of the book in which I reflect on several of the directions that work on teaching writing has taken since 1997. I've also written a coda in which I look at how the teaching of writing is quickly changing in the digital age. And there is now an index to the complete volume.

Academic writing still usually gets taught in the first semester or two of undergraduate study. But the ability to write clearly about complex texts and ideas seems to me less a prerequisite for a liberal education than one of its distinctive achievements. And so, in this book, I look at the first-year writing course not as a site where students *prepare* to do academic work, but where they *begin* such work in earnest. It is where we invite them to join us in our ongoing work as intellectuals.

—JH
Durham, North Carolina
January 2012

FOREWORD(S)
Research and Teaching

This book traces how the teaching of college writing has been theorized and imagined since 1966. I do so by looking closely at how five key words—*growth, voice, process, error,* and *community*—have figured in recent talk about writing and teaching. I believe that in tracing their meanings and revisions I can make a case for composition as a *teaching subject,* as that part of English studies which defines itself through an interest in the work students and teachers do together.

I begin with the 1966 Dartmouth Seminar, where the British theorists John Dixon and James Britton invoked the idea of *growth* as part of an attempt to shift work in English away from the analysis of a fixed set of great books and toward a concern with the uses that students make of language. In chapters 2 and 3, I look at how this interest in the language of students was then taken up by writing teachers in the United States who centered their work around notions of personal *voice* and the composing *process*. In chapter 4, I look at how such approaches have tried (most often with little success) to deal with the problem of *error,* with the nearly unyielding demand that student writings adhere to certain strict standards of usage and decorum. And then, in chapter 5, I show how attempts to rethink error as an index of broader tensions and conflicts in the culture have led to more social views of writing calling on ideas of difference and *community*. I then close by considering some of the limits of these new and often highly politicized approaches to teaching writing.

My aim is not to present a seamless history of composition studies in which one set of terms and interests smoothly gives way to the next—but to get at a set of issues and tensions that continue to shape the teaching of writing. I do this as someone drawn to composition as a place where not only writing but teaching gets talked about in serious and critical ways. At a time in my graduate studies when I was frustrated by what seemed the planned irrelevance of much scholarship, and indeed was thinking of leaving academics altogether, coming across work in composition gave me a way of imagining teaching as an integral part of (and not just a kind of report on) my work as an intellectual. I had never looked forward very much to a career as a scholar writing to a small clique of other specialists, so I was pleased to find a field where so many people seemed to try to speak to the concerns of experts and students alike. I was especially struck by how the writings of students were made part of many books and articles on teaching. Not only did I like the democratic and practical feel of such work, it also struck me as making good sense. If you really wanted to argue for the advanced study of English as something more than a kind of guild activity, the business concern of critics and professional writers, then you would need to look at the uses ordinary people make of reading and writing, and to show how and why they might be encouraged to change them. This book traces some recent attempts to do just that, to rethink the sorts of work students and teachers might do together in a college writing course. In keeping with these efforts, I try to ground what I have to say in close readings of the work not only of theorists and teachers but of students as well—particularly in a series of interchapters that look at how the issues raised in this book inform (and are informed by) specific teaching aims, practices, and situations.

What I have not tried to do is write an account of composition studies as an academic discipline, as a field of inquiry with its own subject matter and methods of investigating it. Others have already done this quite well. James Berlin, for instance, offers a history of composition as a kind of modern offshoot of rhetoric in *Writing Instruction in Nineteenth-Century American Colleges* (1984) and *Rhetoric and Reality* (1987), while in *Textual Carnivals* (1991), Susan Miller pays closer attention to the institutional contexts that gave rise to the modern study and teaching of writing. And in books whose titles hint at their differences in emphasis from mine, Louise Wetherbee Phelps builds a careful and elaborate theory for the study of writing in *Composition as a Human Science* (1988), while Stephen North offers an overview of the competing research methods in the field in *The Making of Knowledge in Composition* (1987).

I have looked here instead at composition as a teaching subject—as a loose set of practices, concerns, issues, and problems having to do with how writing gets taught. To put it another way, my interests in this book have less to do with how knowledge gets made and tested than with how teaching practices are formed and argued for. And so when I turn in these pages to the work of researchers like Janet Emig or Linda Flower or Sondra Perl, I am less concerned with how their studies have shaped theories of composing than with how they have influenced the work of writing teachers. I regard composition as a kind of style of doing English, as a set of attempts to change some of the practical ways we represent writing, reading, literacy, and literature to our students and ourselves. Indeed, composition is the only part of English studies I know of that is commonly defined not in relation to a subject *outside* the academy (to literature, for example, or to culture or language) but by its position *within* the curriculum—by its close involvement with the gatekeeping first-year course in writing. And so even while the concerns of many people now working in composition studies have gone well beyond simple questions of what to do with their freshmen next Monday, for me the most interesting work in the field continues to center around the kinds of day-to-day practices that go on in college classrooms and departments in the name of teaching reading and writing. I intend this book, then, as a sympathetic counterstatement to recent work that has stressed composition as a knowledge-making discipline, as an attempt to reassert ties to the classroom that have sometimes seemed to grow less strong as the field becomes more professionalized. (Although not absent: I think, for instance, of Phelps's valuing of "practical wisdom" as the goal of study in composition, and of North's affection for the "teaching lore" that long characterized most work in the field.)

I have struggled with a set of ironies or tensions in making this argument. For although I want to argue for a view of composition that centers on the first-year writing course, I also realize this is a book most likely to be read by graduate students and their teachers. And while I want to speak in the name of teaching, this is not a book on how to teach better. I have mixed feelings about moves to make composition into a new scholarly subfield, but I am also deeply implicated in such efforts. All my work as a scholar has been in composition studies. The writing of this book helped gain me tenure at a research university. I edit an academic journal on teaching composition. I know that reading work in composition studies has helped me rethink what I do as a teacher in powerful ways, and I strongly support the professionalizing of the field. But I do not want that professionalization to come at the cost of the close ties to teaching that are what give so much work in the field its political and intellectual edge.

There has long been a dissenting tradition in English that has argued for looking closely at the uses students and ordinary people make of language. Its roots go back at least to the early 1900s and the likes of George

Brown, Fred Newton Scott, and Gertrude Buck. Its themes and ideas run through the work of teachers like Louise Rosenblatt and Theodore Baird in the middle of the twentieth century, and appear once more during the 1960s in the talk at Dartmouth. I think they can be seen now in the work of many in composition. In this book I hope to add my voice to theirs.

1
GROWTH

In the late summer of 1966, some fifty American and British teachers met at the three-week Seminar on the Teaching and Learning of English at Dartmouth College (the Dartmouth Seminar). The seminar was organized by the Modern Language Association (MLA), the National Council of Teachers of English (NCTE), and the British National Association of Teachers of English (NATE), and funded by the Carnegie Corporation; its aim was to define English as a school subject and to outline the ways it might be best taught. The participants at Dartmouth proved in fact unable to agree on much in either theory or practice, but this lack of consensus did not limit their impact on the work of many teachers then and since—for whom Dartmouth has symbolized a kind of Copernican shift from a view of English as something you *learn about* to a sense of it as something you *do*. After Dartmouth, that is, you could think of English as not simply a patchwork of literary texts, figures, and periods (*The Fairie Queen,* Swinburne, the eighteenth century) but as the study of how language in all its forms is put into use—from gossip to tragedies to advertising to the talk and writings of schoolchildren. An old model of teaching centered on the transmission of skills (composition) and knowledge (literature) gave way to a *growth model* focusing on the experiences of students and how these are shaped by their uses of language.

Or that at least is the heroic view of Dartmouth—one that can be traced in large part to John Dixon's eloquent, influential, and highly skewed report on the seminar, *Growth through English,* published in 1967 and reprinted twice afterward. Dixon was himself a leading British growth theorist, and his report offered less an account of what was argued at Dartmouth than a brief for a particular view of teaching. His aim was to draw from the seminar "such ideas as are directly relevant to my own work in class" (xi), and so he made little attempt to account for the subject-centered views held by many Americans at the seminar, except to suggest that they were perhaps a necessary step toward his own position. The result was an articulate and contentious book, but one that tended to report Dixon's own views as the findings of the seminar—and thus in its pages Dartmouth began to seem less a debate than the starting point of a new consensus about the aims and methods of English teaching.[1]

A number of other international conferences on English teaching followed Dartmouth—at York in 1970, Sydney in 1980, Ottawa in 1986, Auckland in 1990, and New York in 1995—but none have yet had its impact. Several of the leading speakers at these conferences had been among the participants at Dartmouth, and so many of the themes and ideas of these meetings often seemed reworkings of those first articulated there. The 1987 English Coalition Conference at Wye billed itself as a kind of all-American successor to Dartmouth, and its report shows that most thinking about teaching has changed little since 1966. As Wayne Booth, a participant at both Dartmouth and Wye, remarks in an otherwise enthusiastic foreword to the Coalition Report: "There was nothing radically new in this enterprise" (1989, x).

But although they continue to shape the kinds of talk about teaching that go on at conferences and in journals, the Dartmouth ideas have probably had less impact than might be hoped on what actually goes on in many classrooms. Rather, the day-to-day work of most teachers, in both America and Britain, from preschool to the university, seems only too often to have continued on after Dartmouth much as it had before—marching lockstep to the demands of fixed school curricula standardized tests, and calls for improved skills and increased cultural unity.[2] And, in any case, most of the actual recommendations of the Dartmouth Seminar were remarkably vague—statements it is hard to imagine anyone disagreeing with and thus equally hard to imagine anyone acting on: "The wisdom of providing young people at all ages with

---

1. The seminar also commissioned an American, Herbert Muller, to report on its proceedings. In an effort to do justice to the various competing views articulated at Dartmouth, Muller produced a fair-minded but forgettable report called *The Uses of English* (1967).

2. Arthur Applebee documents the present situation in America in his 1984 *Contexts for Learning to Write*; Sharon Hamilton-Wieler offers an overview of current British classroom practices in her 1988 "Empty Echoes of Dartmouth." Both show that the kinds of drill and memory work Britton and his colleagues saw and deplored in the 1960s still characterize most work done in English classrooms today. By and large, students of all ages are asked to do very little writing, and most of what little they do consists of writing to the teacher-as-examiner, with the sole aim of proving that they recall facts drilled in previous lessons (see Britton et al. 1975, particularly 175–98). Still more accounts, if any are needed, of the ongoing emptiness of most school lessons can be found in Powell, Farrar, and Cohen's *The Shopping Mall High School* (1985) and Sedlak et al.'s *Selling Students Short* (1986).

significant opportunities for the creative uses of language. . . . The significance of rich literary experiences in the educative process." And so on.[3]
The few recommendations that were more pointed—like those against
tracking and standardized testing—have been for the most part ignored.

Even still, most comments about Dartmouth have been nostalgic.
Despite its lack of practical effect on teaching, Dartmouth has often been
invoked as showing what, in a better time and world, work in English
could be. An antinomian streak colors this talk, as institutional politics
and academic vanity are cast as the real blocks to reform in teaching. By
1974, for instance, James Squire and James Britton were to remark that
"the impact of the Dartmouth ideas—perhaps the Dartmouth ideal" was
to be found not in programs but "in the enterprise of individuals, in the
new insights of young teachers" (x). Similarly, in his 1974 *Tradition and
Reform in the Teaching of English*, Arthur Applebee described the growth
model as the "better alternative" among current approaches to teaching, yet admitted that most American teachers stuck to traditional, subject-centered views of their work (228–32). A few years later, in 1979,
Robert Parker argued that the reforms suggested at Dartmouth never
stood a chance of competing against the federally funded programs of
the 1960s Project English. Writing in the same issue of *English Journal*,
Ken Kantor suggested more simply that the ideas of Dartmouth were
too "romantic" and "revolutionary" to be widely accepted. And in 1988,
Sharon Hamilton-Wieler worried that we seem left now with only "empty
echoes of Dartmouth" as students and teachers once again bow to the
pressures of uniform tests and curricula.

There is truth in all these comments, and I don't mean in any way
to defend the dreariness of much schooling from its critics. But I do
think that such views make the lessons of Dartmouth seem a little too
simple. Many seminar participants were unconvinced by the arguments
for the growth model, fearing that a kind of loose talk about feelings
and responses would displace the serious study of language and literature—a view argued by Wayne O'Neil in his acerbic 1969 conference
report in the *Harvard Educational Review*, in which he concluded that
the seminar "misconceived what it is that needs doing and along the
way wasted a good deal of public (Carnegie) money" (365). And since
then the growth model has drawn critics from both the left and right.
For instance, by as early as 1971, Ann Berthoff was to accuse the growth

---

3. See Shugrue (1968, 73–74) for a full list.

theorists of neglecting the social uses of language in favor of an almost total (and in the end trivializing) interest in personal expression. Many others have followed Berthoff in making this charge—most recently James Berlin in 1982 and Peter Griffith in 1988.Whereas in 1980, working from a very different set of concerns, David Allen anticipated more recent conservative attacks on schooling when he argued that the emphasis on personal growth at Dartmouth had led to a devaluing of the claims of the larger culture.

This ongoing debate echoes tensions present at Dartmouth itself. For what one finds in the papers and books that came out of the seminar is not a unified sense of what English is and how it should be taught but a series of conflicts and tensions much like those that divide us now.[4] So rather than reading Dartmouth as the scene of a heroic shift in the theory and practice of teaching, I want to look at it as a moment when many of the conflicts that drive work in English—and particularly those having to do with the relations between teaching and research—were dramatized with unusual clarity.

The plan of the seminar was to begin by bringing all the participants together to address the question, "What is English?" Once having defined their subject, they were then to split into separate study groups and working parties that would take on particular issues in teaching—questions of tracking, testing, curriculum, and the like. The hope seems to have been to give some clear shape to what many thought an almost formless subject of instruction. This did not occur. In the first paper given at the seminar, Albert Kitzhaber invoked the familiar triad of language, literature, and composition in order to define the subject matter of English. The problem, as Kitzhaber saw it, was how to join these three concerns. His aim was to form a view of English as "an organized body of knowledge with an integrity of its own" (1966, 12). What was needed, he argued, was a definition that did not "[turn] out to be but the lengthened shadow of a specialist's personal interest," but that instead collected the various facets of English into a single coherent subject of study (16).

---

4. *The Working Papers of the Anglo-American Seminar on the Teaching of English at Dartmouth College (Dartmouth Seminar)* are archived online at http://www.eric.ed.gov/, ED 082200 to 082216. Many of these papers were collected and published by NCTE in *Drama in the English Classroom* (ed. Douglas Barnes 1968), *Sequence in Continuity* (ed. Arthur Eastman 1968), *Language and Language Learning* (ed. Albert Marckwardt 1968), *The Uses of Myth* (ed. Paul Olson 1968), *Response to Literature* (ed. James Squire 1968), and *Creativity in English* (ed. Geoffrey Summerfield 1968).

Speaking in response to Kitzhaber, James Britton next argued that one cannot define English by determining its proper subject matter. Rather, you must first ask what the function of English is in the curriculum and in the lives of students. For Britton the key question was not "What is the subject matter of English?"—but rather "What do we want students and teachers to be doing?" His answer was to define English as that space in the curriculum where students are encouraged to use language in more complex and expressive ways. They were to learn to do so through reading, writing, and talking about issues related to their own personal experiences, making the English lesson

> the area in which . . . all knowledge must come together for the individual. It is, in fact, the integrating area for all public knowledge. My mother used to make jam tarts and she used to roll out the pastry and I remember this very well—I can still feel what it is like to do it, although I have never done it since. She used to roll out the pastry and then she took a glass and cut out a jam tart, then cut out another jam tart. Well we have cut out geography, and we have cut out history, and we have cut out science. What do we cut out for English? I suggest that we don't. I suggest that is what is left. That is the rest of it. (1966, 12)

This opening exchange between Kitzhaber and Britton set up a conflict between what came to be known as the American and British positions at Dartmouth, although in fact there were strong differences of view among the participants from each country. Kitzhaber and the Americans were concerned with defining English as an *academic discipline*, a body of knowledge. Such an approach, as Britton noted, suggests that the real focus of work in English is something "out there," some kind of information to be gained or set of skills to be mastered (1966, 5–6). But if the American hero was the scholar, then the British hero was the teacher.

The conflict between the American and British positions was shown clearly in the ways they chose to describe their work. The actual jobs held by most of the participants at Dartmouth seem to have had very much in common. Most worked in university departments of English or education and were in some way involved with planning school curricula or training teachers. Yet by and large the Americans identified themselves as *scholars* and the British as classroom *teachers*. John Dixon was to state this opposition quite bluntly in his 1969 "Conference Report," arguing that while there "will be a tendency for the university professor to dominate the work of the schools . . . where there is any strength in the school tradition of English teaching, that tendency can be overcome" (367).

The two positions can be seen as differing responses to what Jurgen Habermas (1975) has called a legitimation crisis. Habermas argues that a profession needs to justify its work to both an audience of experts and to the public at large. Since these groups have differing needs and interests, the work of professionals will often seem to be pulled in two directions at once. And so, on the one hand, there is a continuing need to legitimize English as an academic field with its own specialized subject and methods of study. On the other hand, English has long been valued precisely because it seems more than just another specialized area of study, because it offers a place where different kinds of knowledge can be brought together and related to personal experience. Britton's jam tart metaphor puts the problem well. The importance of English lies in its ability to connect separate kinds of learning and experience, but in doing this it can seem stretched thin, with little substance of its own. One can view the American position at Dartmouth, then, as an attempt to justify the study of English to other university experts, and the British position as trying to place such work in relation to the needs and concerns of students. I have already suggested another way of defining this tension in terms of the troubled relations between research and teaching. My point here is that this conflict cannot be resolved simply through admonitions to do both well or to have one inform the other, since scholars and teachers address competing needs and audiences.

For the Americans at Dartmouth, the task at hand thus seemed one of defining and consolidating the subject matter of English. As a former president of NCTE and chair of the Conference on College Composition and Communication (CCCC), Kitzhaber had long argued for the need to ground classroom practices in formal research on writing and learning, and his 1963 *Themes, Theories, and Therapy* was a groundbreaking study of composition teaching in American colleges. In his opening talk at Dartmouth, Kitzhaber derided what he called "progressive" attempts to turn the English classroom into a "catch-all" space for discussing whatever happened to be on the minds of teachers or students. Citing Northrop Frye in *Design for Learning*, he argued against confusing "educational and social functions," and insisted that our "subject matter must be defined more clearly than it has in the past" so we can then "[bring] forward a 'New English' to take its place alongside the 'New Mathematics' and the 'New Science' now being taught in many United States schools" (1963, 12–13).

This appeal to the Sputnik-motivated New Math and New Science is revealing. Many of the Americans at Dartmouth were involved with the attempts of the federally funded Project English to design a sequenced or "spiral" curriculum for the study of language and literature from kindergarten to college. Project English had been inspired by the success of the National Defense Education Act programs in science and math, and the case for its funding made by a 1961 NCTE report ominously called *The National Interest and the Teaching of English*, which had argued for more "focused" and "articulated" teaching in the place of the current "hodgepodge" of activities that were said to make up many English lessons. The theory of education driving the work of Project English had been powerfully stated at the 1959 Woods Hole Conference—whose principal aim, as its chair Jerome Bruner reported in *The Process of Education*, had been "to examine the fundamental processes involved in imparting to young students the substance and method of science" (1960, vi). This stress on process was salutary. Students were to learn science not merely by reading about it but by doing it, and in this Bruner held much in common with the growth theorists at Dartmouth. But his thinking also led to a two-step theory of education, in which one first defined "the substance and method" of a subject before looking for the "processes involved in imparting" it. As Bruner put it, the problem of teaching could thus be seen as "one of representing the structure of [a] subject in terms of the child's way of viewing things. The task can be thought of as one of translation" (33). The scholar discovers the structure of his subject; the teacher transmits some version of that structure to students.

Another effect of Woods Hole was to make the aims of teaching less general and more disciplinary. Bruner had argued that "the foundations of any subject may be taught to anybody in some form," and so the point of teaching at even the earliest grades came to be seen as introducing students to the rudiments of subjects that some (but not all) would later go on to study at more advanced levels (1960, 33). The curriculum, that is, was thought of less as a plan of study for the whole child and more as a loose amalgam of separate skills and disciplines.[5] It

---

5. In the years after Dartmouth, Bruner himself moved away from this emphasis on the "structure of knowledge" and toward a concern, much like that of the growth theorists, with the *uses* students were able to make of what they learned in school. He talks about the reasons behind this change of heart in his 1971 "*Process of Education* Revisited."

followed that the content of most teaching should then be determined by subject specialists, usually university scholars. The work of Project English was planned in this top-down fashion, as was the Dartmouth Seminar, with its opening attempt to define English as a subject before considering issues in its teaching. In setting up the first two legs of their tripod subject, Project English scholars had turned to Chomskian linguistics and the archetypal criticism of Northrop Frye. A number of conflicting attempts were also made to establish a similar base for the teaching of writing, as a revived interest in classical rhetoric competed with approaches drawing on behavioral psychology and the new "generative" rhetorics of Francis Christensen.[6]

Linked to these attempts to define the "substance and method" of the field was the call of the 1958 Basic Issues Conference to reconceptualize English as a "fundamental liberal discipline"—which it then went on to define as "a core of experience, a body of knowledge, and a set of specific skills to be attained" by students (Basic 1959, 13). Funded by the Ford Foundation, this conference was made up almost entirely of scholars and teachers from elite colleges and prep schools. Their report sketched an Arnoldian view of English as the study of "the best thought and expression of their own time and the cultural heritage which is rightfully theirs," and fretted repeatedly that the "civilizing value" of literature was being "watered down" by misguided attempts to make its study relevant to students raised on mass media and preoccupied with their future careers (3–4). Progressive theories of education had softened and corrupted teaching, the report went on to argue, turning many English classes into *"ad hoc* training in how to write a letter, how to give a radio speech, manners, dating, telephoning, vocational guidance" (4). There was to be no more of that. "We must distinguish between the passing and the permanent," intoned still another report, this one sponsored by the College Entrance Examination Board (CEEB) in 1965 and gravely titled *Freedom and Discipline in English* (3). The CEEB went on to argue, following cliché with threat, "that the scope of the English program be defined as the study of language, literature, and composition . . . and that matters not clearly related to such study be excluded from it" (13).[7]

---

6. Robert Parker offers a useful history of these trends in his 1979 "From Sputnik to Dartmouth."

7. Arthur Applebee gives a much fuller account of teaching practices in America before Dartmouth in his chapter on "An Academic Model for English" in *Tradition and Reform* (1974).

Project English, the Basic Issues, *The National Interest, Freedom and Discipline*: together they voiced a remarkable consensus over the "civilizing value" of literature and the need to formalize its study. So many of the Americans who came to Dartmouth believed that the answer to "What is English?" could be found much the same way you might go about responding to a question like "What is organic chemistry?" First one defines a subject and then identifies a set of principles for use in its study. Wayne O'Neil was again to sum up this view of English in his report on Dartmouth, arguing that "schools in their talk ought to be organized around . . . areas of knowledge" and that the "data" of literary studies were too ill defined to support a coherent plan of teaching (1969, 365–66). For O'Neil and many other Americans, the best model for the study of English was a discipline like linguistics, with its clearly defined subject matter and methods of inquiry.

This subject-based curriculum came under sharp attack at Dartmouth. Many of the British seminar participants had studied at Cambridge with F. R. Leavis—whose hand could be felt in their insistence on the value of lived experience and on the importance of language in bringing order to that experience. Still others, particularly James Britton and his colleagues at the University of London, had been influenced by movements in the teaching of drawing and painting that saw each child "as an artist in his or her characteristic and un-adult fashion" (1989, 59). Both groups had fashioned an approach to teaching that took the work of students as seriously as that of poets or novelists. Denys Thompson (1966) for instance, argued against creating a "pseudo-content" for English when its real subject could be found in the learner. Frank Whitehead warned against letting "teaching about literary forms and techniques" stand in the place of helping students come to their own terms with the books they read (quoted in Squire 1968, 62). And John Dixon rejected "overarching theory" in favor of starting "from detailed experience in the classroom" (1969, 369). All in some way echoed Leavis's concern, voiced in his 1943 "Sketch for an English School," that literature not be reduced to yet another three-hour examination subject but that its study instead serve as the starting point of an ongoing criticism of life and culture.

One of the most striking features of this position was a renewed interest in personal and expressive forms of talk and writing. The growth theorists argued for an acceptance of the individual's own language or dialect, with a resulting de-emphasis on teaching correct or standard forms. The content or focus of most English lessons was not to be the forms of language but lived experience, as shown either in literature or in the writings of students. Language was not so much to be studied as used. Growth in skill was expected to occur in an incidental fashion, not through direct training in stylistic or grammatical exercises (mocked by Britton and Dixon as "dummy runs") but as a natural outcome of meaningful practice in writing and reading. The English lesson was to be less about literature than in it. Students were encouraged to do in their own way what poets did—"bring a new, simplifying order to the complexity of life" (Dixon 1967, 27–28).

This joining of the work of student and artist was rooted in a theory of literature as "language in the spectator role" proposed at Dartmouth by James Britton. Central to this view was a distinction between the roles of the *participant* and the *spectator* in our uses of language. The difference between the two, Britton argued, is like that between work and play, between using language for some practical effect and simply enjoying it for the pleasure it brings. As spectators, then, we use words to gossip, trade stories, tell jokes, share rhymes, and, in its most developed forms, write poetry or fiction. In the years after Dartmouth, Britton rephrased and elaborated on this idea of the spectator role in several books—most especially *Language and Learning* in 1970 and (with Tony Burgess, Nancy Martin, Alex McLeod, and Harold Rosen) *The Development of Writing Abilities* in 1975—that were to have a strong impact on the teaching of writing. In these Britton linked the distinction between the roles of participant and spectator to a more familiar contrast between *transactional* uses of language to move the work of the world along and those more playful or *poetic* uses of words that characterize both gossip and literature. That is, participants use words to get things done; spectators swap stories and poems. While this linking of the spectator *stance* and artistic *work*, role and genre, is in many ways a troubled notion, it offered Britton a way of connecting our informal and everyday uses of language with the more highly structured and celebrated work of poets and fiction writers.

Britton and his colleagues also defined a third *expressive* function of language that consists of those informal utterances "that stay close to the speaker," which have yet to be molded to the demands of a task or audience (1975, 82). This expressive function, Britton argues, underlies all our mature uses of language. According to this theory, then, most learning should have its beginnings in some sort of expressive talk and writing—in language in which ideas and feelings are still being sorted out rather than being phrased as facts or conclusions. Yet in the 1970s, when Britton's research showed that almost no expressive talk or writing went on in the schools, this state of affairs was seen not as an argument against the validity of his categories but as evidence of the need for a new kind of teaching practice (138–73). In speaking of the value of intimate and expressive uses of words, Britton appealed to some of the deepest beliefs about language held by many teachers, who were thus inclined to act on his ideas *despite* the evidence of his schools' survey. Britton influenced their work not because he offered an unbiased view of how children learn to use language but because he was able to make a convincing case for the value of a certain kind of learning. His theory described not what was but what ought to be; it was justified through the teaching practice it gave rise to. And so, even while he failed to offer the map of language learning he promised, Britton still succeeded in changing how many teachers worked in their classrooms.

I think such gains were the point of doing theory for Britton and his colleagues. Whereas the scholars of Project English had looked to theory for a kind of conceptual grid, a comprehensive view of their subject, the growth theorists took a more rhetorical or performative view of it as a means to an end, a form of reflection-on-action whose aim was to change teaching in direct and immediate ways. As James Moffett was to say of his own theory of discourse, "[It] is meant to be utilized, not believed. I am after a strategic gain in concept" (1968a, 15).

The best way to sense the power of this view of English is to go to an example. Let me turn, then, to a passage from John Dixon's 1967 report on Dartmouth, *Growth through English*. Early in his book Dixon argues that in learning to write, children take on and identify with any number of roles or personae—using as an example a poem written by a six-year-old girl just after she had witnessed the death of a kitten. Dixon notes how the writing of the poem (a powerful one) both allows the girl to identify with the pain of the kitten and to separate herself from its tragedy. He then goes on to comment:

We come here to the border country between scholarship and the intuitive understandings of observant and sympathetic teachers. Ideally the one kind of evidence should feed the other. . . . We might recall Joan in David Holbrook's *English for the Rejected*: timid, plain, with thick pebble glasses. Her I.Q. was 76; there was nothing surprising in her primary school record—"has no originality or imagination." Yet after a year's encouragement to creative work in language and drama, she wrote this (in the course of an exam):

A poem
A little yellow bird sat on my window sill
He hop and poped about
He whiseled he cherped.
I tried to chach my little yellow bird
but he flew into the golden yellow sun,
Oh how I wish that was my yellow bird.

> Work such as this has given us a new right to talk about the creative poten-
> tialities of all children. Consider not only the beauty but the complexity of
> Joan's achievement. The bird is alive, quick and jaunty; we feel her longing
> too. But despite its immediacy the poem surely suggests another level for the
> yellow bird and the golden yellow sun—a level not to be spelt out, but just
> as certainly to be felt. For language, like drama, has the capacity to bring
> elements from experience into a structure that stands for life not merely in
> particular but in general. . . . This might be called the poetic work of lan-
> guage. (27–28)

Dixon moves from this to cite T. S. Eliot ("approach to the meaning restores the experience/in different form") and then to argue for
Britton's theory of the spectator. I quote him at some length here to suggest the extraordinary range and flexibility of this approach to English,
as he quickly and characteristically draws together ideas from criticism,
psychology, and poetry and then links these to a close reading of the
writings of schoolchildren in order to form a working theory of language in use. The strength of Dixon's work springs from the way he suggests how the same sort of attention one might give to the poetry of Eliot
can also be brought to the reading of, say, a fourth grader's journal in
science lab—since poem and journal alike are uses of language to give
shape to experience. In doing so he offers a view of doing English that,
at its best, brings together the work of artist, critic, teacher, and student.

Much as many of the Americans at Dartmouth were reacting against a
vision of their past (which saw the teaching of English as having degener-
ated into a contentless pandering to the wants of the "whole child"), so
too the growth model had been proposed in response to a view of how
English had once been taught in Britain. At the start of *Growth through
English*, Dixon argues that past teaching in his country had either
emphasized rote training in the functional skills of reading and writing

or centered on building a sense of national unity through appeals to the greatness of English literature. Both approaches tended to represent English in terms of a certain content—either skills or literature—to be transmitted. Language learning was thus presented to a schoolchild as a passive acquiring of information largely unrelated to the other parts of her life and study. The aim of the growth model, in contrast, was to build on the child's previous mastery of language, to develop her ability to shape experience into words, to connect disparate events and ideas. What was needed to make work in English more pointed and coherent, then, was not a more complete understanding of the structure of literature or linguistics but a better grasp of how students learn to make full and expressive use of language.

Not all of the British at Dartmouth wholly agreed with this, as became clear in the years after the seminar when a number of scholars associated with Cambridge attacked what they saw as the devaluing of literature by the London growth theorists. Their argument was, in effect, that there was more to the "cultural heritage" model of teaching than Dixon and Britton were willing to allow.[8] Part of what was at stake can be seen in how the meanings of *growth* differ from those of *maturity*—the term valorized by Leavis and applied to teaching by Frank Whitehead and David Holbrook. To be mature is to have adapted to the demands of society; the term suggests compromise in ways *growth* does not. In arguing for the personal growth of the student against the acculturative goals of most schooling, Dixon, Britton, and their colleagues implied that the two were often in conflict. Where Leavis had made a higher order of experience ("fine living") the aim of study in English, they centered their work in talk about the ordinary experiences of schoolchildren. Linked to this was of course a valuing of precisely those "social functions" that Kitzhaber and Frye had wanted to bracket away from the formal study of English. An irony of Dartmouth was thus that the British were reacting against almost precisely the view of English that the Americans were trying to achieve. In turn, many of the Americans at the seminar balked at the ideas of growth theory because they seemed so much like the very kind of progressive schooling they had built their own sense of English against.

---

8. See, for instance, Frank Whitehead's "Continuity in English" (1975) and "Stunting the Growth" (1976), Glyn Lewis's "Postscript to Dartmouth" (1968), and David Holbrook's critique of Britton in *English for Meaning* (1979). All three were members of the British delegation at Dartmouth. David Allen restates their arguments against a focus on language and for the centrality of literature in the first two chapters of his 1980 *English Teaching Since 1965*.

And so from the start Dartmouth pitted two conflicting views of English against each other. In its talk about the teaching of literature, for instance, there was, in the diplomatic words of a seminar working-party report, "disagreement . . . over how much knowledge [the student] should have about literary forms" (Squire 1968, 61). Benjamin DeMott put the issue more bluntly when he complained of how hard it was to shake most of his American colleagues "out of the vacuum of taste and genre talk" (1968, 38). In general, it might be said that the Americans argued for the teaching of *literature* whereas the British wanted to focus instead on the *responses* of students to their reading. Similarly, although almost all the participants argued against making a fetish of good grammar, many Americans believed that the forms of Standard Written English could and ought to be taught explicitly; the British felt that such issues were of marginal concern and should not be the focus of teaching at any level. "Leave their language alone!" was said to be a frequent cry of the British at Dartmouth, and David Mackay summed up their stance when he quipped that "to prescribe is no answer at all when what one is finally required to do is produce" (1968, 30). On the other hand, Albert Marckwardt spoke for many Americans when he argued that, given a choice between taking a "stand against" incorrect usage, "ignoring" it, or "treating" it, his "preference would be for the latter" (1968b, 19).

And yet one of the most influential advocates of the growth model turned out to be an American, James Moffett, whose 1968 *Teaching the Universe of Discourse* powerfully shaped the teaching of writing for years to come. Moffett came to Dartmouth while in the middle of a two-year research sabbatical at the Harvard School of Education, during which he finished writing both *Teaching* and a textbook, *A Student-Centered Language Arts Curriculum, Grades K–13* (1968b). He has said he was unaware of the work of the British growth theorists until Dartmouth, and that even though, like Britton, he often invoked the work of social scientists like Piaget and Vygotsky, he had "always worked much more intuitively," and had only really cited such figures "to gain credibility with a society that believes only authorities in white lab jackets" (1981, 62). Piaget gave sanction to an idea that Moffett had already come to through his reading of literature—that one could map the uses of language on an I-you-it spectrum in which "you keep increasing the distance between the speaker and his listener, and the speaker and his subject" (Moffett and McElheny 1966, xii). In the study of literature, this means beginning with interior monologues, then moving on to works using first person and dramatized narrators, before ending by looking at more detached third-person accounts of events. (Moffett works out such a teaching scheme in *Points of View*, an anthology of short stories that he and Kenneth McElheny published before Dartmouth in 1966.) In the teaching of writing, it means starting with jotting down inner speech and dialogue ("what is happening"), moving to memoir and biography ("what happened"), and concluding with speculative or argumentative pieces ("what may happen"). This is the structure Moffett lays out in *Teaching the Universe of Discourse*. Like a modern Ramus, he devises a system that can order and chart all the possible uses of language on a single page (1968a, 47).

Moffett had already been working with such ideas some ten years before while writing a prize-winning senior thesis at Harvard entitled "The Relation of Inner and Outer Lives in the Works of Virginia Woolf" (1981, 133). Underlying what might seem the social-science ed-school sort of discourse of his early work, then, were strong literary tastes and inclinations. Like Britton, Moffett was convinced that our uses of language (and thus our thinking) grow from an inner expressive base. *Teaching the Universe of Discourse* offers an eloquent and weirdly erudite (Moffett is capable, for instance, of linking the work of Piaget and Basil Bernstein) elaboration of that hunch. If Britton and his colleagues had provided a powerful argument for teaching expressive language, then Moffett sketched a compelling way of doing so.

But while several other Americans—James Miller, James Squire, and Benjamin DeMott among them—were also drawn to the thinking of the growth theorists, the political and intellectual conflicts between the two factions proved too sharp for ready compromise at Dartmouth. At least one American, Wayne O'Neil, dismissed the British as "Sensitive People . . . pretty much turned off by coherent and rational discussion, turned on by feelings and Lawrence," and it seems a good guess that others felt the same way (1969, 361). The attitude of the British toward many of the Americans, with their Project English charts and exercises and diagrams, is suggested in an anecdote told by James Miller:

> One of the dramatic moments of the conference came during a heated exchange on the teaching of linguistic grammar, which the Americans haltingly and hesitatingly defended while the British clucked and deplored. One of the more arrogantly aggressive of the Englishmen rose in all of his aristocratic bearing, walked over to a table and plucked off a page of junior high Project English materials that was covered with strange hieroglyphics, the cabalistic

formulae of Chomsky's transformational or generative grammar. Holding this unreadable and baffling page aloft, the Englishman said in the meticulous accents of his controlled rage (I quote in approximation only, from a fading memory): "I would not carry this material into any classroom at any level of the curriculum. It represents an affront to the mind and an insult to the imagination; it is beneath contempt and beyond discussion." There followed a stunned silence; present among us Americans were the makers, supporters, or approvers of those materials. But there were none among us willing or able to explain those occult and arcane equations, or to demonstrate how seventh or eighth graders might be lured into curiosity about them, or to show how they benefited once they had mastered the esoterics of their formulation. Silence begat silence, and a shift of focus; and the raw and painful moment was gradually soothed over by the steady flow of talk. (1971, 105)

There is more to this moment, I think, than a simple conflict of styles and personalities (although there is surely that too). I see it as a point where two opposing ideas of English—one centered on a loyalty to a certain kind of knowledge, the other rooted in a certain view of the classroom—met head on and found that they seemed to be talking about different subjects. The Americans tried to define the subject matter of English apart from the ways it is taught; the British saw the work of teachers and students as an intrinsic part of what that subject was. The first view saw English in terms of the thing to be studied—literature, criticism, theory, rhetoric, and so on. The second looked at English much more loosely as a set of teaching moves, practices, and concerns. Unfortunately, the result of their confrontation seems to have been not negotiation but withdrawal into separate camps, and since Dartmouth their conflict has been less resolved than continually displaced.

In *Professing Literature* (1987), Gerald Graff traces much of the growth of English as a field to its tendency to absorb rather than confront dissenting views and methods. A result is that many departments end up as odd confederacies of new critics, deconstructionists, compositionists, new historicists, feminists, film theorists, and the like—with none of these specialists having much reason or occasion to speak with any of the others. My sense is that the dissenting view of English articulated at Dartmouth has been co-opted in a similar way. Many of the concerns and methods of the growth model have by now been accepted as parts of an almost official pedagogy. Talk about the writing process, uses of freewriting and drafting, work in small groups, and the like, are now a common part of undergraduate study in English—or at least in

This more social view of the self informs the writings of Basil Bernstein and Lev Vygotsky, both of whom are cited by Britton and Moffett. But such insights tend to get lost when what one most values are highly personal and expressive uses of language—or when one is more interested in the *activity* of writing (as a means of learning or self-discovery or even as a kind of therapy) than in the actual texts that students come to write. There is an odd moment in *Teaching the Universe of Discourse* when Moffett urges his readers to view the complex Piagetian scheme of language growth he has been elaborating as "essentially a hallucination," and then goes on to admit that "at every turn of the road" what a student learned "seemed to depend more on his out-of-school language environment and previous school training" than anything else (1968a, 54–55). But having said that, he then continues on with an account of language learning that consistently downplays the social in favor of the psychological. Following this lead, in the twenty years after Dartmouth, the study of writing took a strong individualistic turn in the work both of teachers concerned with helping students find their authentic voices and of researchers interested in documenting the mental processes involved in composing texts. Only in the last few years have social and political issues once again begun to figure strongly in much work in composition.

Yet for all this it must be said that in many ways the aims of the growth theorists were radical ones. The idea of personal growth proved a powerful if flawed tool in contesting the sort of top-down disciplinary view of teaching found in the spiral curricula of Project English, and it also helped democratize the view of culture and learning offered by Leavis and Cambridge. Perhaps most importantly, the growth theorists—Dixon, Britton, Moffett—proved that one can do serious work in English not only by studying literature or criticism but also by looking closely at the talk and writing of students. They offered not only a set of ideas about language and learning but a way of linking the concerns of scholars with those of students and teachers—and thus of reimagining what work in English might be.

POSTSCRIPT, 2012: STUDENTS AS WRITERS

For the most part *growth* is no longer a much-contested or even much-used term in our field. In 2007, John Trimbur published an essay on "The Dartmouth Conference and the Geohistory of the Native Speaker" in which he (correctly) faults most accounts of Dartmouth, including mine here, for glossing over its boosterish support of an emerging global industry of English teaching and its unexamined celebration of the "native speaker" as the consumer of that teaching. Trimbur argues that we now need a pedagogy that can inform our work with students who often speak many languages and have roots in several cultures. In pointing to the shift from a national to global context for teaching writing, he offers one reason Dartmouth has begun to fade from our view.

But he also notes another reason—the extraordinary success of the conference in shifting the attention of many teachers from reading to writing, and particularly to the writing of students. To work in composition—as opposed to literature, or perhaps even rhetoric—is now almost by definition to be involved with the study of student writers and texts. In our field, at least, the argument that raged between literature and writing at Dartmouth has been over for some time, and the position held by Britton, Dixon, and Moffett has prevailed. This book, with its frequent use of student texts, is itself one example of their influence.

But that argument has been followed by a debate over *how* teachers and scholars should cite student texts. This debate has had several aspects. *Legal*: How do we secure permission from students to reproduce their writing? *Ethical*: How do we make sure students grant that permission freely? *Procedural*: How should student writers be identified and how should their texts be listed in scholarly works? *Intellectual*: What is the status of student writing in composition scholarship? Is it simply an object of study, something to be described and explained? Or might it be viewed as intellectual work in its own right, calling for citation and response?

My sense is that these questions grow more difficult in the order I've listed them. With the increasing role played by Institutional Review Boards (IRBs) in vetting all sorts of research projects, the legal questions involved in securing permission to use student work have become more cut and dried—if also often much more cumbersome. For instance, in 2008 Andrea Lunsford and Karen Lunsford replicated a 1988 study (conducted by Robert Connors and Andrea Lunsford) analyzing patterns of error in papers written by students in colleges across the nation. Lunsford and Lunsford note that the process of securing permissions to review student papers for the first error study took only three months—even though this study was done in the mid-1980s, before the widespread use of word processing or email. But obtaining a similar set of permissions for the follow-up study in 2008 took over *eighteen* months—because the authors were forced to apply for separate approval to the IRB of almost every one of schools in their study. And note that Lunsford and Lunsford were not asking to draw blood or administer drugs, but simply to look for patterns of errors in anonymous student papers. The upside of IRBs is that they have made us more aware that we need to *ask* students for permission to study their work. The downside is that IRBs may well discourage many scholars from doing so.

In the 1990s several scholars began to press our field to think not only about the legal but ethical issues involved in using student texts in our work. In 1998 Paul Anderson noted that a growing amount of work in composition had become *person-based*, by which he meant research drawing on interviews with and unpublished writings by students and others—including, for instance, the sort of work with student texts that appears throughout this book. Anderson suggested that many composition scholars working in English departments had, in effect, failed to notice that their research methods had begun to diverge from the more exclusively text-based studies of their colleagues. He argued that our field thus needed to develop protocols to inform our own distinctive person-based work with student writers and texts. In response, CCCC established its 2003 "Guidelines for Ethical Conduct in Research in Composition Studies," which urge scholars to comply with IRB standards, to obtain written permission to quote from student texts, and to take special care in asking to use work by students in courses they are teaching.

This last point strikes me as key, since it returns us to the scene of teaching. While some uses of student writing in composition result from planned studies in which researchers have deliberately mapped out the data they will collect and the methods they will use to analyze it, others are more serendipitous. A teacher remembers an essay written by a student the semester before, or stumbles upon a paper written in a class taught by a colleague, and thinks . . . *this connects with the piece I'm trying to write.* While this might strike some as a haphazard form of research, I think such *ad hoc* uses of student writing mark out an important form of work in our field. None of the student texts I quote in the interchapters of this book, for instance, were collected as part of a planned study. They were all, rather, pieces that I remembered, that helped me think about certain issues in teaching, and that I only sought permission to quote long after they had been written and submitted in class.

Taking students seriously as writers defines the intellectual work of composition. And thinking in public about the work students have done in your courses helps you become a more reflective and self-critical teacher. I thus think we need not only to allow but also to encourage teachers to cite and use student writings much as they might draw on critical essays or novels or poems—that is, as part of the repertoire of texts they've read and that have informed their thinking. The question is how to cite student texts without infringing on the privacy or trust of their authors. It might well be hard, for instance, for a student to feel she really can refuse a request from her teacher to have her writing used as part of a talk, article, or book. How do we avoid commandeering their work for our purposes?

Paul Anderson returned to this issue in a 2010 essay he cowrote with Heidi McKee on "Ethics in Teaching with Student Texts." In this piece Anderson and McKee argue that most of the safeguards we should put in place for using student texts in our scholarship also apply to using them in class. Students should be asked before we use their work. They should have some sense of how we plan to talk about their writing. They should know where their work is likely to be read and discussed—in class, on a blog, in a journal article, and so forth. And they should always have the choice to opt out, to ask that their writing not be used or discussed.

In 1994, as the editor of *CCC*, I published a set of guidelines for citing student work in the journal. To my knowledge this remains the only time such an editorial policy has been articulated in the pages of one of our journals. I told contributors they must secure written permission from any student whose work they wanted to quote in *CCC*. I also suggested they "allow students to read a draft of the article in which their work appears so they can see how their writing will be quoted and what will be said about it" (439). This is a practice I've followed in my own work for the last twenty years. While I suspect that showing them how I plan to use their texts in my writing strikes most students as simply a gesture of politeness, since no one has ever declined my request to quote their work, I feel sure that knowing the authors of the texts I am discussing will read what I have to say has encouraged me to approach their work with care and respect.

So far, so good. But I also went on in the *CCC* guidelines to say that student texts did not need to be included in a Works Cited list, and I suggested that in most cases student authors should be given pseudonyms. My worry was that as scholars of writing we often work with the incunabula of academic discourse—with the notes, drafts, and other work in progress of students who are often inexperienced and unpolished writers. We needed, I thought, to find ways of taking the work of *developing* writers seriously. My *CCC* policy was an attempt to respect the privacy of students while still encouraging scholars to attend to their writing.

Amy Robillard (2006) has criticized the paternalism of that approach and I've come to agree with her. It now seems to me that the best thing to do, if you're not sure how the writer of a text you're quoting may want to be identified, is simply to ask. Rather than trying to settle the question of how to cite student texts with a single fixed policy, then, I think we need to become more open, in the actual writing of our articles and books, about our aims in quoting from unpublished student texts, how we've obtained permission to do so, and why we've chosen (or not) to name their authors.

And so, for instance, what I can say about this book is that every student whose work I quote has read the chapter in which his or her writing appears and has given me permission to use it. If I could do it again, I'd ask each of the student writers if they wanted to be identified by name, but for the reasons I've mentioned, I decided at the time to use pseudonyms. More important, I was intent on responding to student texts in this book because I hoped to show that my views on teaching do not stem simply from my reading of work in the field—that instead my work with student writers has always driven my approach to the work of fellow scholars.

Perhaps I seem to have drifted here into a fretting over editorial minutiae. But I believe that such procedural issues grow out of the concerns of Dartmouth—that they point to an ongoing effort in our field to figure out *how* to take the writing of students seriously. In their incisive historical study of the "The Figure of the Student in Composition Textbooks" (2010), Mariolina Salvatori and Patricia Donahue link the frequent failure to name student writers to the kinds of uses that get made of their work. They show how when textbook authors cite student texts simply to illustrate some lesson in writing—to serve, that is, as examples of either good or ineffective prose—then the writers of those texts are rarely identified. And that, unfortunately, is how student texts have most often been used in our field—*as examples*. We cite students to make our points. Salvatori and Donahue argue that this practice encourages a habit of reading student texts not for any specific insights their authors may have to offer, but rather for how they typify some general principle about writing. The individuality of the student author is erased by the use of her or his writing as a nameless example of some prior claim.

Many writing scholars and teachers have begun to respond to these concerns. A key tenet of what has come to be called the writing studies movement is that we can and should ask students to do real research on writing, and an interesting new journal, *Young Scholars in Writing*, has emerged to showcase such work. Amy Robillard (2006) and Doug Downs, Heidi Estrem, and Susan Thomas (2010) offer enthusiastic overviews of this approach to both teaching and research. I applaud how they see students as colleagues, as writers whose ideas and insights we can learn from. I'm not convinced, though, that we need to ask students to do work in writing studies—that is, to become apprentices in our own field—in order to accord them such respect. What matters is not what students write about but how we approach their work. I am reminded of a story that James Slevin (2006) tells of the comments he received on the first essay he wrote as an undergraduate:

> The paper was a three-page, double-spaced close reading of *Moby Dick*. The teacher's script was legible and gentle, sloping. The comment went like this.
>
>> Here [arrow to a sentence] you make Melville sound like Plato. Here [another arrow to another sentence] he sounds like Aristotle! Which is he? Which are you?
>
> While not exactly Chapman's Homer, this comment was news to me. What had been a straightforward, required paper with no one really in it was suddenly populated by a small crowd: Plato, Aristotle, Melville, [my teacher], Slevin. We were all gathered there in that tiny little 1-inch margin, on erasable paper, my writing inexplicably transformed into an object of cultural attention and gentle interrogation. (11)

What Slevin shows us here is a teacher addressing a student as a fellow intellectual, asking him not for a performance but a perspective, a point of view. That's the sort of conversation we need to learn how to have with student writers.

INTERCHAPTER

In coming to college, students are often pictured as entering a new sort of community whose interests and concerns are for the most part separate from their own. Put broadly, the world outside the university is usually seen as a place where people do and feel things: where they work, play, fight, cry, laugh, eat, drink, make friends, make love, raise kids, drive cars, run errands, hang out . . . and college is imagined as a place where people talk and read and write about things. The world of action and the world of the mind. One response to this split (by the growth theorists and many others) has been to have students write and talk about their experiences outside school. While I don't object in principle to this, I do worry that such an approach actually *reasserts* the gap between experience and intellect at the very moment it tries to bridge it. These are different things, different worlds, such teachers seem implicitly to say, but we will try for the time not to keep them so very far apart.

My instinct is to argue against the split altogether. I do so for not only theoretical but practical reasons. On the one hand, a college is a place where people *work*—either as students or in their jobs as teachers, administrators, secretaries, janitors, electricians, security officers, and the like. It is thus not something separate from the world of actions and events but an integral part of it. (Think of what would happen to the economies of many towns and cities if the colleges in them were to close down.) It is a place where things get done or don't get done, and where the consequences of doing them or not are often felt in material ways—grades and degrees are awarded or withheld, tenure is given or denied, references are given, contacts are made, grants and salaries and offices and assistantships are apportioned. It takes a kind of willed blindness (although also a very common and useful one) *not* to think of the academy as such a workplace.

And it takes a similar effort not to picture the many kinds of reading that make up much of our experiences outside the university. Watching television, listening to the radio, playing tapes or CDs, reading the paper, glancing through magazines, checking out ads on busses and billboards and in stores, scanning supermarket tabloids, going through the mail, playing video or computer games, following recipes or directions, filling in forms . . . That's a lot of reading without ever setting aside time to pick up a book. And this doesn't count the kinds of reading that form a regular part of many jobs, or the ways we read the meanings of things that are perhaps less often thought of as being texts—clothes, buildings, cars, appliances, haircuts, gestures, bodies, and so on. Our media culture is saturated with texts. Much of our experience is bound up with reading. And, again, I don't mean reading in a loose or metaphorical sense. I mean that we all spend much of our time decoding and interacting with texts. This may be either a bad or good thing, a symptom of the hegemonic functioning of late monopoly capitalism or an instance of postmodern playfulness. I don't know. But I do think it is a given in current American culture. Or at least I have never met a college student whose life was not taken up in large part by the sorts of reading I have just described.

One way to help such students imagine themselves as intellectuals, then, is to ask them to look closely at how they *already* go about reading the many various texts they meet from day to day—both in school and outside of it. For this reason, I often ask students to think and write about the uses they make of the texts and discourses of popular culture, to consider the ways their sense of themselves as persons has been shaped in part by the music, movies, advertising, television, and fashion they look at and listen to everyday. One way I do so is by having them read Dave Marsh's introduction to his collected writings on rock and roll, *Fortunate Son* (1985), in which he tells of how as a kid growing up in a white working-class neighborhood of Detroit, Michigan, his discovery of soul music not only gave him a sense of a wider and different world, but also helped him question some of his own racial biases. "The depth of feeling in that Miracles record," Marsh writes, "which could have been purchased for 69 cents at any K-Mart, overthrew the premise of racism, which was that blacks were not as human as we, that they could not feel—much less express their feelings—as deeply as we did" (xxv). I don't expect many of my students to testify to moral epiphanies of this sort, but I have found that reading Marsh helps many of them begin to think about songs that have somehow mattered or meant something to them, and I ask them to write an essay in which they talk about some of the ways music has entered into and affected their lives. (If they're not into music, they can of course write about movies or television or fashion or whatever does matter to them.) Here is one response by David, written in 1989, when he was a freshman at the University of Pittsburgh:

> When I was in about the ninth grade, I was a somewhat of an insecure person. I was fat, somewhat funny-looking, and I didn't go out on the weekends. In short, I was a geek. Sure, I had a lot of friends and I got along with everybody, but nonetheless, I was still a geek.

There was a reason for this though. As I said earlier, I stayed home a lot. But when I stayed home I watched a lot of television, especially MTV; and there was a particular type of video I liked to watch, dance videos. People like Michael Jackson and Janet Jackson were *my* favorites. Unfortunately, they were the only dance videos MTV would play. I then started to listen to WAMO, Pittsburgh's, for lack of a better term, "black station. " And when listening to this music, it is only inevitable that you start to dance. I was not very good at first, but it was a lot of fun trying. Even though I became alright at it, I still stayed at home.

Now you have to understand something about the place I grew up in, Brentwood. Kids from Brentwood were into heavy metal bands and hard rock. Groups like Led Zeppelin, the Doors, and Motley Crue were definitely mainstream Brentwood. Unfortunately, I didn't get into these groups like everyone else. Sure, I had listened to these groups before, and I could even somewhat tolerate them. But *my* friends knew everything about them, words from every song and group member. As I said before, I was listening to New Edition, LL Cool J, and Kool Moe Dee and that made me different.

Another thing, Brentwood is somewhat prejudice. There was only one black kid in the entire high school. Listening to WAMO was social suicide.

One evening at one of the few football games I attended *my* sophomore year, I danced. We were playing Clairton, who is a predominately black school. It was halftime and everyone was making fun of Clairton's drum major who was dancing. Keeping with the fun, I imitated him. For the first time, I danced in public. I became the center of attention for a minute and I liked it.

In time, I decided to go out more often. I also found a new group of friends who were interested in the same type of music as I was. Although we were the minority, we didn't care. We considered everyone who listened to heavy metal to be stupid, dirty, and dope heads. Hey, what did we know, we were young.

As time went by, dance and rap became popular in Brentwood. And if you could dance well, you became pretty popular. So, every chance I got, I danced when a good jam would come on. Sure, I was showing off. What would you do? I had the chance so I took it. When we went to dances or to parties or to Hubcaps, which is an under 21 dance place, everyone expected me to know all the new moves. Once again, the center of attention, I liked it.

I also started to look and act differently. I wore ties, vests, and dress clothes compared to the t-shirts and jeans everyone else was wearing. People told me it was a waste of time and even called me vain. I did not care what they said, though. It was their opinion. Like Bobby Brown said, it was my prerogative.

I find this piece intriguing—and in fact am inclined to believe that, through his wary sketching out of both the connections and gaps between his tastes and allegiances, David draws (or at least hints at) a fuller and more nuanced account of the politics of music listening than Marsh offers with his tale of a quick and decisive conversion. (Of course, Marsh tells his story from a distance while David talks about something he has only just lived through. The clarity that time offers can often come at the expense of detail, especially conflicting detail.) But there is also a way in which David is too wary. For while he suggests early in his piece that his liking for black music set him out of synch with his friends and school-mates in white Brentwood, we see little real evidence of what this might have cost him. Instead, a new group of friends comes along at precisely the right time and what originally seemed a problem turns out to be the key to success. The kid can dance! Questions of race get turned into simple matters of taste. It's his pre-rogative to dress and move this way, and since Brentwood somehow seems to be getting a lot cooler too (what happened to all those slam dancers?), it turns out to be not such a big issue after all. Indeed, it never becomes clear if his taste for dance music led David to rethink his attitudes about African Americans in any way. (Actually it's not clear what his attitudes were at any time.)

Similarly, the turning point in his piece comes when David tells of a moment when the very thing that once excluded him from the Brentwood in-group becomes a means for him to gain their applause, as he gets up at a football game to parody the moves of another school's African American cheerleader. Who can easily say what the politics of such a gesture are? Has David somehow crossed over metaphorically from white to black to white again? And is that better or worse than being a straight-out Zeppelin freak, smoking dope with the older white boys? And what are we to make of the fact that while David closes by quot-ing the words of crossover singer Bobby Brown as though they were his own, midway through his piece he speaks of listening to rappers like New Edition, LL Cool J, and Kool Moe Dee? Surely in a dying steel town like Brentwood, PA, where racial tensions can often run very high, listening to crossover megastars like Brown or the Jacksons ("it don't matter if you're black or white") must be one thing and following hip hop another. But David obscures such issues by turning them all into a simple question of style or taste, of their opinion against his pre-rogative. He thus never really offers the insight into race and music that his paper at first seems to promise.

The problem with his piece is not that David fails to give a full or frank account of his experiences. He could perhaps give some more imagistic details in his nar-rative—but what for, really? What happened at the game is clear enough already, as is the conflict between his tastes and those of his friends. And I don't think one can really complain that we don't know his feelings about finding himself placed somewhere between two musical worlds, one black and the other white. It seems fairly clear that he's ambivalent about it; like everyone else he wants both to be different and accepted at the same time. Instead what I think David needs to do with this piece is to say more about what he thinks his experiences *mean* or add up to, to move from narrative to idea, to show how what he has to offer here is something besides one more zero-to-hero story. In my comments I urged David to try to do so by relating his story to the one told by Marsh. I told him my sense was that he did not want to make the same direct connection which Marsh does between liking black music and rethinking racism, but it wasn't clear to me yet what he wanted to use his story to argue for instead.

In his piece, the need to be accepted, to have friends, to feel part of his school and neighborhood seem placed in tacit opposition to the more liberal discourses of MTV and the radio (which is itself something for knee-jerk critics of the media to think about). But David does not so much resolve or even confront these conflicts as sidestep them. The problem simply ceases to be a problem; Brentwood gets funky and the kids dig his new moves. And so the consequences of style, of choosing between black and white music, never really get explored. Doing so, it seemed to me, would be the next real step for David to take as a writer.

I expected students in this particular class to revise each of their writings in response to my comments and our talk in class. But other than attending to some small matters of phrasing, David made few changes to his second draft. I was disappointed but not much surprised. David had already written a fairly frank and complex account of his dealings with black music. To really do something more with this story he would have needed to make some very hard intellectual and political choices—and that's a lot to ask of anyone. My guess is that for any number of reasons he simply didn't want to choose then and there between the demands made on him by friendship, neighborhood, race, music, and fashion— or that he didn't care to reveal the choices he had made to his writing teacher. And so I offer his piece here not as a classroom success story but as an example of the kinds of issues students often must struggle with when they are asked to write about the uses they make of popular texts. Despite its difficulty, the value of such work, it seems to me, lies in how it pictures students (and encourages them to picture themselves) as people who bring not only experiences but ideas to the classroom, whose work as intellectuals does not begin and end in school but continues on outside of it.

2
VOICE

Picture two writing classrooms. In the first, students have simply been asked to write about something that interests them. In class they break into small groups and begin to read their texts aloud to one another. After a student has finished reading her piece, the members of her group begin to question and advise her about what she has written. The writer takes notes on what her readers have to say and perhaps asks them some questions back. In this way the group works through the writings of all its members, in each case first comparing what the writer intended to say with what she actually ended up writing, and then trying to find ways of bringing the two closer together.

The second class also focuses on student writings, but in a different way. In it the members of the class have been given copies of the same student essay. There is no name on the text, and although its author is sitting somewhere in the room, the custom of the class is that she stay silent and anonymous. The students here have done the same readings and written in response to the same assignment, so they raise and discuss these questions: In what ways does this text respond effectively to the issues raised by the readings and assignment? What moves does its writer make, what strategies and conventions does she draw on, to lend authority and interest to what she has to say?

The ways these two classrooms are set up reflect important contrasts in how writing teachers have imagined their subject. The first classroom links writing closely to speech. It brings readers and writers face to face, dissolving the gaps in space and time that usually separate them, and makes the subject of their talk not so much the writer's text as what she *wants* to say. The text is thus seen as a kind of imperfect extension of its author. And so what really counts is what the writer means, not what her text happens now to say—since that can always be changed. The job of her readers centers on helping her get those meanings straight. As its many advocates have made clear, the goal of this sort of classroom is less to analyze writings than to work with writers, who in this context are not seen as very different from speakers or even thinkers.

The second class deals more with writing as writing. It does not ask if a text accurately expresses what its author might have wanted to say, since that author and her intents are unknown. Instead it looks at how this writing responds to other texts (in this case, the readings and assignment) and at how it draws on the peculiar commonplaces and conventions of its form of written discourse, at the moves and gestures that place it as part of the field of, say, criticism or sociology or autobiography. The power and meaning of a text is seen to stem largely from the stance it takes toward other texts. The task such a class defines for the student is one of finding her way into a written world, of gaining control over a set of textual conventions that often differ widely from those she uses as a speaker.

I'd like to use these scenes as instances of two powerful and competing ways of imagining the voice or self of a writer. The goal of the first workshop is to move *beyond* the text to get at the thoughts and feelings of its author; the aim of the second seminar is to define and talk about the person implied *in* the phrasings of the text itself. Both of these ways of conceiving the voice or self of the writer have figured strongly in composition in the years after Dartmouth. I think their differences have often been blurred and confused, though, and I want to show here what I see as their competing strengths and limits.

"The underlying metaphor," writes Peter Elbow, "is that we all have a chest cavity unique in size and shape so that each of us naturally resonates to one pitch alone" (1981, 281–82). This natural resonance Elbow calls *voice*, which he then goes on to define as what gives the work of some writers "the sound of 'them'" (288). As Elbow uses it, voice often refers to something like style or tone—writing with "real rhythm and texture" (290). But while such terms suggest that the problem facing the writer is a technical one, a question of phrasing or diction, voice hints that matters of selfhood are also at stake. It implies breath, spirit, presence, what comes before words and gives them life. And so it becomes both the most vital and mysterious part of writing. Elbow calls it a kind of "juice" or "electricity" that makes a text "real" (283–86), and argues that without voice, writing "is dead, mechanical, faceless" (287). But yet its exact workings can never be pointed to or defined, since to do so would be to reduce them to a kind of mechanical trick, a matter of style or technique—and voice is precisely what transcends all that. It is something felt rather than analyzed, "a matter of hearing resonance rather than being able to point to things on a page" (299).

In imagining voice in concrete and physical terms, as something that comes from *inside* a writer and makes her work somehow more real, Elbow speaks for most of the theorists and textbook authors who have used the term after Dartmouth. One after the other identifies voice as what makes writing honest, authentic, personal, original, human. Students are exhorted to stand naked and speak the truth, to renounce English and jargon and the five-paragraph theme.[1] In his 1987 "Voice as Juice': Some Reservations about Evangelical Composition," Irvin Hashimoto warns against the messianic underpinnings of such a rhetoric of authenticity, arguing that while some teachers and students "may *like* to believe that honest human voices do not reveal themselves in academic terminology, certainly very little scholarly work of much value could go on without such terminology" (78). I agree, and my debt to Hashimoto is clear throughout this chapter. But I also think we should not downplay the extent to which work in our field has long been infected with a kind of missionary zeal. Since the time of Matthew Arnold, one of the strongest appeals of English has been that its study involves more than just technical training in the skills of reading and writing, but instead deals with the growth of students as whole persons. (Recall Britton's insistence at Dartmouth that English be seen as "the area in which . . . all knowledge must come together for the individual." I perhaps also ought to add that, although I might phrase it in different terms, I too share in this sense of a social mission, that there is a political as well as intellectual edge to my interest in teaching.) The study of literature in particular has long been defended in therapeutic and quasireligious terms as offering students a way of growing somehow more sensitive, whole, cultured, critical, or humane. Literature was to help them become not just better readers but better people as well.

In "From Astor Place to Kenyon Road," Myron Tuman shows how these aims and values were adapted to the teaching of writing by early NCTE reformers like Edward Holmes and James Hosic, who argued

---

1. One sign of how strongly a rhetoric of authenticity continues to shape the teaching of writing is the remarkable number of textbooks published since the 1960s whose central aim is to urge students to find their own personal voices as writers. Some characteristic instances of this genre are Albert Guerard et al.'s 1964 *The Personal Voice*, Ken Macrorie's 1968 *Telling Writing*, Donald Murray's 1968 *A Writer Teaches Writing*, Donald Stewart's 1972 *The Authentic Voice*, Peter Elbow's 1973 *Writing without Teachers*, Lou Kelly's 1973 *From Dialogue* to *Discourse*, Jim Corder's 1973 *Finding a Voice*, James Miller and Stephen Judy's 1978 *Writing in Reality*, Toby Fulwiler's 1988 *College Writing*, and Jeffrey Sommers's 1989 *Model Voices*.

against the focus of many nineteenth-century instructors on the forms of public speech and rhetoric, and began to urge students to strive instead for a poetic self-expressiveness in their work. Anticipating many of the aims and phrasings of the growth theorists' by more than fifty years, Holmes wrote in 1911:

> I mean by composition the sincere expression in language of the child's genuine thoughts and feelings. The effort to express himself tends, in proportion as it is sincere and strong, to give breadth, depth, and complexity to the child's thoughts and feelings and through the development of these to weave his experiences into the tissue of his life. (quoted in Tuman 1986, 345)

And in 1917 Hosic argued:

> The development of the expressional power of the individual pupil should be the aim of the teacher rather than the teaching of specific forms and rules. Each year of a pupil's life brings a broader outlook through added experience and mature thought. . . . Only from a realization on the part of the teacher of this growth of personality can an adequate course in composition be organized. (quoted in Tuman 1986, 346)

For both men, developing the student as a writer and as a person were inextricably linked. A similar concern with the languages, thoughts, and feelings of individual students (rather than with "the teaching of specific forms and rules") has been a defining concern of most liberal attempts to reform English teaching since—from the efforts of Fred Newton Scott and Vida Scudder to those of Louise Rosenblatt and James Britton. So when in the 1960s and 1970s teachers once again began to speak of the centrality of personal and expressive kinds of writing, they had a long tradition of dissent in English to call on.[2]

They also had the events of their time to respond to. These were, after all, the 1960s, the years of Kennedy, King, Vietnam, urban riots, student protests, and Watergate. Open admission programs, community colleges, and increased forms of financial aid made higher education more available to many nontraditional students—adults returning to school after years in the workplace, people of color, kids from working-class or poor families, speakers of English as a second language, and so

---

2. Arthur Applebee traces the work of this dissenting tradition in full and sympathetic detail in his 1974 *Tradition and Reform*. James Berlin also surveys many of the social and disciplinary forces behind the 1960s renaissance of composition in *Rhetoric and Reality* (1987, 120–79).

on—whose often widely varying levels of training and experience with writing seemed to call for new sorts of teaching practices. At the same time social critics like Neil Postman and Charles Weingartner (1967) argued for teaching as a subversive activity, a way of undermining establishment thinking. The personal was the political, and to help students find their own voices seemed one way to protest a system run amok. And so, for instance, Ken Macrorie began *Uptaught*, his 1970 polemic against English and inauthenticity, by describing a police assault on a student-occupied university building, and Peter Elbow opened his 1973 *Writing without Teachers* by observing:

> Many people are now trying to become less helpless, both personally and politically: trying to claim more control over their own lives. One of the ways people most lack control over their own lives is through lacking control over words. (vii)

And so while expressivists like Macrorie and Elbow have often been criticized since for their supposed navel-gazing tendencies, there seems no doubt that at this point their aims were aggressively and self-consciously political.

A comparison with another emerging academic field in the 1960s, that of film studies, might help here. One of the decisive moments in the systematizing of the study of film was the formulation by a number of young French critics of the *politique des auteurs*, in which they argued that the director of a movie should be seen as its "author," whose characteristic themes and styles could then be catalogued and interpreted—a move that paved the way for the serious study of what was then the undervalued work of Hollywood directors like Hitchcock, Ford, and Hawkes. While this "auteur theory" has since fallen out of favor with many academic critics due to its (intended) neglect of the various social and economic forces that impinge on filmmaking, it is worth keeping in mind that it was first phrased not as a theory but as a *politique* on behalf of the directors working within the Hollywood movie factory.[3] Similarly, we need to see many 1960s expressivist teachers of writing not as fleeing from politics but as engaged in a political defense of the student in her struggles to assert herself against what was seen as a dehumanizing corporate and university system.

---

3. Peter Wollen tells the story of the beginnings and later uses of the auteur theory at length in *Signs and Meaning in the Cinema* (1969, 74–115).

As with auteurism when it moved from being a *politique* to a theory of film study, much of the political charge of expressivism has by now faded. Still an (often very loose) linking of personal writing to programs for social change continued throughout the 1970s and 1980s. In his 1981 "First Person Singular, First Person Plural, and Exposition," for instance, Allan Brick argued for "an increased awareness of [our] traditional calling as teachers of the language to persons rather than teachers of mechanically determined skills to a standardized mass" (508). To do so, Brick argues (following Moffett and Britton, although he cites neither) that we should have students write from their own observations and experiences, drawing whatever conclusions they can from them. Note that Brick sees this emphasis on the personal as part of our "traditional calling," and later in his essay he argues once more that to reinvigorate teaching we need a new "confidence in our own humanistic literary traditions," along with an increased control over our work in the classroom (515). As an example of how this control might be gained and exercised, Brick then points to the work of Paolo Freire with illiterate Brazilian peasants, effecting a peculiar linking of Arnold and Marx, self-liberation and political resistance. (But remember that Leavis too had cast his form of humanism as an *alternative* to Marxism, a different means to the same end.) In making this connection, Brick was on the crest of a wave of citations, as throughout the 1980s a striking number of defenders of personal writing began to invoke Freirian support of their views, as if in doing so they might recover the political edge of such teaching.[4]

The advocates of voice also had ties to the work of literary critics interested in how the language of a text could be said to indicate the character or *ethos* of its writer. Among such critics were Wayne Booth, who in 1961 brought out his landmark study of the implied author in literary works, *The Rhetoric of Fiction*, and Walter Ong, who in 1962 published *The Barbarian Within*, a series of essays on the relations between the mask or persona assumed by a writer and his or her real self. A few

---

4. Freire has been cited in a remarkable number of books and articles on composition in the last fifteen years by writers ranging from Ann Berthoff and Peter Elbow to Ira Shor. Although what Freire is said to stand for varies widely, he is almost always cited approvingly and used to lend a sense of social urgency to whatever the writer happens to be proposing, from nurturing personal voice to teaching ideological critique. The volatility of Freire as a symbol of political commitment is further shown by the tendency of those who cite him to claim his other readers have gotten him wrong, have somehow missed or neutralized his activist agenda.

years later, Walker Gibson took on the similar question of how an author might be said to set up an imaginary relationship with the reader in his 1966 *Tough, Sweet, and Stuffy* and 1969 *Persona: A Style Study for Readers and Writers.* As its subtitle suggests, the aim of this later text was to help students use what they learned as readers in forming their own voices as writers. The notion of voice or persona was thus used as a kind of bridge between the study of literature and the teaching of composition. Implicit in such a move was the recognition that student writings could be read as a kind of literature, that they could be valued, as Holmes and Hosic had argued long before, not simply for their correctness or persuasiveness but for the "breadth, depth, and complexity" of their expression. A central goal of literary study thus became not only the writing of criticism but the deepening of students' own creative powers, as can be seen in the many approaches to teaching since the 1960s that have urged students to find their own voices (at least in part) through reading and imitating the poems, stories, and essays of others.

Some of this work again grew out of the government-funded Project English. In 1968, for instance, at the University of Oregon Curriculum Study Center, Albert Kitzhaber drafted a twelfth-grade course called The Personal Voice: The Rhetoric of Literature that involved students in analyzing the style and tone of various literary works and then applying what they had learned to their own work. At about the same time, John Hawkes and Albert Guerard launched the Voice Project at Stanford University, an attempt to get students to realize that "the sound of his voice conveys something of his personality" (Hawkes 1967, xii). (Some years before, Guerard had also supervised James Moffett's undergraduate honors thesis on Virginia Woolf's rendering of inner life.) Hawkes and Guerard took a more self-consciously experimental approach than Kitzhaber; they audiotaped students as they spoke, for instance, and then asked them to describe the pitch and intonations of their own voices, and they also gave a striking amount of close critical attention to classroom talk and student writings. But like Kitzhaber, they returned in the end to literature as a model of what writers could do and to a kind of literary analysis as a method for describing and assessing their voices—as can be seen as well in a reader and textbook, also called *The Personal Voice*, that they cowrote in 1964 with Maclin Guerard and Claire Rosenfield.

This linking of a rhetorical criticism of literary works with the developing of students' own voices—where students are asked to apply what they have learned from reading Virginia Woolf or Tom Wolfe to their own efforts as writers—has proved an enduring textbook genre. Jim Corder added to it with his 1973 *Finding a Voice*, in which he groups stories and essays around various social or political issues but ultimately points students toward a kind of personal writing, as have more recently Nancy Sommers and Donald McQuade in their 1986 *Student Writers at Work and in the Company of Other Writers*, in which they collect a set of prize-winning student papers along with some more standard literary selections. The message such books offer students (and I imagine it is as daunting to some as it is liberating to others) is essentially that *you can do this too*. As Tuman argues in his piece on Holmes and Hosic, such teaching aims to join literature and composition by asking students "to accomplish in prose what only a hundred years before had been the goal of romantic poets—to transform ordinary experience and ordinary language into self-sustaining literate texts" (1986, 347).

But in moving from the study of the persons implied in texts to a valuing of students' own authentic voices, a distinction between what might be called the real and the literary self of a writer was often blurred or contested. In *The Rhetoric of Fiction*, Wayne Booth had insisted that "it is only by distinguishing between the author and his implied image that we can avoid pointless and unverifiable talk about such qualities as 'sincerity' or 'seriousness' in the author" (1961, 75). This view was echoed by writing teachers like William Coles, who explained in his 1972 "An Unpetty Pace":

> The self I am speaking of here, the one with which I am concerned in the classroom, is not a mock or false self, but a literary self, a self construable from the ways words fall on a page. The other self, the identity of the student, is something with which I as a teacher can have nothing to do. (379)

But I suspect that much of the allure and power of a certain kind of teaching springs from a decision to more or less ignore this distinction, and to suggest instead that the real concern of a course in writing should be the relation of a text to its actual author. For instance, in a 1989 piece on "The Pleasures of Voice in the Literary Essay," Peter Elbow grants the difference between reading for the sort of person implied "in" the language of a text (which is what I take Booth and Coles to be talking about) and what he calls the much more "presumptuous" attempt to talk about the "authentic voice" or self of the writer that lies "behind" its phrasings (224–26). But Elbow then goes on to argue that "good reading and good teaching depend on the ingrained human tendency to make these dangerous inferences" (226). Students like and understand talk about voice, he argues, in ways that they don't respond to discussions of stylistic matters or *ethos*. (While this may be the case for some students, my guess is that it probably says even more about the ongoing desire of many English *teachers* to talk more in terms of persons and experiences than skills or techniques.) Elbow is after "more sense of contact with the author"; he wants the face not the mask, the teller not the tale (232). And so he more or less rejects the distinction Coles makes between a false and literary self, arguing instead that

> [Aristotle] notes that we are *not* persuaded if we sense that the "trustworthiness" is a matter of "conscious art." He clearly implies that we need to experience that trustworthiness as inhering *in* the actual writer. Indeed we *distrust* a writer to the extent that we sense him as a clever creator of personas. (232)

Driving this sort of talk is a belief in a self that stands outside or beyond language and culture. That is both its central appeal and flaw. The metaphor of voice lets the teacher imply that there is more going on here than just another language game: questions of selfhood are also at stake. The task of the student is no longer simply to write clear and acceptable prose, but to find her own voice and speak in it rather than in one imposed by her job or school or field of study. As Leo Hamalian put it, somewhat melodramatically, in 1970, "Once the student finds his own 'voice,' he attains an honesty of selfhood in his prose that distinguishes it from the duty-driven drivel that he sometimes submits as a theme" (228). Writing thus begins to be valued more as a form of self-discovery or self-expression than as a way of communicating with others.

This is shown strikingly in the later work of James Moffett. As I've noted before, in his 1968 *Teaching the Universe of Discourse*, Moffett offered a compelling plan for starting the work of a course by having students experiment with personal and expressive uses of language and then having them move from there to more formal and public kinds of writing. In subsequent years, though, Moffett's interests came to center more exclusively on those beginning personal uses of writing. By the 1980s he was arguing for writing as a form of "discursive meditation" much like the spiritual exercises of Loyola and the practices of Zen and yoga. "By external speech," he wrote, "individuals communicate to each other, and by inner speech each informs himself" (1981, 139). Composing is a powerful way of controlling the monotonous and obsessive tendencies of such speech, Moffett suggested, a "counterspell" whose forms can "subject my inner speech to conditions not of its own making and hence cause it to alter itself" (1985, 307). The goal of composition is thus "composure," a disciplined self-understanding and control (306).

One of the pleasures of reading Moffett is his mix of modes and styles, and many of his phrasings seem drawn as much from the 1960s counterculture as the practice of yoga. "The composition process can be [a] kind of mental trip," he argues, as "a part of our self that wants growth and change finds a way to subvert the inner establishment" (1985, 307). It speaks to both the integrity and eccentricity of his vision that he should be writing such lines in 1985, moving as it were in the opposite direction of much other work in the field, which was by then shifting away from a concern with personal writing and toward an interest in the politics of teaching academic discourse. And Moffett does still concede that writing has something to do with readers. After reaching a state of internal composure, he argues, a writer can then "[work] up a final revision, for an audience and a purpose, of those thought forms that have surfaced to the realm of inner speech" (1981, 134). But it seems clear that such communicative issues are almost an afterthought to "the composing of mind" that he now sees as the real aim of writing (134).

Where Moffett drew on his practice of meditation, Elbow called on his experiences as part of a therapy group (1990, 17). In both *Writing without Teachers* (1973) and *Writing with Power* (1981), Elbow offers a rich sense of how he has students share their work in class and respond to what each other has to say. In contrast to most academic seminars, the job of a reader in his workshops is not to argue with or critique the position taken by a writer but simply to describe how she experienced her text—what words or phrasings she liked and what ones she did not, what images or associations the text evoked for her, and so on. Elbow calls this sort of reading "giving movies of your mind" (1973, 85–92). Similarly, he tells his writers not to argue with what their readers say to them, but simply to listen and then later on to use those responses that seemed helpful and to ignore those that did not (101–06). As in some forms of therapy, the point is more to share feelings and reactions than to argue out positions.

This therapeutic impulse can be seen even more clearly in John Schultz's story workshop, a method for teaching writing that he originated at Chicago's Columbia College in 1965, and refined and elaborated throughout the next twenty years. In what seems to have been the manner of many kinds of group and encounter sessions, the story workshop joins liberationist rhetoric with a directive style of teaching. As Schultz describes it in his 1977 "Story Workshop Method" and 1982 *Writing from Start to Finish,* a typical workshop lasts at least four hours, most of which involves the teacher putting students through a set of verbal and written exercises meant to augment their "telling voices." The emphasis is almost always imagistic, sensual, gestural, intuitive—and throughout his own telling of the workshop Schultz leans heavily on exclamation points for effect: "Give the gesture! Play it over! See what each word gives you to see! Now listen to your voice!" (1977, 414–19). Students are pushed to tell and retell images and stories, to read aloud, and to listen to each other, but there seems to be fairly little dialogue encouraged among them, little arguing out of competing views or readings. "The Story Workshop director instructs participants to save discussion for an appropriate time" (416). Like much work in literature since Lawrence and Leavis, then, the story workshop betrays a kind of fear of experience-distant language, of theory or abstraction. "The reflective/analytic reflects upon nothing unless the content and presence of the perceptual/intuitive lives immediately before it" (416). In trying to regain such a sensual content and presence, to recover the physical voice of the writer, the story workshop ends up deferring other more critical sorts of talk and argument to some more "appropriate" time. *Voice* serves as a key term in what thus becomes an anti-intellectual project.

Elbow is much more given to working through the ambiguities and tensions in his valuing of voice than Schultz, and for this I find him much more interesting as a teacher and writer. But I think his main differences from Schultz may have less to do with aim than tone. For instance, Elbow helped pioneer the use of group work in writing classrooms (as did Moffett). So he was right to insist on the "concretely social dimensions" of his teaching (1990, 17). Yet I can't agree with him when he goes on to argue that his goal in teaching has been to "stick up for the personal in such a way as to simultaneously foster the social" (17). Instead he seems to me to move in almost the opposite direction, to use the social to foster the personal. For there is an odd way in which the students in his workshops, like those in Schultz's, do not seem to be held answerable to each other as intellectuals. Readers are simply asked to say what they felt about a text, not to offer a convincing case for their readings of it; writers need only respond to those questions about their work that strike them personally as interesting or useful. Students in such a class serve more as sounding boards than as interlocutors. The aim of their work together is more to help a writer figure out what *she* thinks or feels than it is to help her compose a text that will seem persuasive to a certain group of people at a certain time. Writers thus once again seem imagined more as poets, speaking to whom they know not, than as rhetors, trying to make their positions prevail in a public exchange of views.

I have been part of workshops set up along the lines suggested by Elbow, and I've seen how such groups can help people form a powerful sense of who they are or want to be as writers. But I think that the rhetoric of authenticity also sets up a situation where a certain kind of talk or teaching becomes next to impossible. For if what counts is less what a writer has to say than how much she really means or feels it, then the measure of good writing becomes its genuineness or sincerity. And how do you tell *that?* As Elbow admits, "Real self. Real voice. I am on slippery ground here" (1981, 93). What happens if a student does not feel the resonance of a passage? Or if she finds a certain kind of writing authentic and her teacher does not? Or how might you show somebody who doesn't know already how the voice of a writer is real or fake? Elbow says his strategy as a teacher is simply to point: "I began to mark these passages with a line in the margin, and I simply told students that these passages seemed to me to have strength, resonance, power" (283).

But in the name of recognizing a student's own voice, such a practice might end up giving more power and mystery to the teacher than ever, since it lets her name various passages as real or powerful without having to say why. As Elbow concedes:

> I have been nervous about the charge that what I am calling "real voice" is just writing that happens to tickle my feelings. . . . If I experience resonance, surely it's more likely to reflect a good fit between the words and *my* self than a good fit between the words and the writer's self; after all, my self is right here, in contact with the words on the page, while the writer's self is nowhere to be found. (300)

Indeed. (Again, one of the things I most admire about Elbow is his willingness to think through opposing views seriously and at length; in fact, it often seems to me, as it does here, that he states the position he is against better than the one he is trying to argue for.) In recent years

Elbow has worked hard to give more evidence for what he means by voice (or the lack of it) in writing. In his 1989 "Pleasures of Voice," for instance, he lists a set of stylistic maneuvers—like imitating the rhythms and syntax of speech, or calling attention to the act of writing—that can help give "the *illusion* of presence" in a writer's work (233; emphasis in original). Then in his 1991 "Reflections on Academic Discourse," he associates voice with a "*kind* of nonacademic discourse . . . that tries to render experience rather than explain it" (136; emphasis in original). And in his forward to a special 1990 issue of *Pre/Text* he edited that focused on personal expressive academic writing, Elbow begins to map out the features of such writing as a kind of discursive genre. Among other things, he speaks of the *form* of expressive writing as being characterized by a personal tone of voice and a loose organization that lets a writer "imply more and spell out less," by an openness to talk about the feelings and experiences of the writer, and by an attentiveness to the reader, even though it has "no tradition of citation" (1990, 9–10).

This interest in defining personal writing as a *type* of discourse is echoed by several of the contributors to the special *Pre/Text* issue, some of whom actually stop in their writing to ask if this is really the sort of piece Elbow was looking for. And so Mara Holt, in a public exchange of letters with John Trimbur, remarks, "But Peter wants from me in my letter to you *the kind of thing* I wrote in my letter to him, and I'm not sure if that's possible (1990, 48; emphasis added). And Stephen North wonders, "Am I being 'expressive' or 'personal' here, now, as I write this? How should we decide? Ask me? Take a poll? Look for certain textual features?" (1990, 106) I appreciate such attempts at precision. But I think that in trying to define the personal or expressive as a certain *kind* of writing, or even as a certain well-defined set of stylistic moves, Elbow and his cohorts give up the game. For it makes little sense to me to try to imagine one discursive genre—one set of inherited social codes and expectations for using language—as being somehow more authentic than another. It's like saying blue jeans are more genuine than business suits. You can find saints and con artists wearing both. And surely it is as easy to fake a piece of personal writing—my abortion, the rose of Auschwitz, dancing with tears in my eyes—as it is to hide your own voice and feelings in a research paper. Irvin Hashimoto offers a hilarious account of this problem in his 1986 "Toward Honesty," in which he writes of his difficulties in figuring out if his students are really and truly sharing their authentic feelings with him or not:

> I told Gump that while his paper certainly deserved no better than a C- for mechanics, I would give him an A for revealing his honest feelings about Jews, wimps, nurds, and queers. And Gregory sneered at me and said that seeing as he had lied about his feelings about Jews, wimps, nurds, and queers to begin with, he probably couldn't take what I had said seriously, either. (15)

And so on. Many of the student essays in the 1985 *What Makes Writing Good?* show the same problem. The editors of this book, William Coles and James Vopat, asked forty-eight teachers of writing to submit what they thought was one of the best student papers they had ever received and to say why. Many of these writings turn out to be autobiographical in some way, yet the supposed authenticity of these pieces often fails to make it very hard to predict either what their writers have to say or how they will say it. Instead several seem to have been chosen precisely because they conform so closely and well to that familiar genre of school prose, the personal essay. And so, for example, one student writes of being moved by a West Texas sky that is "vain in its immensity, shameless in its ambiguity" (41), while another just happens to notice "a rose, left by a mourner, caught and dangling from the wire" that encloses the old death camp at Auschwitz (83). This he goes on to interpret as a symbol of the conflict between "love and progress through peace" and "the evil of their own race" (83). Still another student begins his piece by noting that "outside my window there stands a tree preparing to sleep through the cold storms of the year's final season" (191). Is it any surprise that he closes by invoking the "cyclical seasons of life" (193)?

My point is not that any of these pieces are particularly bad but that they are very conventional—and their conventionality shows the problem with supposing that certain kinds of writing are intrinsically more personal or authentic than others. The personal essay, the essay that renders rather than explains experience, the essay based on direct observation, the essay that moves through an association of feelings and images—these are all as much *social* forms as the business letter, the scholarly article, and the five-paragraph theme. As a teacher I share the goal of helping students form a sense of their own voices as writers and intellectuals. But I think there is a contradiction in trying to get them to do so by asking them to produce a certain *type* of prose. What we need to do instead, I would argue, is to make students more aware of how they can work not only within but against the constraints of a given discourse—of how they can take its methods and use them for their own aims, inflect its usual concerns with their own.

Such teaching requires us to rethink the metaphor of voice in what may at first seem an odd or awkward way. Instead of starting with the idea of a personal voice that comes from within, from "a chest cavity unique in size and shape," we need to begin with the idea that our culture speaks to us through many competing voices, among them those of the home, school, neighborhood, and place of worship; of work and leisure, childhood and parenting, youth and age, friendship and love, individualism and community; of nation, gender, class, and race; as well as those of the various fields and methods that make up our ways of knowing. We need to think, that is, of a voice as a way of speaking that lies *outside* a writer, and that she must struggle to appropriate or control. Her voice as a writer will thus come out of the stance she takes toward these other social codes and voices, in the ways she makes use of the languages and methods of her field or culture.

I am aware that there is a kind of postmodern ring to such phrasings, and in a different context I would be glad to call on the likes of Barthes, Bakhtin, or Derrida in stating my case.[5] But what I have to say here really draws less on their work than on an approach to teaching writing that can be traced back to Amherst College in the 1930s, where Theodore Baird and his colleagues pushed freshmen[6] to define their own stances as writers in response to a dense series of questions and perspectives on a single (often deceptively simple) topic: on lying and telling the truth, for instance, or on amateurism and professionalism, or on correctness in language. While Baird himself wrote little, his influence can be seen in the work of teachers and theorists of writing like William Coles, Walker Gibson, and Roger Sale—each of whom taught near the start of his career at Amherst, and then went on, in his own distinctive ways, to center much of his later work on the question of how a writer *constructs* a voice or self out of the languages and materials offered her.

---

5. Susan Miller has made perhaps the most sustained attempt to use the language of poststructuralist theory in order to reclaim a notion of the writer's self. See both her 1989 *Rescuing the Subject* and 1991 *Textual Carnivals*. Lester Faigley has also argued for a postmodern view of the writing subject in composition in his 1992 *Fragments of Rationality*. Kurt Spellmeyer asks similar questions of subjectivity in his 1989 "Foucault and the Freshman Writer"; Don Bialostosky has tried to forge a Bakhtinian notion of voice in his 1991 "Liberal Education, Writing, and the Dialogic Self." And I have had a go at these issues myself in my 1987 "The Plural Text/The Plural Self."

6. And they were indeed all *freshmen* at that time at Amherst, as were almost all of its English faculty, a fact which might go some way toward explaining the combative tone that infects the work of this group of teachers.

In his 1974 *Seeing and Writing*, for instance, Gibson presents students with a series of assignments that seem to begin simply enough by asking them to describe the world they see around them, but then quickly move to have them consider the ways in which different conceptual lenses and vocabularies shape and limit what they see, to reflect on how seeing as a scientist differs from seeing as a historian or novelist or biographer. Similarly, in his 1974 textbook, *Composing*, Coles starts with a set of assignments that at first seem to invite students to make some hard and fast distinctions between real and rote learning, but then go on to present them with a series of readings and exercises that force them to reflect on how their prior experiences and assumptions continue to shape what they do as students and writers. The effect is to turn the question about the differences between rote and real learning into a complex rather than simple one. As Coles puts it in a companion volume, *Teaching Composing*, near the start of the course he expects that "students' attitudes towards rote learning as they express them in their papers will emerge as almost totally rote-learned—and this with virtually no consciousness of the ironic self-indictment that such a stance implies" (1974b, 28). The aim of his course is thus to help them form a more ironic or reflexive awareness of how they are situated and framed as users of language, of how, paradoxically, a writer must always draw on the words and methods of others to create her own sense of a text or an issue or even herself.

Baird did write about his own work as a teacher once, though, in a brief 1952 piece on "The Freshman English Course." In it he says:

> The assignments are our leading questions, yet a list of them does not give an adequate idea of what goes on in the course until it is made quite plain what function they serve. We begin our thinking by saying that writing is an action, it is something the student does, and the teacher aims at putting the student in a position where he can do it. The assignments are our means of locating that situation in which the student knows what he is talking about. (1)

The emphasis here is all on action and context. While the aim of the course is phrased as one of getting students to know what they're talking about, this is seen not as a problem of simply telling the truth or spilling their guts, but of locating a situation that they can speak from, a position where they can see or do something new. In a 1985 biographical essay on Baird, Walker Gibson points out that this interest in how a writer is positioned was once hypostasized in a series of assignments that began by asking students what it meant exactly to read a road map and how they went about doing it, and ended by raising the question of what a map was after all. "The answer (of course)," Gibson notes, "was that it is a set of directions, a guide for certain kinds of human action. It is not an expression of terrestrial reality" (1985, 140).

So too a writer's text can be seen not as an expression of some inner reality, some authentic self, but as a kind of performance, a working through of the various roles and possibilities that her language and situation offer her. In "Freshman English," Baird suggests that the assignments in his courses are best viewed "like a scenario rather than a syllabus" (1)—that is, not as a finished argument but as a series of prompts to action, rephrasings of context, invitations for students to take on various roles as writers. Over and over the student is asked to define who he is *in relation to* a shifting set of voices, concerns, and texts. As Baird put it in a headnote to one of his assignments,

> Grammatically, it would seem that "I" am a user of prepositions. "I" see something as above or below, to the left or the right, before or after. (quoted in Coles 1983, 248)

The self is here imagined not as an essence but as a set of perspectives, as something that can only be seen in relation to something else. It is a self defined in and by words rather than outside of them—what William Coles has called a *plural I*: "He with his languages is who he is; I with mine am I" (1974b, 108). To articulate any strong sense of this self, then, it follows that a writer needs to use words in complex and distinctive ways. His style—not his sincerity or authenticity—will be the best sign of who he is as a writer. Where the Amherst teachers tended to look for evidence of voice in a piece of writing, then, was in its details, in what might seem fairly small points of phrasing or word choice. Given that a student writing a paper for his English class was likely to come up with much that was familiar, they looked for the ways he still might be seen as subverting or transforming the usual conventions of school prose, as not only writing a theme but doing something else as well.

Roger Sale offers some striking examples of this sort of analysis in *On Writing* (1970). Sale is interested in what might be said to be at stake in the way a writer uses seemingly trivial connective words: *and, but, yet, although, however.* "The life of any writer," he argues, "is expressed in his sense of small, moment-to-moment relationships" (73). How a writer chooses to relate two words, phrases, clauses, or sentences will tell us much about how he relates ideas and feelings, builds a sense of the world and his place in it, forms a sense of himself as a "user of prepositions." To make this point, Sale reads through a paper in which a student talks about the connection (or lack of one) between his stated principles and his everyday life. The essay begins,

> There is a great portion of my life which education does not seem to touch. And I am beginning to believe that much of my life does not touch my listed noble principles. I do have these principles, they do matter to me, but so often they don't seem connected with anything I am doing. A saint will find a way to serve the Lord in all he does. I am no saint. (76)

Sale pauses after each of these sentences to ask if it might have been preceded by an imaginary *and* (does this thought follow smoothly as an example or continuation of the one before?) or an imaginary *but* (does it somehow question, qualify, or complicate what was just said?). Asking such questions, Sale argues, lets you see how this particular writer gets in trouble when he tries to defend what doesn't need defending.

> It is clear in which direction he wants to go: the unreality of his principles is not going to bother him, because such unreality is normal. But . . . having written that his principles don't seem connected with what he is doing, he seems to think that fact needs a defense, so he writes an implied "but." Better, I think, would have been an implied "and," and an example of the way his life leaves him disconnected from his principles. (76)

What we are offered by this student text, then, is not a sense of its writer as someone willing to live with a certain level of moral ambiguity so much as the image of a frat boy whose answer to the problem of leading a principled life is simply to say, "Hey, but I'm no saint." In the spaces between his sentences the stance or voice of the writer emerges—and in this case betrays him. The power of this sort of approach, it seems to me, is that in looking at the ways a writer relates the various elements of a piece, the teacher or critic can achieve a kind of precision about what she is calling voice *without* reducing it to a fixed set of stylistic moves or techniques.

William Coles offers an extraordinarily rich and detailed sense of the day-to-day work that makes up such teaching in *The Plural I* (1978), a novelistic account of a writing course he taught after leaving Amherst. Near the start of the book (and the course it describes), Coles offers a characteristic and telling instance of how as a teacher he confronts the issues of theme writing and voice. The class is reading a student paper on the merits of amateurism that includes passages like these:

> Amateur athletics, for example, offer as much intrinsic enjoyment as the professional games which are widely publicized and acclaimed. The number of interested fans at college and high school competitions would readily testify that amateur athletics are as exciting, if not more so, than many professional sports.
>
> Another example would be the field of scientific research. Many of the basic experiments which later led to important discoveries were for the most part completed by amateur experimenters who made their own equipment, wrote descriptive reports, and kept accurate records of their findings. Although many lacked formal education, they compensated with long hours of intense and formal study. (1978, 20)

Coles says that many of his students tried to praise this paper for its clarity and use of examples. He calls their bluff, though, arguing back:

> —Specific and Concrete examples—except when you notice that for "amateur athletics" you could just as easily read "amateur-made bread which contented eaters of homemade bread throughout the country would readily testify is just as successful as professionally made bread."
>
> —What?
>
> —Take out the term "scientific research" in the third paragraph. If you plug in the term "medicine" or "chimney making" or "textile development" do you have to change anything else in the paragraph to have it go on making sense— particularly when you've got terms like "for the most part" and "many"? (23)

The problem, then, is that this student has failed to make his use of examples in any real way distinctive or his own. He is following the formula for a certain kind of school essay, slotting in the appropriate nouns and adjectives when needed. In calling attention to the interchangeable quality of the terms in it, Coles thus also points to the emptiness of the passage. And so what may seem at first to be a simple fussing over style turns out to deal directly with the position (or lack of one) the writer has taken.

Somewhat later in *The Plural I*, Coles sketches out another version of the same teaching move, as he presents to his students what he calls a "portmanteau essay" that he has assembled by stringing together individual sentences from several of their papers (1978, 34–37). The montage reads remarkably like an average and conventional student essay, which is of course Coles's point. He wants his students to see they have written pieces that were for the most part indistinguishable from one another, which allowed him as he moved from one to the next to feel he was reading the same generic theme. *Voice* thus becomes the quality of a writer's work that resists such easy kinds of appropriation, that somehow marks a phrasing or sentence as the writer's own.

So where the key to finding your own voice for many expressivists was to somehow get *outside* the conventions of academic writing, for the Amherst teachers it was more a question of working *against* such constraints. This shift in emphasis is even more clearly marked in the work of David Bartholomae, a colleague of Coles at the University of Pittsburgh since the mid-1970s. Bartholomae has a fondness for the language of critical theory that Coles does not share, but he freely and often admits the influence Coles has had on his thinking, and in many ways his work can be seen as continuing a line of inquiry about writing begun at Amherst.[7] Part of what interests Bartholomae is how a student can learn to take on the languages and methods of the university in order to form a more critical stance toward the stock notions and attitudes of common sense and the common culture. This has led some critics of his work to cast him as a kind of enemy of personal writing, but this criticism seems to me wildly off target. His own writings are at once allusive and anecdotal, chatty and learned. And the writers he most often speaks of admiring—Emerson, Burke, Rich, Geertz—are those who cross borders, blur genres, mix story with argument, who "seek out the margins" and take on not an easy but "a hesitant and tenuous relationship to the language and methods of the university" (Bartholomae and Petrosky 1986, 41).

This is also what Bartholomae asks students to do. The books he and Anthony Petrosky have written for use in teaching are characterized by a kind of double move: students are asked both to take on the method or ideas of other writers *and* to draw on their own experiences in responding to what those writers have to say, to use what they read for their own ends. And so, for instance, in the course described in their 1986 *Facts,*

---

7. A distinctive feature of what I have been calling here the Amherst school is the way its ideas and concerns have been formed and passed along as much through classroom teaching as scholarly books or articles. Before coming to Pittsburgh, Bartholomae had studied with Richard Poirier at Rutgers, who had himself done his undergraduate work at Amherst and had then taught for a time at Harvard with Reuben Brower, a former colleague of Baird's. Similarly, I first read *The Plural I* when I was studying at New York University with Gordon Pradl, who had taken English 1 at Amherst with Coles. Behind this particular view of writing, then, lies a set of classroom concerns and experiences that lends those ideas much of their force. What I am trying to describe, then, might be described as less a traveling theory than a traveling practice.

Artifacts, and Counterfacts, Bartholomae and Petrosky ask students to read through a series of writings on adolescence as part of a semester-long project in which they draw on both what they have read and their own experiences in constructing their own theories of growing up. Similarly, a typical assignment in their textbook, *Ways of Reading,* asks students to read Adrienne Rich's autobiographical essay, "When We Dead Awaken," and then to "tell a story of your own" that extends or responds to what she says in it. In doing so, students are urged to "imagine that this assignment is a way for you to use (and put to the test) some of Rich's key terms" (1990, 711). Far from asking students to forgo personal writing, then, Bartholomae and Petrosky insist that they draw on their own experiences and tell their own stories. But they also ask that those stories be placed in relation to a set of readings and issues that the class as a whole is dealing with. Like Baird and Coles, they listen for what a writer has to say against a stereophony of competing voices.

What Bartholomae *does* argue against is the notion of some sort of free and untrammeled private space in which a writer can work, a space that is somehow beyond the reach of convention or history, where she can say what she really wants and really feels. Instead, he argues that all writing will in some way show "the pressure and presence of the institution in the work of an individual" (Bartholomae and Petrosky 1986, 39). The question for a writer is thus how to define her own voice and interests in response to such pressures. In his 1985 "Inventing the University," Bartholomae reads through a number of essays by beginning college students and argues that the "more successful writers set themselves against what they defined as some more naive way of talking about their subject" (153). Those who were unable to position themselves in (and against) such a way of speaking, to claim or forge a kind of critical distance, instead slipped "into a more immediately available and realizable voice of authority, the voice of a teacher giving a lesson or of a parent lecturing at the dinner table" (136–37). But here I might just as well have quoted Theodore Baird, who in 1952 was writing this:

> Certainly the student who comes to Amherst has been well talked to—and by all sorts of people in varying tones of voice. He has been told now this and now that about his duty to serve his country, he has been told whom he should hate, he has been given heroes to imitate, and he has been urged to buy. (1)

Baird goes on to argue that the work of a writing course should be to get such students to draw on their own experiences in responding to (rather than simply imitating) these voices of authority. In doing so, he both looks forward to our current fascination with rhetorics of resistance and struggle, and back to a view of the intellectual as the sensitive alien or outcast in her own society. (But perhaps the romantic and isolated poet, the alien intellectual, and the resisting reader are versions or recastings of the same role?)

I am not trying to argue that there are no differences among Baird and Coles and Bartholomae. But I do want to suggest that we don't need to turn to recent continental theory for a decentered view of the self, that there is instead a line of thought within composition that has long imagined the self of the writer in highly social terms. I make this point for two reasons. First, I want to argue against how the relations between theory and practice are usually imagined—which is, to put it simply, that the one leads to the other, that first one figures out what the theory is and then applies it in the classroom. For what I think we see in the work of the Amherst school is how a certain kind of teaching has long enacted the very sorts of insights about language that are now too often talked about as if they were invented by poststructuralist theory. Richard Poirer makes much this point in "Hum 6, or Reading before Theory" (1990), in which he describes a beginning course in critical reading at Harvard, designed by a colleague of Baird's, Reuben Brower, after he moved there from Amherst, and taught by a staff that included not only Poirer himself but Paul de Man—whom he quotes as remarking that "my own awareness of the critical, even subversive power of literary instruction, does not stem from philosophical allegiances but from a very specific teaching experience" (19). Poirer wants to show some of the excitement and rigor of that experience, and in doing so "to help disrupt the calendar of theory and loosen its intimidating hold" on the profession (16).[8] Similarly, Gordon Pradl has recalled what it felt like to be a student in English 1 at Amherst, noting in particular how the course anticipated current concerns with "shifting contexts and loyalties" and a "variety of selves and social roles" (1987, 30). I would push this point to argue that the social view of the self enacted in this sort of teaching offers a compelling dialectical

---

8. Brower and Poirer offer a sense of the wide range of work that went on in Hum 6 in their 1962 collection of critical essays, *In Defense of Reading*. Of perhaps most interest in the volume is Brower's own piece on teaching, "Reading in Slow Motion." Poirer also brilliantly illustrates a fluid and social view of the writing subject in his 1971 study of modern American literature, *The Performing Self.*

alternative to both a romantic hope (in which writers speak free of all social constraints) and a neo-Foucauldian despair (in which systems of power determine in advance all that can be said).

Second, I want to argue against the sort of narrative of progress that still informs many histories of composition. In *Rhetoric and Reality*, for instance, James Berlin suggests that in the 1960s a new sort of epistemic rhetoric began to appear that imagined the writer in original and powerful ways. What were these?

> Communication is at the center of epistemic rhetoric because knowledge is always knowledge for someone standing in relation to others in a linguistically circumscribed situation. . . . Language forms our conceptions of ourselves, our audiences, and the very reality in which we exist. Language, moreover, is a social—not a private—phenomenon. (1987, 166)

And so on. While I don't object in any way to what Berlin has to say about the workings of language here, I am troubled by how he contrasts this view with that of "leading expressionists" like (and these are his examples) Macrorie, Gibson, Coles, Murray, and Elbow (151). In lumping these disparate figures together as advocates of a single naive and romantic expressionism, and in then suggesting that a new and more complex epistemic rhetoric has now superseded theirs, Berlin is able to construct a theoretical victory out of what I see instead as an ongoing struggle among conflicting practices and philosophies. This has the odd effect (since Berlin writes as a leftist historian) of depoliticizing his analysis. Coles and Elbow are seen as figures of the past (they appear in a chapter called "Major Rhetorical Approaches: 1960–75") rather than as advocates of current (and competing) ways of imagining the aims and methods of teaching. Similarly, when in a 1989 essay, "Images of Student Writing," Louise Wetherbee Phelps claims to identify a new Bakhtinian approach to reading student texts "through [their] relationships to a context or *field* of discourse" (55), she fails to see how this sort of reading has long been a strategy of many teachers, even if they have not always described their work in poststructuralist terms. (I think of the teacher Coleridge describes in his *Biographica Literaria* who would go through the work of his students and tear up those pieces that held more than one sentence "that might not have found as appropriate a place under this or that other thesis" [1926]. Surely this was reading texts as part of a field of discourse.) Once again a political and intellectual choice is masked as a theoretical advance.

Poststructuralist theory has offered us powerful ways of rethinking and elaborating our views of voice and self. I don't in any way mean to argue the contrary. But I think we need to be wary of talking as though theory can solve problems in teaching, when at best it can only rephrase or clarify them. And so my aim in this chapter has not been to show how the teaching of writing can be improved through taking on a particular theoretical stance, but to suggest how an ongoing debate about the nature of the self in writing has been reflected in and revised by various approaches to classroom work. Once again, then, I have no story of progress to tell, no account of a shift from a naive to a theorized practice, but instead have only a set of competing theories of voice and writing to offer, a series of choices I believe individual teachers and students must still face for themselves.

For instance, in reading over an early draft of this chapter, I noticed that I had, without much thinking about it, placed quotation marks around the term *real* almost every time I had used it, so that real voice always figured in my text as "real" voice and real self as "real" self. I decided in revising to get rid of such scare quotes, both because they struck me as condescending and because I felt they let me off the hook too easily, that I was using them to imply something I needed to argue for. But I mention them now because I think that in a way the crucial question here is whether you want to put quotes around a term like *real* or not. As I've argued at a number of points already, a driving impulse behind much work in English has long been the belief that the study of literature and writing offers us a chance to regain some of that sense of wholeness and individuality that otherwise seems to come under such repeated assault by the rest of our culture. And it's easy enough to see how talk about the self as the intersection of various cultural fragments and discourses might pale beside such a belief. If you think you have something like a real self and you want to use language to get at it as fully as you can, then becoming immersed in the intricacies of an academic or critical discourse may seem at best a distraction from (and more likely an obstacle to) doing so. You'd be more likely instead to want to say what you really think and feel in a kind of nonspecialized common language. This is what I think Peter Elbow is trying to get at when he says he is

> particularly concerned that we help students learn to write language that conveys to others a sense of their experience—or indeed, that mirrors back

to themselves a sense of their own experiences from a little distance, once it's out there on paper. I'm thinking about autobiographical stories, moments, sketches—perhaps even a piece of fiction or poetry now and again. (1991, 136–37)

But if you think of the "self" as something formed (in large part) through the pressures of various social discourses and institutions, you'd be more likely to agree with David Bartholomae when he argues,

> I think it is wrong to teach late-adolescents that writing is an expression of individual thoughts and feelings. It makes them suckers and, I think, it makes them powerless, at least to the degree that it makes them blind to tradition, power and authority as they are present in language and culture. (1990, 129)

These contrasting views of what ought to go on in a writing classroom stem from deep and conflicting intuitions about how language and the self are related. I don't think there is a way of disproving one or the other, any more than there is a way of proving or disproving the existence of God. But I don't think they can be easily reconciled either, for much the same reason. The differences go too far down. They involve founding insights, beliefs, axioms, precisely what neither side wants or is able to question.

But these two views also hold much in common—most importantly, a sense that the *subject* of composition is not only writing but the person who writes, that in changing how they use language students can also change their sense of who they are. There lies both the excitement and danger of such teaching. In "Judging Writing, Judging Selves" (1989), Lester Faigley argues that how you interpret a text will always have something to do with the person you sense in or behind its phrasings, that the one cannot be separated from the other. This hints at a reason for the almost obsessive concern of many teachers and theorists in the 1970s with the writing *process*, since a focus on *how* students went about writing offered them, among other things, a way of sidestepping many of the moral and political problems involved with actually reading and responding to *what* got said in their papers. Much as some teachers may have once avoided dealing with what their students had to say by turning the reading of their texts into a grueling hunt for errors and solecisms, so too a preoccupation with prewriting heuristics and revising strategies can serve as a way of deferring talk about what makes writing good and who gets to decide. In the next chapter I argue that in once again diverting attention away from what students might have to say and onto their *behaviors* while writing instead, the process movement actually helped contain many of the political challenges raised by attempts to take student work seriously. For now, though, I simply want to say that what I most admire about both the expressivists and the Amherst school is their continued willingness to take on, in their varied ways, the tangled relationship between the self of a writer and her text.

And tangled it is. To show why let me return with different emphasis to the sentence I quoted earlier from Mara Holt: "But *Peter wants from me* in my letter to you the kind of thing I wrote in my letter to him" (1990, 48; emphasis added). Is this what the teacher wants from me? Have I expressed (or forged) the sort of personal authentic self I was supposed to? Physical exams, court appearances, confessions, parole board hearings, loan applications, revival meetings, Maoist self-criticism groups. Where else but these and the writing classroom are people asked to reveal the whole unflinching truth about themselves to a figure of authority? It should come as no surprise that such situations don't always feel empowering, even when you've been told that it's all being done for your own good.

"You're not just telling us what we wanna hear, are you, boy?" says the warden to the convict in *Raising Arizona*, "Cause we don't wanna hear that." For the missionary, the problem is figuring out whether the natives really believe their prayers or are just mouthing the words. Or as Hashimoto says of his exchange with the Jew-, wimp-, nerd-, and queer-hating Gump: "How in the world could I respond spiritually if I didn't even know what was going on in his twisted demented head?" (1986, 15). For the natives, the problem is finding the right words to convince the missionary that they really do believe what they're saying—whether they do or not. The demand is thus not simply to be sincere or honest, but to compose a self that seems somehow both authentic and appropriate to the occasion.

Stephen Carr (1990) has traced the workings of this double bind back as far as the first English novel believed to be written expressly for children: Sarah Fielding's 1749 *The Governess, or The Female Academy*. Fielding's novel is about life in a small boarding school for girls (run by a Mrs. Teachum) and was probably also meant for use in teaching itself. It begins with a squabble among the girls over some apples. To put a stop to their ill feelings, the eldest among the girls, Jenny Peace (a pedagogical surrogate for Mrs. Teachum, who is never seen throughout the novel), suggests that they read a set of fairy tales together and share their responses to them. Each of these tales is thus followed in the novel by a personal story from one of the girls that in some way applies the moral of the tale to her own experiences. In this way, the girls simultaneously learn a little about each other and the proper responses to what they are reading. By the end of the novel harmony has been restored among them.

In many ways *The Governess* offers a sophisticated and appealing model for teaching reading and writing. (In fact, it bears a striking similarity to William Coles's 1988 *Seeing through Writing*, also a novel meant for teaching use that follows the work of students in response to the assignments of an unseen instructor.) But its setting and method are just unfamiliar enough to begin to problematize what otherwise might seem routine. For what the girls in the novel do *not* realize is that Jenny Peace has been reporting their stories to Mrs. Teachum. (Jenny's reports form the text of the novel.) And so what each of the girls has to say serves a number of purposes: to offer a reading of a story, to share and interpret their own experiences, to create a sense of goodwill among themselves, *and* to certify to their teacher that they are making proper progress as she judges it. Their stories serve at once as a means of self-discovery and a form of surveillance or control. The girls are thus subjects in both the common and Althusserian sense of the term—that is, they are shown both as individuals who act and speak as they wish, and as persons whose actions and desires have been molded or "subjected" to the demands of an authority.

I can't imagine how one might teach writing without in some way addressing this tension between freedom and constraint. *Voice* has been used as a key term in describing both sides of this tension—in naming both what is thought to belong uniquely to a writer as well as those cultural discourses that are seen as speaking through her words or text. But there remains a curious gap between these two conceptions. For while writers are often pictured as either trying to express the voices they have inside them or as trying to enter into or appropriate a certain way of speaking that lies outside them, they seem rarely to be imagined as responding to other actual and specific persons. That is, voice tends to be conceived as either a personal attribute of the writer or as a kind of totalizing discourse that she must submit to. There is little in between. This has led theorists as different as Don Bialostosky (1991) and Martin Nystrand (1990) to argue for reimagining voices as embodied not only in discourses but in other people too. For whereas it is one thing to be familiar with the gestures and commonplaces involved in writing a critical essay, it is quite another to know how to deal with the ideas and phrasings of a particular critic—or even to know which critics one most needs to respond to. And while students do need to invent the university, in the sense of entering into a new sort of discourse, they can only learn to do so through responding to the voices of individual teachers, texts, and assignments. Similarly, although it may seem impossible to alter an entire way of speaking, to transform a discourse, it is easier to imagine affecting the shape and tone of a particular argument, changing the minds of specific persons.

The point is not to reduce the complexities of writing to a sorting out of personal influences and politics, but to suggest that writers deal not only with codes but people, not only with genres but situations. The culture does speak to us, and perhaps even through us, but its discourses and commonplaces are heard through and inflected by the voices of individuals. This argues for the power of inviting students of writing to see themselves not simply as taking on a set of discursive strategies or conventions, as entering into a kind of abstract discourse, but also as responding to what other real people—writers, teachers, classmates— have had to say to them, as building on the projects of some individuals and arguing against those of others. At the same time, it still seems to me crucial that we recognize certain ways of speaking which cannot be located in individuals, but belong, as it were, to the culture as a whole or to certain discourses within it: what a student or teacher can say, what a man or a woman can say, what a literary critic or a composition theorist can say. All these and many more roles are determined by habits, traditions, and expectations that go well beyond the power of any individual to change or transform. It is for me precisely in that tension between the issue or argument at hand and the ways we have of arguing—between the voice of an individual and the demands of the discourse of which she is part—that much of the interest of teaching writing lies.

POSTSCRIPT, 2012: INTENSIVE ACADEMIC WRITING

I was surprised in rereading this chapter to discover that I don't discuss the famous debate on voice and academic writing between Peter Elbow and David Bartholomae. This exchange took place at meetings of CCCC in 1989 and 1991, and was documented a few years later in *CCC*—see Elbow (1995) and Bartholomae (1995). I no longer recall why I decided not to comment on this argument. Perhaps I felt it had already been analyzed to death. (You can now even buy Elbow vs. Bartholomae term papers online.) But still there are few quicker or surer ways to locate yourself in our field than to define your stance on the issues raised in this debate. Do you picture students as writers or academics? Do you ask them to write about their lives and experiences, or about texts and ideas? Do you assign them personal essays or critical papers?

Of course, the actual positions taken by both Elbow and Bartholomae are far more nuanced. Elbow is, after all, a critical essayist who has spent much of his career dissecting the views of other academics, while Bartholomae is an accomplished stylist whose prose is often more evocative than precise. (What does it mean, exactly, to "invent the university"?) So the one does not simply stand for freedom and the other for convention. Still, their positions in this exchange resonate powerfully with choices writing teachers need to make. Elbow wants students to form their own voices; Bartholomae wants students to reflect on the voices that form them. Do you teach writing as a means to express the self or as a way to enter the academy?

J. Brian Schwartz suggests that such questions echo the ways our culture already tends to think about writing and writers. In a 2007 essay on "Fear of Narrative," Schwartz looks at how writing teachers are portrayed in two short stories—"Cats and Students, Bubbles and Abysses," by Rick Bass (1988), and "Fenstad's Mother" by Charles Baxter (1989). The story by Bass centers on a young macho teacher of fiction writing who believes fervently that writers need to have a story of their own and to tell it straight and true. Schwartz jokingly calls him "Elbow Unbound" (431). Baxter's story tells of a smart but ineffectual teacher who wants to help his underprepared students learn the conventions of academic writing but is unable to connect to their interests and concerns. Schwartz labels him "Beyond Bartholomae" (431).

I need to be careful here. Schwartz is *not* saying that either of these fictional teachers accurately represents the views of Elbow or Bartholomae. He instead presents them as types, stock figures. There is the writing teacher as artist, rebel, truth seeker. And then there is the writing teacher as schoolmaster, the person who knows all the rules and conventions. Schwartz suggests that these two stock figures—the poet and the professor—are already part of how our culture understands who writing teachers are and what they do. It thus becomes easy to cast Elbow and Bartholomae in those preset roles, to read the one as a romantic iconoclast and the other as a learned guide.

To move past this impasse we need to shift the terms of argument. A 2008 essay by John Guillory, "How Scholars Read," might offer us one way to do so. Drawing on work by several historians of the book, Guillory distinguishes between *extensive* and *intensive* modes of reading, mapping these two modalities on the "axis of speed" (11). Extensive reading is quick—either for the purposes of pleasure (as in reading a "page turner") or to meet the demands of research. Intensive reading is slower, closer, exegetical—the style of reading we think of as quintessentially academic. Except, as Guillory notes, no working academic could afford to read intensively all or even most of the time—there are always simply too many books and articles to get through. To keep up, academics thus need to learn how to scan, to absorb as much as they can as quickly as they can while still remaining alert to signals to slow down, to read certain texts, or sections of texts, more slowly. They must learn, that is, how to alternate between extensive and intensive modes of reading.

Guillory suspects that this demand to read both widely and deeply promotes the writing of texts that "beg to be skimmed" (2008, 14). It's crucial to note, though, that Guillory is referring here to texts that are written not badly but efficiently. Extensive reading prizes texts that are clear, concise, and well organized—in brief, that allow for smooth processing. Small wonder that these have also been the values of generations of writing teachers, who must week by week read and respond to a quantity of student texts that would daunt the most assiduous of scholars. And so the working conditions of both scholarship and teaching lead to a valuing of prose that, as Guillory puts it, can be read "gratefully, but quickly" (9).

But neither Elbow nor Bartholomae participates in this ethos of clarity and efficiency. Instead, each argues for a version of what, following Guillory, I'll call *intensive academic writing*. By this I mean the writing of texts that ask to be read slowly, that resist easy summary, that draw attention not only to their content but also to their language and construction. Certainly Elbow and Bartholomae disagree about what such texts ought to look like. Elbow calls for experience-rich writing, Bartholomae for reflective and critical prose. But both their views stand in sharp contrast against those of an academic culture that, for the most part, prizes extensive writing—that thrives on speed, clarity, and efficiency.

I think that recognizing this gap between intensive and extensive views of writing can help us better understand the debates over error I discuss in chapter 4 of this book. In that chapter, I quote from an interview with the philosopher Richard Rorty in which he opines that the main task of a writing course should be "just to get [students] to write complete sentences, get the commas in the right places, and stuff like that" (Olson 1989, 85). When our colleagues in other fields talk in similar ways about grammar and correctness, I suspect what they're telling us is that they have little interest in considering the performative aspects of student writing, they just want to get to the content. And I can understand where they are coming from. For most academics, student texts are simply things to be gotten through—marked, graded, corrected, the quicker the better. Our colleagues thus assume that our job must be to teach students to produce the kinds of texts that will make the onerous task of grading a little easier—that we will help students learn how to write clear, brief, extensive prose. From their perspective, then, an interest in encouraging students to create more intensive, writerly texts must seem, at best, somewhat beside the point.

I don't claim here to have reconciled Elbow and Bartholomae. The differences between them run deep. But I do think that to take either side in their debate is to commit yourself to explaining to others outside our field why undergraduates should be required, in the first place, to take a course in *intensive* academic writing (rather than one simply training them to produce clear, extensive prose). To some degree, this seems to join both camps in an argument for a different sort of attention to student writing *as writing*.

I'm not sure, though, that this sort of broader argument for the value and interest of student writing has often been made. The closest thing I know to it is the 2000 WPA Outcomes Statement for First-year Composition. But the tone of this statement—with its talk of outcomes, processes, skills, and knowledges—is far more instrumentalist than either Elbow or Bartholomae. Indeed, its opening list of admonitions— "Focus on a purpose," "Respond to the needs of different audiences," and so on—seem to describe a course geared toward having students produce extensive prose. The WPA Outcomes Statement doesn't rule out first-year courses centering on either personal or critical writing, but it doesn't make a case for such work either. A volatile argument *within* the field over personal and academic writing thus gets erased in a bland attempt to speak *for* the field.

But I think what we're all about is teaching intensive academic writing— writing that repays a second reading. And I think we can argue convincingly for such work in the terms offered by either Elbow or Bartholomae.

Indeed, in my own teaching I draw on both sets of terms. I set up my first-year courses as introductions to academic writing very much along the lines suggested by Bartholomae, and I also teach courses in creative nonfiction that take up the concerns about voice and expression raised by Elbow. But I don't think either sort of course is well described by the bureaucratic descriptions of "rhetorical knowledge" or "knowledge of conventions" in the WPA Outcomes Statement. We need to find better ways of talking to colleagues outside our field about why we want students to produce not just efficient prose but thoughtful and reflective writing.

We also need to hold our own writing to higher standards. One of Guillory's complaints is that we have fallen into a habit of writing more to be cited than to be read (2008). As evidence, he calls on a 2008 paper by the sociologist Andrew Abbott, who claims that while the number of average citations per academic article has risen fivefold since the 1950s, the percentage of citations that refer to *specific pages* has gone down (Guillory 16, Abbott 8). In other words, we're citing more but quoting less—which Abbott interprets as a sign of a "substantial decline in the seriousness with which scholars are reading each other's work" (9). While I'd like to avoid the cantankerousness of their tone, I have to say I think Guillory and Abbott are on to something. Too many references in our books and articles are of the "see also" type, or are simply lists of names in parentheses tacked to the ends of sentences. While I understand the pressure to be comprehensive, I think we have to become more willing to slow down, to become more selective in the works we cite, and to engage with those works more fully.

I'm not arguing here for fine writing so much as close reading. Rather than approaching books and articles in our field as artifacts to be mined for data or ideas, we need to read them as we would a piece of student writing—that is, as a text whose form contributes to its meanings. Some of the best work in our field calls for this sort of intensive reading through its experimentation with genres, voices, and formats—pieces like Ellen Cushman's "Rhetorician as Agent of Social Change" (1996), Richard Miller's "The Nervous System" (1998), or Michael Spooner and Kathleen Yancey's "Postings on a Genre of Email" (1996). And there is a distinguished line of scholars of color in our field who have skillfully switched codes and registers to drive home their points about race and writing—from Geneva Smitherman in *Talkin and Testifyin* (1977), to Keith Gilyard in *Voices of the Self* (1991), Victor Villanueva in *Bootstraps* (1993), and Adam Banks in *Digital Griots* (2011).

But scholarship can take more conventional forms and still repay a close and intensive reading. I think, for example, of the meticulousness with which Bruce Horner unpacks the possible meanings of terms like *work* and *tradition* in *Terms of Work for Composition* (2000). Or of the close and sympathetic regard Richard Haswell offers both student writers and fellow scholars in *Gaining Ground in College Writing* (1991). These are books that look closely at the languages of their subjects and, in doing so, ask us to attend with similar care to their own phrasings.

My aim here is not to create some sort of personal best-of list, but rather to point toward the kind of writing that, as a field, we want to stand for, practice, and teach. *Intensive academic writing* is an inelegant and clumsy phrase. But perhaps its strangeness can help us push past the deadlock of the Elbow-Bartholomae debate. Intensive academic writing does not have to be personal or experimental, although it can be. Nor does it have to adhere to the conventions of a particular discipline, although it might. But it does need to do something more than efficiently deliver information. That something more—however each of us may define it—must drive our work as writers and teachers.

not tell Heather what she thinks her point about writing is or should be. She gives no specific directions for how Heather might recast her paper. But she does speak as though she thinks Heather can write such a new paper, that she has not just a story to tell but a point to make. That is, her comments call for a *response* from Heather and not simply for a set of corrections or additions to her text. And this is what Heather wrote in reply:

I feel very strong about the way I write, whether it be an essay, a letter, or a news story. Whatever I write on that piece of paper you know it's me. My news articles are the equivalent to my picture or my signature. My writing is my identity. When I give someone my article to read I get a feeling of anticipation, because I want to hear what they have to say about it. Whatever they say, good or bad, will affect me deeply. That's how important writing is to me.

As they read my work, I watch their eyes go from line to line. I watch their facial expressions and try to read if they are good or bad. Sometimes the anticipation is so great I have to leave the room. While I am outside in the hall, I ponder about what is going through their heads and I can honestly say I have no idea. It drives me crazy! The minutes it takes them to read it seems like hours. Though after my readers give me their opinions I get a flow of relief that rushes through my body.

I take my readers opinion very seriously and very personal. Which probably is a bad trait to a certain extent. For example, when I got on the front page of my school newspaper I would hear what my readers would say about my work. There were people who really liked it, which made me feel like I did a great job; but then there were also people who didn't like it and their opinions went through my heart like a cold steel stake. They were criticizing my work, which to me was just as bad as criticizing me. True, sometimes my writing can be wild and unruly, but it still hurt. I decided that this was a problem that I had to correct. I started by trying to look at my readers not as critics, but as uninformed people who just wanted to read my work. I began to feel more relaxed and I was able to stay in the room while they read it. It was hard to correct, but this class has helped me a lot, too. By us discussing other people's papers I found out that everyone makes mistakes. I think I can now hear what my readers have to say and not feel that they are against me, but for me and also for my writing.

A story in Rose's book that I think sort of parallels to my story is the story of when he made the kids, who needed help in their reading and writing, look at pictures and write about them. Then he typed them out and put them on the cafeteria wall (page 96, Rose). Now I am sure that these kids were a little scared at what the other kids would say about their writing since they were thought of as the "stupid" ones. It reveals on page 96 that they were not ashamed of their work. Rose said, "The real kick came when I walked through the cafeteria a few days after our lesson and saw two of my kids showing their poster essay to a third child who was not in the group." God, I would be terrified if my work was on the cafeteria wall. I would be trying to listen to every conversation to hear what all my readers thought about my work. That is one thing these kids have over this college student, they can handle other people reading their work. To sum up this paper, the obstacle that I had to overcome was the relationship between my reader and me. And I did.

Although this draft is in some ways less polished than the first, it interests me far more. The success story has turned into an essay on the relations between a writer and her readers. The narrative that makes up the whole of her first draft now serves as an example of a larger point Heather wants to make about the intensity of her feelings about her writing and the problems this causes for her when it is read. Note how paragraph four now begins: "*For example*, when I got on the front page of my school newspaper . . ." And notice, too, how while in her first draft Heather said her writing "*was* wild and unruly" at the start of the term, she is now willing to admit, "True, sometimes my writing *can be* wild and unruly." And so although she still tells a success story of sorts, it is no longer as clear cut or simple as before.

But what I most like here is how Heather has changed the use she makes of Rose. Now she draws on him not merely to support but to complicate what she has to say. Rather than simply suggest, as she did in her first draft, that she and Rose have had similar experiences with writing, Heather now imagines herself as part of a scene he has described and shows how it would be different for her: "God, I would be terrified if my work was on the cafeteria wall. I would be trying to listen to every conversation to hear what all my readers thought about my work." And so, even though Heather insists at the end of this draft that she has "overcome . . . the relationship between my reader and me," she leaves us with a new view of the cafeteria scene—which is that the relations between writers and their readers might sometimes be far more complex and anxious than Rose suggests. Heather has moved here from the ventriloquizing of her first draft to a much more critical use of quotation. Through this contrast between her own anxiety and the easy pride of the kids Rose talks about, she achieves a kind of distance and control over both her and his stories, which means she now has something to say about each.

I like the person that emerges in this piece. I like the quiet defiance of her first paragraph, in which she repeats in several different ways how much she identifies with her writing—and which I read as implying, at least in part, that she was indeed stung by Rashmi's response to her first draft. But I also admire how she used those remarks to revise her work in intelligent and independent ways, much as I admire Rashmi for saying what needed to be said. One of the things I often tell students is that you want to *do* something with a passage you quote, to talk back to it somehow—that you don't want simply to let someone else speak in your place. What I think we see here is a writer beginning to form her own voice through such an active and critical use of quotation.

3
PROCESS

All men can not be consider equal in America base on financial situations. Because their are men born in rich families that will never have to
worry about any financial difficulties. And then there are another type of
Americans that are born to a poor family. And this is the type of Americans
that may always have some kind of financial difficulty. Especially today in New
York, The way the city has fallen into fin-debt. It has become such a big crisis
for the working people, in the If the working man is able to find a job, especially a city The way city fin-sition is set up now, He'll probably lose the job
a whole lot faster than what he got it. When he loses his job he'll have even
more fin-difficulty. And then he'll be force to go to the city for some fini-assi.
So right here you can see that all men in America are not created equal in
the fin-sense. (Perl 1979, 336)

This brief, strained, and, I think, quite moving text was written almost
twenty years ago by "Tony," a young ex-Marine from the Bronx with a
wife and child, who was at the time a student in a New York City community college—and the key subject in Sondra Perl's influential 1979
study of "The Composing Processes of Unskilled College Writers." Tony
was given about ninety minutes to plan, draft, and edit an essay in an
"extensive" (that is, roughly, expository) mode on the topic of "Society
& Culture," which Perl notes was drawn from a sociology class he was
then taking. Tony was observed by Perl as he wrote. He was also asked
to "compose aloud"—that is, to read out his text (and any changes he
made to it) as he drafted it. His "writing performance," as Perl puts it—
when he planned, wrote, paused, crossed out or added words, worried
over spellings, and the like—was thus made available for detailed tran-
scription and analysis, along with the actual text he wrote.

Perl of course was studying Tony, not teaching him. And, as a
researcher, she was more interested in *how* he went about writing than
in what he had to say as a writer. Even her transcriptions of his texts are
coded in an attempt to show how they were physically composed. (Her
version of Tony's text, for instance, includes even those words he crossed

out.) Her article was published in *Research in the Teaching of English* (*RTE*), a journal that publishes work that often aspires to the status of social science, and her own stance as a writer, for the most part, is that of a detached observer. But not quite always. For Perl, like many other writers in *RTE*, also wants to argue that her research has certain "implications" for teaching—and so the language of advocacy creeps into her article as well.

> The conclusion here is not that Tony can't write, or that Tony doesn't know how to write, or that Tony needs to learn more rules: Tony is a writer with a highly consistent and deeply embedded recursive process. What he needs are teachers who can interpret that process for him, who can see through the tangles in his process just as he sees meaning beneath the tangles in his prose, and who can intervene in such a way that untangling his composing process leads him to create better prose. (328)

I don't agree with the teaching practice Perl suggests here, and I will say why shortly. But what I want to point to first is how Perl uses the notion of *process* to make powerful moves in two directions at the same time. For on the one hand, her focus on Tony's behaviors while composing allows her to claim standing as a social scientist who is observing and defining a certain "highly consistent and deeply embedded recursive process." But on the other hand, this idea of a composing process that can be "interpreted" and "untangled" by qualified teachers quickly becomes the key term in a classroom practice that promises to rescue students from the condescension of others who believe they can't really be taught to write. And here it hardly seems coincidental that Perl had chosen to study much the same sort of students that Mina Shaughnessy had written so powerfully about just two years before in her 1977 *Errors and Expectations*, residents of "one of New York's racial or ethnic enclaves" who were now aspiring to a level of education that had long been closed to most members of their race or class (3). Much as the idea of *process* gave compositionists like Perl hope for a new and more respected place among university researchers, it also promised their students a way of entering at last into the languages of the academy. The process movement thus seemed to offer both students and teachers of writing a kind of power they had lacked before.

The story of how a growing interest in the composing process galvanized a new research agenda for composition scholars in the 1970s and 1980s has been told and retold many times by now—perhaps most famously by Maxine Hairston, who in a 1982 article, "The Winds of Change," argued that the ways we thought about writing and its teaching had by then undergone a nearly total "paradigm shift." Such narratives of transformation sparked an almost immediate series of critical responses—most arguing it was by no means clear what the new paradigm for composition was, since various teachers and researchers invoked the notion of process in strikingly different ways. Both Lester Faigley (1986) and Patricia Bizzell (1986a), for instance, identified three main strains of process thinking (expressive, cognitive, and social); James Berlin (1982) counted four (classicist, positivist, expressionist, and new rhetorical).[1] What such counterstatements shared with the narratives they were responding to, though, was both an implicit sense of progress (the last category of process he or she defined always turned out to be the one the writer wanted to argue for) and a certain level of abstraction. That is, while almost everyone involved in the process debate invoked the centrality of teaching to work in composition, very few offered sustained analyses of classroom scenes, student writings, or even textbooks. (Paul Kameen's 1980 "Rewording the Rhetoric of Composition," a close reading of the metaphors underlying several influential textbooks in the field, was a striking exception.) Instead they tended to respond to views of the writing process suggested in the research of fellow scholars. And so, as the field of composition grew more "disciplined," the arguments in its journals came to be less about teaching than about research or theory—even as they testified to the value of classroom work. Perhaps this had something to do with how an attention to "process" (of whatever sort) had quickly become the marker of an informed or progressive stance toward teaching writing. For all the dispute over which theories best described the composing process, so far as teaching went there were really only "process people" and "current-traditionalists," and no one wanted to be counted among the latter—or at least this is how it seemed to me when I entered the profession in the early 1980s, and it was certainly the view of the field offered by Maxine Hairston when, as chair of CCCC in 1985, she called on compositionists to "break their bonds" with literary studies and to "reaffirm their connections" with one another as teachers and scholars of writing.

---

1. The very titles of these three influential articles dramatize a shift in the 1980s toward historical and metacritical work in composition, as all of them announce the field itself as their subject of study: Faigley's "Competing Theories of Process: A Critique and Proposal" (1986), Bizzell's "Composing Processes: An Overview" (1986a), and Berlin's "Contemporary Composition: The Major Pedagogical Theories" (1982).

But I don't want to become entangled in the intricacies of the arguments over process theory, and thus to prolong what seems to me an increasingly tiresome professional debate. My aim here instead is to try to get at what it might have meant to *teach* writing as process, not product. For while it seems clear that the process movement helped establish composition as a research field, it has never transformed the actual teaching of writing as dramatically as advocates have claimed. For instance, in trying to explain why Tony and her other subjects have such difficulties with composing, Sondra Perl argues that they "wrote from an egocentric point of view" which "took the reader's understanding for granted" (1979, 332). From her perspective, then, the goal of teaching is to guide students out of such egocentrism through "untangling" their composing processes in ways that will allow them to state what they mean more clearly and persuasively. And yet Perl seems to pay very little attention to what her subjects actually have to say. My reading of Tony's text, for instance, shows him as quite clearly worried that his reader will not understand or agree with his claim (with its troubling echo of the Declaration) that "all men in America are not create equal in the fin-sense." Note how he spends so much of his short text trying first to state and then to refute the possible objection that the poor man could even up the odds by getting a job (no good, since given the "way city fin-sition is set up now, he'll probably lose the job a whole lot faster than what he got it"). Even the persistent concern that Tony shows for spelling (where most of those crossouts that Perl includes in her version of his text come from) suggests not a lack of reader awareness but an overriding anxiety about how his text will be judged by others, a disabling hypercorrectness that it is easy to imagine as stemming from the internalizing of a reader who is more interested in surface form than meaning. And the irony is that he is right; for all her sympathy for Tony, even Perl is still more interested in counting miscues and crossouts than in responding to what he has to say.

This is not to downplay the problems Tony has as a writer. They are clearly many and significant. But I think it is misleading to see them as stemming from some sort of egocentrism, from an inability to understand the likely concerns or doubts of his readers. I would instead argue that Tony is trying to say something (there's more to getting ahead than just working hard) that often doesn't go over very well in school. What he needs, it seems to me, is not a teacher who can "untangle his composing process," as Perl suggests, but someone who is willing to take his ideas and phrasings seriously, to work with him on ways of testing and elabo-rating his thoughts in writing—a reader rather than a composing coach. The problem with the older current-traditional approach to teaching writing, as has been argued over and over, was its relentless focus on the surface correctness of student texts, so that writing was reduced to an empty tinkering with verbal forms.[2] But the advocates of process did not redirect attention to what students had to say so much as they sim-ply argued for what seems to me a new sort of formalism—one centered no longer on textual structures but instead on various algorithms, heu-ristics, and guidelines for composing. This new formalism has proven little different from the old, as those versions of process teaching that don't work toward a very familiar set of therapeutic and expressionist goals instead work toward an equally familiar set of technocratic ones. Both versions tend to move backward, as it were, from an ideal vision of the composition student: either the mature individual of one kind of humanist teaching or the expert practitioner of another more technical sort. The aim of teaching thus becomes to coach students toward either an emotional and intellectual maturity or an expert-level performance. What gets lost in this concern for development toward a known ideal are the actual concerns and perspectives students bring with them to their writing. In the rest of this chapter I try to show how this loss happens through looking closely at the work of two of the scholars most associ-ated with the process movement: Janet Emig and Linda Flower.

Before I do so, though, I want to allay suspicions that I am some sort of composition equivalent of a flat-earther. There is no question that it is useful for students to learn to distinguish among the activities of draft-ing, revising, and editing texts, as well as to understand that texts are not always written all at once, or from an outline, or from start to finish without blotting a line. But I don't think that such insights began with the 1970s process movement—that infamous New Critic, John Crowe Ransom, for instance, wrote a textbook in 1935, *Topics for Freshman Writing*, that focuses extensively on revision—and I also don't think it takes very long to foster an awareness of writing as a technology that in many ways differs from speech. That is, it seems to me that a teacher can fairly quickly explain the various aspects of composing, schedule plenty of time in the semester for students to revise and edit their work

---

2. John Mayher offers both a compelling critique of current-traditional methods and an engaging argument for process teaching in his 1990 *Uncommon Sense*, a book that use-fully sums up progressive approaches to teaching English through the 1970s and 1980s.

thoughtfully, and then get on with the main business of the course: to help students articulate, extend, and perhaps rework the positions they take up in their writings. So my criticisms in this chapter are not aimed against the proposition that writing is a process—which, again, strikes me as a claim that is true, banal, and of a real if limited use—but against a view of teaching that places some vision of the composing process (rather than an interest in the work of students) at the center of a course in writing.

Janet Emig's 1971 NCTE monograph, *The Composing Processes of Twelfth Graders,* was the first sustained observational study of how writers go about producing texts.[3] Before her study, as Emig is quick to note, descriptions of the writing process had been inferred from the memoirs of and interviews with well-known authors, from early drafts of published works, from theories of creativity (themselves often based on little more than introspection or intuition), and from the prescriptions of rhetorics and handbooks—but rarely had they been drawn from the notes of someone who had sat and watched other people as they wrote and asked them about what they were doing (7–28). That is what Emig set out to do. In the summer of 1967 she met four times apiece with eight students who would soon be entering their senior year of high school. In their first two meetings, Emig asked these subjects to draft a short text while "composing aloud"—that is, while vocalizing as much of what they were thinking about while they were writing as they possibly could. For their third meeting, Emig asked them to bring any writings they had saved since childhood and to draw on these materials in discussing with her their "writing autobiographies." For their last meeting, Emig asked her subjects to write a brief "imaginative" piece beforehand, to bring all drafts of this piece with them, and to talk about how they went about composing it with her (29–31). Although Emig fails to say why she did not ask her subjects to compose this last piece aloud, as they did all their other writings for her study, my guess is that it had to do with her strong valuing of "reflexive" or poetic writing over other types of discourse—about which I will soon have more to say.

But if few people had been much interested in documenting the composing process before Emig, many were after her. The technique of "composing aloud" proved of immediate and practical use to an entire generation of compositionists—including Donald Graves, Sharon Pianko,

---

3. Emig's study began as a 1969 dissertation at the Harvard School of Education, supervised by Priscilla Tyler, herself a former chair of CCCC.

Sondra Perl, Nancy Sommers, Carol Berkenotter, and Linda Flower and John Hayes.[4] This no doubt had to do with its flexibility as a research tool: studies soon came out that looked at writers of differing ages and abilities, or that placed subjects in altered circumstances, or that gave them varying tasks to complete—and to some degree these all offered varying accounts of the composing process, and thus gave both their authors and the new field of composition studies an increasing claim to its own brand of knowledge and expertise. The format of the case study also directed attention to the writing behaviors of individuals, with a resulting emphasis on the value of seemingly idiosyncratic detail and the thick description of experience that must have felt congenial to many people working in English (and in education in general). And, finally, an interest in process could be readily aligned with the attempts of many in English since Dartmouth to shift attention to the experiences and perspectives of students. For instance, when Donald Murray spoke in 1972 of "teaching writing as process not product," a phrasing that was quickly to gain the status (and perhaps nearly the meaninglessness) of a mantra, the first three implications he listed as following from this shift in stance had to do with a renewed focus on the student's "own writing," "own subject" (or "own truth"), and "own language" (91). It is in this highly charged and somewhat contradictory context—a new field trying to legitimate itself in the academy, a set of reformers trying to change the schools—that Emig's work takes on such importance and interest, since she was at once committed as a teacher to the therapeutic value of writing as a mode of self-expression and as a researcher to the need to study the means (or process) of that self-expression with a scientific detachment and rigor.

The terms that Emig herself used to mark this tension between expression and science were *reflexive* and *extensive*, yet another rephrasing of the distinction between literary and nonliterary discourse that has structured

---

4. Almost all the classic process studies saw print between 1975 and 1983: Graves in 1975 on young writers; Perl in 1979 on unskilled writers; Pianko in 1979 on reflection; Sommers in 1980 on revision; Flower in 1981 on writer-based prose; Berkenotter and Murray in 1983 on professional writers. These studies were also often among the first major research articles published by their authors, many of whom have since gone on to become eminent figures in the field. In a very real way, then, the process movement helped composition come of age as a research discipline, a moment of transition that can be traced in the programs for the annual meetings of CCCC in the early 1980s that featured young scholars like Linda Flower, Ellen Nold, Sondra Perl, and Nancy Sommers speaking together in ballroom sessions on topics like "Research in the Composing Process" (1980) and "Research on Composing: From Theory to Practice" (1981).

work in English since its very beginnings. The distinction Emig drew between these two uses of language was almost identical to that made by James Britton in his discussion of the poetic and transactional functions: *reflexive* writing is personal, imaginative, and artistic; *extensive* writing carries out the business of the world, gets things done. Emig was perhaps even more insistent than Britton that reflexive writing must have a personal and "contemplative" quality; it was the insights that such writing could offer into the self that she most valued (1971, 36–37). Like Britton, too, Emig was convinced that schools should make more room for self-sponsored and self-expressive forms of writing, and one of her aims was to show that the experience and value of reflexive writing for students differs in kind from (and is in many ways superior to) that of the other-directed work most often assigned them in school. But since none of her subjects actually *chose* to compose in the reflexive mode, if she did not directly ask them to do so, this belief in the intrinsic worth of reflexive writing remained largely a matter of faith for Emig that, much as in the case of Britton, only seemed to grow more strong for lack of evidence.

Emig has herself rather scrupulously observed the distinction between these two forms of discourse: on one hand, she is a published poet; on the other, much of her scholarly work is stylistically tedious: unornamented, detached (she calls herself "the investigator" throughout *The Composing Processes*), and given over to diagrams and lists in a very deliberate and social-scientistic mode. (Britton veered similarly between the studied impersonality of *The Development of Writing Abilities* and books of poetry and autobiography.) The conception of the ideal writing researcher held by Emig, that is, seems much on the order of Eliot's perfect critic: a writer who restrains his own creative impulses in order to help set up the conditions for poetry to flourish. In this case, the writing researcher (working exclusively in the extensive mode) makes knowledge about the composing process available for teachers to use in encouraging students to write more expressively or reflexively. Science enables art.

In thus defining one sort of discourse (reflexive) as self-sponsored, imaginative, contemplative, and exploratory, and another sort (extensive) as school-sponsored, assignment driven, and geared toward efficiency, Emig seems to leave out the possibility that some kinds of critical and scientific writing may often hold real personal worth for their writers. At various points in *The Composing Processes*, Emig speaks of her disappointment that none of her subjects expressed much "joy or satisfaction" in their work for her. Referring to their composing-aloud protocols, she remarks,

At no time does any of the students ask aloud any variants of the questions: "Is this subject important to me? Do I care about writing about it?" (1971, 89)

Although I find it hard to feel surprise that her subjects—teenagers asked to do some writing for a university research study while a stranger takes notes and asks them about what they're doing—decided to write on topics that seemed fairly impersonal or "easy" (Emig's term), I also think Emig's desire to find moments of intimacy or self-revelation in their work blinded her to much else that seems to have been going on. For instance, Emig interprets the reluctance of two of her (male) subjects to write a poem as a sign that they are "fearful of expressing feelings" (81). Yet she also reports that one of these boys handed in what she labels "a piece of obscenity" and told her, "Here; I doubt if this is what you want but it's what I wanted to write" (81). Is such behavior really evidence of a "fear of feeling" on his part? Or is it instead a fairly open expression of the wrong sort of feelings, of a growing resistance to Emig and her project? Emig does admit that, as a middle-aged woman, "the investigator" may have "reminded the boys too much of all the teachers of comp they have had in high school," but then quickly rejects this explanation in favor of one that argues that they simply believed writing poetry was "unmanly" (82). By thus psychologizing their resistance to her assignment, Emig puts herself in a position where she no longer has to respond to what might have been seen as her subjects' legitimate mistrust of school-sponsored forms of self-expression—that is, of being required to reveal their feelings to a teacher or researcher. And this then means she has no need to explain why she thinks it is indeed a good or manly thing for boys to write poems (of a nonobscene sort) on demand.

In a similar way, in her anxiousness to see her principal subject, Lynn, conquer *her* "fear of feeling" (1971, 71), Emig fails to hear much of what this young woman does in fact value about writing. Emig wants Lynn to view writing much as she herself does—as a complex and sometimes painful yet ultimately self-revealing process. When it becomes clear that Lynn does not see writing this way—she instead views it as a fairly simple task, as a means to an end and not much more—Emig interprets this self-confidence as the sign of repressed neurosis. That this hostile and condescending reading of Lynn's character went for years unremarked in the profession testifies to how effectively Emig used her persona as "the investigator" to firm up a set of literary and expressionist beliefs about writing. Her research, that is, seemed to discover what many teachers of composition and English already believed: the teaching of writing as commonly practiced was "essentially a neurotic activity" that fostered unfeeling and uncommitted students (99). With her emphasis on feeling and introspection, and her frequent recourse to metaphors of machinery to describe the sort of society and schooling she opposed, Emig's language had strong Leavisite colorings beneath its educationalist veneer. Schools were churning out not feeling beings but "unsophisticated computers" who were "so thoroughly programmed to a single species of extensive writing that they can readily and comfortably compose no other" (81–82).

And who were these miseducated and unsophisticated computers? As she describes them, the students Emig worked with actually seem a rather bright and articulate lot, able and willing to provide her with detailed accounts of what they were thinking about while writing. And Lynn, the only one of her subjects whom Emig reports on in detail, and who thus serves for her as a kind of archetypal figure of the student writer, seems in many ways an ideal focus for such a case study—fluent, self-aware, and forthcoming, even when there are strong hints that her dealings with Emig were at times strained. Emig devotes by far the longest chapter of *The Composing Processes* to a detailed account of Lynn. (The single chapter discussing her other seven subjects is less than half as long.) She also appends the full transcripts of Lynn's writing autobiography and second attempt at composing aloud to the end of her study, so that Lynn ends up the focus of most of her monograph.

These transcripts remain among the most interesting and ambiguous glimpses into the composing process that we have yet been given. The picture that emerges of Lynn as a person and writer is a conflicted one. Emig describes her as "very vivacious" (1971, 45), "dutiful and disciplined" (56), and "extremely amiable, efficient, and well-organized" (56)—phrasings of the sort that tend to appear on lukewarm letters of reference, and there are indeed several points in her transcripts where Lynn comes off as a little too clever, too eager, and too unbearably cute. This is a girl, for instance, who after inveighing against "soppy" and "trite" topics (129), chooses herself to write on the reactions of visitors to a two-foot-high cardboard cutout of Snoopy, the dancing dog from Peanuts, that she keeps in her parents' living room, and who then titles this vignette "Terpsichordean Greetings." And so when Emig notes her "sophistication, hovering near cynicism, about teachers and their ways" (45), it is tempting to write Lynn off as a junior version of the sort of character we have grown to know from the stories of Updike and Cheever—someone who already knows how to play the game only too well, but fails to question why she is playing it. Emig makes the most of this cultural subtext. We learn right away that Lynn is Jewish and middle class, the daughter of a lawyer and a high-school teacher, a striver who gets good grades, edits the year-book, and is an officer in a youth organization (45). Indeed, Lynn seems so familiar as a character, a cultural type, that it is a little hard to remember she is not fictional but real.[5] (In doing some rough calculations as I wrote this, I was a little startled to realize that this person whom I think of as the prototype of the adolescent student writer must in actual life now be a woman who is six or seven years older than I am.)

Emig's encounters with Lynn form the heart of her study. In a 1983 interview, Emig speaks of writing an early article, "The Uses of the Unconscious in Composing," as a way "to justify why I find writing such an agony" (1983, 44). In that early article, first published in *CCC* in 1964, Emig distinguishes between two types of writers: "Mozartians" who compose with fairly little effort or anguish, and "Beethovians" who "agonize," "plod," and "lumber" toward what they want to say (1983, 52). While Emig does not openly disparage Mozartians, she identifies her-self as a Beethovian and has some nasty asides in her article about "the human 7090s [another machine metaphor] who fit a lifetime's writing to one program" (49) and the "efficiency expert operating on Western Calvin time" (52). Lynn, on the other hand, is quite clearly a Mozartian. At first, Emig seems to acknowledge the value of such an approach to writing, noting that

> no form of American society requires for success from its members more cognitive and psychic versatility and organization than the American high school. . . . There is no time for mooning or moping or any form of tempera-ment: Writing is a task to be done like any other, and one simply gets on with it. (1971, 56)

---

5. Emig makes an odd and somewhat troubling use of this kind of novelistic detail throughout *The Composing Processes*. For instance, Emig notes Lynn's Jewishness twice on the opening page of the chapter about her and claims that "by far [her] most important extracurricular activity . . . is her work as officer of the Midwest Jewish Institute" (1971, 45), although Lynn never mentions this part of her life in any of the transcripts Emig reproduces. Similarly, Emig makes a point of telling us that the only boy in her study who liked to write poetry and keep a journal was African American— although it also turns out he went to an "experimental lab school" (82). Gradually, perhaps even unconsciously, Emig allows such details of race and class to coalesce into a picture of uptight middle-class white kids whose instincts and feelings have been blunted by their schooling.

But Lynn's "versatility and organization" soon becomes not her strength but her problem ("run, Rabbit, run"). According to Emig, Lynn "marches through Georgia" as a writer, quickly finding a plan for a piece and sticking with it, rather than musing over "a Valeryian 'ligne donee'" (56). For Emig, writing is (should be?) "one of the most complex processes man engages in" (44). For Lynn, it's just a job, although one she does reasonably well. Indeed, Emig's response to Lynn's success at writing is to remark that she "*seems susceptible* to the teaching of composition she has experienced" (73; italics added). She argues that for Lynn "the good student writer is the polite student writer" (72), and suggests that Lynn has been schooled by her teachers into an obsessive concern with the "amenities of writing": spelling, handwriting, titles, and other forms of "technical correctness" and "Madison Avenue" writing concerns (69–73).

In making such claims, Emig leans heavily on a few anecdotes Lynn tells as part of her writing autobiography: about being in the third grade and writing some sentences on the chalkboard for a visitor, only to have that visitor (a school superintendent) criticize her for misspelling a word (1971, 117); about having been penalized in the sixth grade for not writing in the Palmer style (122); and about her high-school teachers' fixation on spelling (121). These are all good examples of the by now quite familiar (at least to process advocates) genre of what-those-damn-teachers-do-to-kids stories—and there seems no question that, for whatever the reason, Lynn is very attentive to matters of decorum in writing. But I'm not sure if this necessarily translates into an *over*-attentiveness to such issues, since Lynn is clearly able to compose fluently and successfully, and Emig herself admits that Lynn also has a sophisticated awareness of and control over nuances of style and phrasing (72–73)—which is surely a positive expression of the same sort of concern with the look and sound of a piece of writing. What I find more troubling, though, is how Emig chooses *not* to remark on a whole other set of stories Lynn tells about her experiences with writing and schooling, stories that consistently show her taking pleasure in a certain kind of intellectual work. For instance, Lynn speaks with pride of crafting "complex" sentences in the fourth grade (104), of a parodic and affectionate essay she wrote in the seventh grade about how a sexy young male teacher "practically jumped" and "banged" on a piano as he played it (110–11), and of collaborating on the script of a play that same year (112). She also talks of how she likes to "write about a specific incident, and use specific facts" rather than "writing fantasy" or other school-sponsored imaginative writings (113), and she points with great precision to her growth in sophistication as a writer. When in writing a piece for her freshman science class she says she

> had to trace the evolution of the organism and I did a whole parallel thing about . . . tracing it along with the embryo and, it was really a very good piece of writing if I could find it I'll bring it in, because, you know, it's, it was the first time I think I ever used a parallel construction, where I actually carried something out in a parallel construction. (113; ellipses in original)

Lynn speaks of a paper comparing Captain Ahab to Machiavelli's Prince as "rather adventurous" (113)—here using the term in quite a different way than perhaps most expressivist teachers would, since the adventurousness she refers to is of an intellectual rather than emotional or experiential sort. She praises a high-school teacher for the length and substance of her commentaries on student writing (121), and suggests that an ideal writing teacher should make students "more aware of styles" (127). Lynn also shows a strong awareness of the differences between proofreading and revision. Here's how she responds to busywork:

> I remember in our freshman year, most of the corrections were technical, and if we had more than three corrections, even if it were three misplaced commas we had to copy the entire them over . . . and, I was looking at some of my friends' copies and second copies, the graded ones and the corrected ones and, there's no difference in the writing. (121)

But that is not her only experience with rewriting:

> I remember starting compositions and then, taking like one paragraph, out of my composition, or one thing I mentioned and then rewriting the entire composition on that one thing. (128)

And, finally, in a comment that mixes flattery with a gentle ribbing of Emig, Lynn also shows that she knows whom she is speaking to, what sort of rhetorical situation she has been placed in:

> It seems all the teachers I had [that] would give us interesting courses were either doing research or working on their Ph.D.'s and I think they're using all our material. (112)

What Lynn does *not* do at any point is speak of writing as a means of expressing feelings or of writing as a complex or agonizing task. This is, I think, what leads Emig to diagnose her as "susceptible" to the influence of "essentially neurotic" teachers. And it is also what reveals the "process" that Emig describes to be in fact a kind of back formation from an ideal *product*. Why should writing be a messy, recursive, nonlinear, anguished, Beethovian kind of activity? Because that is the process that most seems to lead to the sort of self-expressive writing Emig (and countless other English teachers) value above all others. The therapeutic goal of using writing to achieve a fuller sense of self thus prescripts her attempts to describe the composing processes of her subjects from the very start of her study.

Another such prescripting of process can be found in the early work of Linda Flower. A prolific writer and twice winner of the Braddock award, Flower set the pace for research in composition studies through the 1980s. In collaboration first with the psychologist John Hayes, and later with numerous graduate students at Carnegie Mellon University, she elaborated a "cognitive process theory" of composing that went well beyond Emig's observations in both its detail and its claims to generality. Through the use of think-aloud protocols, Flower and her colleagues tried to describe what experienced writers actually do when they sit down to write. The resulting map of the composing process, they reasoned, could then be used as the basis for a pedagogy in which we teach our students to imitate the problem-solving strategies of these experts. The description Flower and others gave of this process was sharply criticized by theorists like David Bartholomae and Patricia Bizzell, who pointed out how their model failed to show how larger social and discursive forces position writers and shape what they can say.[6] I agree with these

6. In their 1993 survey of *CCC* since its first issue in 1950, Phillips, Greenberg, and Gibson count more than twice as many citations of Flower than of anyone else in the field in the years 1980–1993. (This is with the exception of John Hayes, her coauthor!) This remarkable record of citations testifies to how Flower not only influenced a whole set of process studies but also became a key figure for rival social theorists to respond to. Flower's first scholarly work in composition used case studies of novice writers to theorize "Writer-Based Prose: A Cognitive Basis for Problems in Writing" (1979) and "Revising Writer-Based Prose" (1981). She then teamed up with John Hayes to elaborate "A Cognitive Process Theory of Writing" (1981) and "Identifying the Organization of Writing Processes" (1980), which together articulated perhaps the most detailed model of the composing process the field has ever seen. These last two pieces were criticized at length by Bizzell in a 1982 essay-review "Cognition, Convention and Certainty" and Bartholomae in his 1985 "Inventing the University." Both accused Flower's model of failing to account fully for the social and political contexts of writing, and in doing so helped to precipitate the cognitivist/social-constructionist debates that raged in the field through the late 1980s. Flower has tried to incorporate and respond to these criticisms in pieces like "Cognition, Context, and Theory Building" (1989), and in her 1994 book *The Construction of Negotiated Meaning: A Social Cognitive Theory of Writing*. The fourth and most recent (1993) edition of *Problem-Solving Strategies for Writing*, though, suggests her approach to teaching (my focus here) has remained consistent over the years.

criticisms and discuss their implications for teaching in some detail in chapter 5. My aim here, though, is not to go over the theoretical war between the cognitivist and social accounts of composing. That argument is by now well rehearsed and, for my purposes, somewhat beside the point. For what most troubles me about the early work of Flower and her colleagues is not so much their account of the composing process as their single-minded focus on *technique*. Their work rests on the notion that our job as teachers can be usefully defined as helping students to write "better"—with "better" simply meaning technically more able to meet the demands put on them by one institution or the other, to produce better themes, better reports, better memos, better term papers, and the like. Like Emig, then, their descriptions of the composing process are predetermined by a vision of an ideal text—although this ideal now has less to do with self-discovery than with success in the academic or corporate world.

In the fourth edition of her textbook *Problem-Solving Strategies for Writing* (1993), Flower restates her belief that the main difficulty of poor writers has to do with their failure to structure their prose around the needs and interests of their readers. She joins Perl and Emig in claiming that the work of beginning or struggling writers is often egocentric, self-focused (in a limiting rather than therapeutic sense), organized not so much around their ideas as on how they came to think them. What such writers need, then, is a set of strategies for making their work more *reader-based* (162–65). Such a move from egocentric to reader-based prose is often mirrored by a shift from narrative to essay form. Flower warns her students against that kind of writing in which we must "watch the writer's mind at work and follow him through the process of thinking out his conclusions" (169). Academic readers are impatient for the point, she says, and will interpret such narratives of a writer's thinking as confused or evasive. Make sure your ideas are way out in front, she suggests; let your readers know the gist of what you have to say early on (169–77). What all this amounts to, in practice, is more advice about thesis statements and topic sentences and explicit transitions and such. Here, for instance, is a passage that Flower describes as egocentric, writer-based:

> In *Great Expectations*, Pip is introduced as a very likeable young boy. Although he steals, he does it because he is both innocent and goodhearted. Later, when he goes to London, one no longer feels this same sort of identification

with Pip. He becomes too proud to associate with his old friends, cutting ties with Joe and Biddy because of his false pride. And yet one is made to feel that Pip is still an innocent in some important way. When he dreams about Estella, one can see how all his unrealistic romantic illusions blind him to the way the world really works. (170)

And here is its revision into reader-based prose:

In *Great Expectations*, Pip changes from a good hearted boy into a selfish young man, yet he always remains an innocent who never really understands how the world works. Although as a child Pip actually steals something, he does it because he has a gullible, kindhearted sort of innocence. As a young man in London his crime seems worse when he cuts his old friends, Joe and Biddy, because of false pride. And yet, as his dreams about Estella show, Pip is still an innocent, a person caught up in unrealistic romantic illusions he can't see through. (171)

The first draft retells the writer's ongoing response to the novel. It is structured around what she felt and thought as she worked her way through *Great Expectations*, and it offers a fairly interesting account of both her own uncertainty as a reader and, implicitly, the prowess of Dickens in creating and exploiting the ambiguous character of Pip. In her second draft the writer drops this narrative structure for a more hierarchical one, leading off with a thesis statement ("Pip changes . . . yet remains an innocent") that sets an impressively vague and sentations tone, and devoting the rest of the paragraph to a set of particulars that appear to back up that (actually rather vacuous) opening claim. The voice throughout has become sure, firm, authoritative—Academic with a capital A. There is little sense, as there was in the first draft, that this writer ever wavered in her *view* of Pip, whose essential character now seems to have been clear to her from the very start of her reading.

Flower argues that this second draft is better "from a professor or other reader's point-of-view . . . because it clearly shows what the writer learned from the novel" (1993, 171). I wish I could argue more with what such a claim suggests about how and why most professors read student writings, but we probably do read in the role of an examiner too much of the time, and even then far too quickly and superficially. Still, advising students to write theme prose simply because it works, because that is what many of their professors will expect, surely raises as many questions as it answers. And that second draft is indeed theme writing—prose meant less to persuade than simply to sound persuasive. Where, for instance, does the writer actually back up her claim that Pip changes yet remains an innocent? Nowhere, really. What she offers as evidence does not support the claim so much as simply repeat it: Pip steals, but does so through "a kindhearted sort of innocence"; he cuts his friends "yet . . . is still an innocent." The points don't add up. The reason, I suspect, is that the writer is trying to reuse evidence from her first draft to prove a different point in the second. A concern with how and when the reader comes to identify with Pip ("Pip is introduced . . . one no longer feels . . . one is made to feel . . . one can see") runs through and ties together the thinking of her first draft. But the writer simply drops this concern in her second draft and replaces it with vague talk about Pip's true character. She has (or has been given) a new thesis statement but not a new argument. The result is a revised text that sounds more imposing but no longer has much of a point to make.

So it is merely the style of the passage that has changed here, and that for the worse—becoming more sweeping, wordy, aggressive. No more is Pip "an innocent in some important way," as he was in the first draft. Now he instead "always remains an innocent who never really understands how the world works." Similarly, Pip no longer merely "steals"; in the second draft he "actually steals something"—and does this not, as in the first draft, simply because he is "innocent and goodhearted" but because he now "has a gullible, kindhearted sort of innocence." This reworking of her piece, then, shows us the writer being socialized, appropriated, as she struggles to take on the voice of the academy—or at least of her teacher. But I'm not sure that such struggle is always a sign of intellectual decentering or growth, and in this instance, certainly, the narrative of the first draft makes more sense than the hierarchical structuring of the second. As I suppose is clear by now, I *like* the way we see the writer in her first draft begin by forming a view of Pip as an agreeable innocent, then wrestling with events in the novel that seem to contradict that view, and finally deciding that, even at his most dishonest, Pip seems somehow untouched by malice. It reminds me of the sort of talk about books and movies I often have with my friends and family, and that I imagine this student might have with hers. Of course the point of such talk is not usually to come to a critical agreement on issues of form or character, but simply to share our various responses to the text—to retell scenes that have stuck in our minds, to recall what we were thinking and feeling as we saw the movie or read the book.

Such talk is not egocentric; it simply differs from the kind that goes on in most English classes, although it is not hard to imagine the workings of an English class that values the sort of direct response to a text given in the first draft more than it does the mock *Cliff's Notes* styling of the second. The teacher of such a class would be aware, of course, of bucking the tide, of urging her students to avoid what has become a privileged way of talking about books. But that's the point. What we see occurring in these two passages is not a process of decentering—of the writer learning to shape her prose for a reader—but of acculturation, as the student starts to rework her text for a *different* sort of reader than she has written to before.

As with Emig, perhaps what is most revealing is what Flower does *not* talk about. Aside from the nearly meaningless comment that "the passage is full of good ideas" (1993, 170), everything she notes about these two versions of the text concerns their structure. What the writer actually has to say about the novel (and if it is worth saying) never gets brought up. Rather, the second draft is judged better than the first because it *sounds* more like conventional academic prose. Despite all the talk of issues and ideas and logic, what counts in the end is form.

This emphasis on formal tinkering can be seen in most of the instances Flower gives of transforming writer-based into reader-based prose, a process she openly defines as one of the writer *reorganizing* his thoughts and writing for his reader.

> In most expository and persuasive writing, the writer needs to *reorganize* his or her thoughts around a problem, a thesis, or the reader's needs. Writer-based prose just hasn't been reorganized yet. (1993, 165)

The implication is that for the most part the writer first figures out what he wants to say and *then* adapts those ideas for his reader. And, indeed, while *Problem-Solving Strategies* is filled with plenty of reorganized texts, it is notably short on instances of writers changing their minds, reworking the substance as well as the form of what they have to say. And so the revision of a group progress report on The Oskaloosa Brewing Company (166–68) consists for the most part of the inserting of a few headings and topic sentences; there is little evidence that the group ever thought (or was ever asked) to use the occasion of rewriting its document to also reconsider its analysis of the firm. Similarly, while the second draft of an essay on selecting the right kind of running shoes (who gives such assignments? why?) does make the choices open to the buyer more explicit, its

changes are also all stylistic: the same information and same recommendations are repeated from draft to draft (171–72). And although Flower
points out that experienced writers, unlike novices, spend a good deal
of time reworking the gist of what they have to say (186–87), virtually all
of her advice on editing and revising concerns style—with sections on
direct and economical prose, noun/verb ratios, nominalizations, weak
linking verbs, negative expressions, passive constructions, avoiding lists,
embedding simple sentences, common paragraph structures, and the
like (188–219). In sum, then, the shift from writer-based to reader-based
prose involves not so much the reconsidering of what one thinks as the
restructuring of what one has written, of writers "transform[ing] what
they know in order to meet the needs of their readers" (221).

I am indeed troubled by what seem to me the technocratic aims of
such teaching. But my larger point here is to argue that, while they offer
quite different views of the composing process, both Emig and Flower
arrive at their sense of that process in much the same way: through positing an ideal text and working backward from that. The process you
teach turns out to depend on the sort of product you want. The effect
of process teaching thus becomes not an opening up of multiple ways
of writing but an inculcating of a particular method of composing. In
Flower's early work, "process" is conceived explicitly as a form of discipline, a way of asserting control over the unruliness of writer-based
prose.[7] For Emig, too, the process of composing is a discipline, but
in a somewhat more subtle spiritual (neo-Loyolan) or analytic (neo-
Freudian) sense in which writing is seen as a means first to express and
then to reflect on one's feelings and identity. In order to advocate and
teach a certain process of composing, then, both Emig and Flower must
proscribe others: either the "Mozartian" efficiency of Lynn or the "egocentrism" of the author of the Pip paper.

Both the expressivist and technocratic views of process lacked a dia-
logical sense of revision. For theorists like Emig and Flower, that is, the
process of writing *ends* with the creation of a particular sort of text; they
fail to explore in any real detail how writers might change not only their
phrasings but also their minds when given a chance to talk about their
work with other people. To really change the teaching of writing, then,
it seems to me that a view of process must go *beyond* the text to include

---

7. Robert Brooke deftly critiques attempts to link process teaching to theories of textual
   indeterminacy and deconstruction on much these grounds in his 1989 "Control in
   Writing: Flower, Derrida, and Images of the Writer."

a sense of the ongoing conversations that texts enter into—a sense, that is, of how writers draw on, respond to, and rework both their own previous writings and those of others.

And that seems much the direction that Flower's most recent work is taking. In the late 1980s, Flower and her colleagues became involved with a literacy project in Pittsburgh whose aim was to bring various members of a racially and economically diverse community together to define a shared set of issues and concerns and to begin to form responses to them. Students, teachers, and school administrators met, for instance, to discuss why African American students were being suspended from neighborhood public schools at a higher rate than other populations, basing their talk together on the document "Whassup with Suspension?" that the students had written and designed for the occasion. And in another instance, renters, building owners, and community activists met to collaborate on the writing of a workbook for use in tenant-landlord negotiations. (These projects are described by Peck, Higgins, and Flower in the 1995 *CCC* article "Community Literacy.") I very much admire these attempts to enact (rather than simply preach) a liberal politics in the teaching of writing. I am also struck by how the process of collaboration and inquiry these projects foster both includes and goes beyond the writing of texts. For the overarching goal of the Community Literacy Center seems less to teach writing *per se* than to bring people with diverse interests to a common table to sort out differences and act on shared concerns. As a result, the texts that do get written are often stylistic hybrids meant to respond to specific needs and situations—which, ironically, tends to make them less formulaic and more interesting than most of the student writings cited in either *The Composing Processes of Twelfth Graders* or *Problem-Solving Strategies for Writing*. If the idea of *process* is to continue to have an impact on the teaching of writing, it will need to be rethought along these more open lines.

POSTSCRIPT, 2012: TRACK CHANGES

In her great novel about the First World War, *Regeneration* (1992), Pat Barker imagines a series of conversations between two soldier poets, Wilfred Owen and Siegfried Sassoon, while both are convalescing in a sanatorium in Scotland. The younger and, at the time, lesser-known of the two, Owen, has been charged with editing an in-house literary journal, *The Hydra*, as part of his treatment for shell shock. He tentatively approaches Sassoon for a poem. Sassoon agrees to contribute and asks to read some of Owen's work. He quickly sees that the young man has talent, but teases Owen about his reluctance to write about the war. Taking on the role of teacher, Sassoon puts Owen on a strict writing schedule: "It's like drill. You don't wait until you feel like doing it" (125).

In response, Owen begins to draft what will become one of the most harrowing poems ever to be written about war. He brings an early version to Sassoon, leading to this extraordinary exchange between them:

> Sassoon took the sheet and read the whole poem through twice, and then returned to the first two lines.
>
> *What minute-bells for those who die so fast?*
> *— Only the monstrous/solemn anger of our guns.*
>
> "I thought 'passing' bells," Owen said.
> "Hm. Though if you lose 'minute' you realize how weak 'fast' is. Only the monstrous anger . . ."
> "'Solemn'?"
> "'Only the solemn anger of our guns.' Owen, for God's sake, this is War Office propaganda."
> "No, it's not."
> "Read that line."
> Owen read. "Well, it certainly isn't meant to be."
> "I suppose what you've got to decide is who are 'these'? The British dead? Because if they're *British*, then 'our guns' is . . ."
> Owen shook his head. "All the dead."
> "Let's start there." Sassoon crossed out *our* and penciled in *the*. You're sure that's what you want? It isn't a minor change."
> "No, I know. If it's 'the', it's got to be 'monstrous.'"
> *What passing-bells for those who die . . . so fast?*
> *— Only the monstrous anger of the guns.*
> "Well, there's nothing wrong with the second line."
> "'In herds'?"
> "Better."
> They worked on the poem for half an hour. (1992, 141–42)

While this conversation is fictional, it is based on actual events. Sassoon and Owen did meet, in 1917, while both were recuperating at Craiglockhart War Hospital in Edinburgh, Scotland; *The Hydra* was a real journal; and the changes that Barker has Sassoon suggest to Owen do in fact appear, in Sassoon's handwriting, on an early draft of "Anthem for Doomed Youth" (Owen 1984, 249–50). What Barker does here, then, is to dramatize the process of revision by creating a scene that lets us eavesdrop on a writer and teacher as they work on a text together.

That work is of course more incisive than most of us can hope to imitate. Owen and Sassoon focus tightly on a set of word choices—*minute-bells* or *passing-bells, solemn* or *monstrous, our guns* or *the guns.* But each of those choices has a kind of ripple effect. One change leads to the next. As Owen remarks, "If it's 'the', it's got to be 'monstrous.'" The changes they discuss are thus not mere editorial corrections, simple substitutions of one word for another, but revisions that affect the stance and meaning of the poem as a whole.

Such work with texts is, of course, the meat and potatoes of our field. We spend much of our time trying to help student writers think through the implications of using one word or the other, of striking a certain stance or tone, of starting or finishing their essay on a particular note. So you might think our scholarly literature would be filled with nonfictional versions of Barker's imagined conversation between Owen and Sassoon.

It is not. I suspect one reason it is not is that we have been preoccupied with, as it were, Sassoon's side of the conversation. In the early 1980s, Nancy Sommers (1980, 1982) and Lil Brannon and Cy Knoblauch (1982) wrote a set of influential articles arguing for a mode of response in which teachers help students develop their projects as writers rather than simply correct their prose. That was excellent advice then and remains so now. But while each of these articles offers a close reading of teacher *comments* on student work, none of them offers an example of the *uses* students make of such comments. There is no attempt, that is, to *track changes*, to chart the actual work of revision from draft to draft. Instead the focus rests almost exclusively on what the teacher, not the student, has to say. Similarly, in *Twelve Readers Reading* (1995), Richard Straub and Ronald Lunsford collect responses by twelve different teachers to a set of fifteen student essays, but these student texts serve as little more than Rorschach blots for use in analyzing the responses they solicit from the faculty readers. The effect is to suggest that teachers can decide on a style of response in advance of commenting on any particular essay—that our comments are driven not by what students have to say to us but by what we already have decided to tell them about writing. Summer Smith confirms this hunch in a 1997 analysis of over 200 teacher comments on student texts in which she shows that the form of such comments is so depressingly formulaic that they, in effect, constitute a genre of their own.

In contrast, Barker is interested not simply in what Sassoon has to say to Owen but also the (not entirely predictable) uses Owen makes of his advice. After the conversation I've quoted, Owen returns to Sassoon with yet another version of his poem. When Sassoon asks him what draft this is, Owen replies that he's lost count, that after all Sassoon did tell him to "sweat his guts out." Sassoon replies:

> "Did I really? What an inelegant expression. 'What passing-bells for those who die as cattle?' I see we got to the slaughterhouse in the end." Sassoon read through the poem. When he'd finished, he didn't immediately comment.
> "It's better, isn't it?"
> "Better? It's *transformed.*" He read it again. (1992, 157)

But after offering this silent testimony to the power of what Owen has written, Sassoon goes on to argue some more with the direction the poem has taken, worrying that Owen might offer his readers a false sense of consolation for the meaningless slaughter of the war. But Owen objects to this reading of his work, insisting that one can take "pride in the sacrifice" without suggesting it was justified. Indeed, Owen points out, Sassoon makes a similar move in one of his own poems about the war, which Owen reads triumphantly to his teacher (Barker 1992, 157). Sassoon cedes the point to his newly confident student, but still makes one last perspicuous revision, changing *Dead* to *Doomed* in the poem's title (158).

What matters most to me is not how this conversation ends, but that it *is* a conversation, an exchange in which both writer and reader, student and teacher, assert their views about the text they are working on together. Barker shows us a process in which both Owen and Sassoon win and lose and compromise, and through which a better text is forged. If we want to understand writing as a *social* process, we need to cultivate a similar sense of reciprocity, of how a text emerges as part of an ongoing conversation between a writer and her readers.

INTERCHAPTER

Let me offer an example of how I have tried to teach writing as a process in a way that resists casting it as a kind of formula leading to the production of a particular sort of text. I regularly teach an undergraduate course called Writing About Movies at the University of Pittsburgh. The aim of this course is not to train students in a particular method of film criticism or analysis, nor is it to have them reproduce the sort of easy critique of ideology that seems the goal of much current teaching about the media and popular culture. I worry that such approaches leave students' experiences as moviegoers behind, that they ask them less to rethink their ways of talking about film than simply to replace old approaches with new ones. My goal is instead to get students to reflect critically on the ways of talking about movies that they *already* have, and in doing so maybe to learn something about themselves as readers of their culture. The particular value of writing in such a class lies in the ways it can begin to make students more aware of the expectations and values that shape how they already look at movies. Writing allows us not simply to respond to movies but to talk directly about those responses themselves. By centering the work of the course on the writings of the students in it, we can thus talk as a class not only about the films we have seen but also about how particular viewers have come to interpret them.

The focus of the course is thus shifted away from "learning about film" and toward a critical look at ourselves as moviegoers. In line with this goal, the assignments in the course are designed, first, to interfere with students' usual ways of thinking and writing about movies, to make their viewing a little less spontaneous and more self-conscious, and, second, to get them to consider the competing ways in which they are positioned as viewers of film. In practice, this usually starts with questioning the meanings and origins of terms like *entertaining* or *boring*, and so I often begin the semester by having students list on the board the terms they use for talking about and rating movies. Having done so, I then ask them to think about what this list seems to value and to exclude. What do these terms suggest about why people go to movies or about what roles films might play in the rest of their lives? This exercise leads to the first writing assignment, in which I ask students to define who they are as moviegoers—to write on what movies have been important to them in the past, what sorts of movies they go to see now, what sorts they avoid, and why.

We then usually move on to talk about *genre*, using the term to refer not only to the usual categories of comedy, drama, western, mystery, and so on, but also to the less stable but in many ways more suggestive ones of sequels, takeoffs, star vehicles (Murphy, Midler, Schwarzenegger, Stallone), "art" films, slashers, space, martial arts, gross-outs, yuppies with babies, teenagers getting laid, and the like. We talk about how these emerging genres respond to certain concerns of their viewers, and I then ask students to write a second piece in which they name a current television or movie genre they know well, identify some of its members, define its rules and conventions, and speculate on the reasons for its appeal. At some point early on in the term I also have students re-view (that is, go back and look again at) a problematic scene in a movie in order to "read" what happens in it closely. (While this was almost impossible to do when I first started teaching about film in the early 1980s, video recorders have now made it easy.) In doing so, they learn what they might also find out by looking closely at a poem or story: readers and viewers often "see" very different things in the same lines or images, and thus any reading of a text must be argued for rather than simply asserted.

About midway into the semester, I assign a series of writings on the process of moviegoing that I think of as being central to the work of the course. I begin by asking students to write on everything they know about a certain movie *before they have actually gone to see it*—on the way their expectations about the movie have been shaped by ads, previews, the remarks of critics and friends, the prior work of the people involved with the movie, its genre, and so on. In recent years, this writing task has also led to talk about the differences between the experience of going out to a movie and of renting one at the local video store. I then ask them to see the movie and write not a review but an account of the specific ways it met or violated their expectations. (Doing so, many students realize they had brought far more to their viewing than they had previously suspected.) For their third writing, I ask them to locate two or three texts they think will help them better understand what they've just seen—reviews, interviews, biographies, historical or critical studies, information about how the movie was made, other movies or writings by people who worked on it, or the like—and then to talk about how these texts add to or change their view of the movie (or why they do not). Finally, I ask them to review their previous three writings in order to compose an account of how their reading of the movie grew and changed.

Throughout all this, the members of the class read and talk about one another's work—as well as discuss the comments of various theorists on advertising and movies. In the course of thinking and writing about their responses to a single movie, then, students are confronted with an extraordinary range of discourses. But their work does not center on learning to write conventional film criticism in either its academic or journalistic modes. They are not asked, that is, to take on some new language of film analysis, but rather to analyze their familiar ways of seeing and talking about movies. In doing so, they often end up writing both as viewers of a movie and as readers of movie critics, as movie critics themselves and as critics of critics, as targets of advertising and as analysts of advertising's targeting tactics.

The results can be unwieldy but intriguing mixes of autobiography, theory, and close reading—writings that interpret movies in powerful ways even as they transgress many of the conventions of both academic criticism and popular reviewing. And so, for instance, here is how Steven, a student in the first class I taught on Writing About Movies in 1982, sums up his changing understanding of *My Dinner with Andre*:

> In reviewing my responses to the previous sections of this assignment, I find it interesting that where I have said the most is where I say the least. Perhaps I should qualify that statement by saying that where I think I say the most about the film is actually where I say more about how I experience film and the power that preconceived ideas have over the act of viewing a film. . . .
>
> In the first draft of this assignment I wrote of a conversation that I had with a friend of mine. He had seen *My Dinner with Andre* and he told me that the film had a profound effect on his view of life. He then proceeded to tell me what he thought the basic message of the film was. Whether it was a result of a subconscious respect for the authority of my friend's opinion or from some other cause I am not sure but I proceeded to watch the film with this message firmly in mind. I wrote in the second draft of this assignment that what had affected me most while viewing the film was the relationship between what the film was saying and how it was being said. Actually, however, it was the relationship between what my friend said and how the film was saying my friend's opinion of what its message was that had most affected me. Parker Tyler wrote of the viewer only seeing part of the film while viewing it. In narrowing it down it seems all I was seeing was just the words of Andre Gregory. These words corresponded to my friend's view of the film's message and apparently to mine while I was viewing it.
>
> A question to be asked is—what made me aware of the fact that I was viewing the film so partially? Well, I first became aware of the fact that I had unjustly simplified the content of the film after I read Stanley Kaufman's review of the film in *The New Republic*. . . . Just the mere mention of something like the economic relationship of the characters sparked the idea in my head that there was more on the screen than what I was criticizing. . . .
>
> This experience raises the same question that Parker Tyler raised; namely, how can a film be criticized as a whole when it is not viewed as a whole but rather

only as a part or parts of itself? On a different level this raises the question of the theatrical nature of the film experience as a one-time event as opposed to the conception of a film as a work to be studied and viewed again and again. I saw *My Dinner with Andre* once and I was most affected by its comparison to my own prior conceptions. If I see this film again will I be seeing the same film I saw originally?

Thinking about film in this light (and any art for that matter), I am beginning to think that any notion in your mind that you can fully comprehend a work of art or that you understand what it is saying and thus can criticize it—any notion of this kind is the direct result of an initial response that should be regarded with a degree of skepticism and should only be a starting point rather than a final judgment.

There are several things I like about this piece. The first is how Steven draws on anything and everything that he can in figuring out what he has to say—including the remarks of his friend, his own viewing of the movie, Kaufman's review, Tyler's theory, our talk in class, and his prior writings. I am also struck by how the subject of the piece is clearly not *Andre* but Steven's ongoing responses to it, and I admire how he draws on the ways that response changed over time as he begins to form his own theory of what is involved in viewing and understanding movies. And, perhaps most of all, I like how Steven gains a critical distance from his first response to *Andre* without wholly disowning it. The lesson he draws from his shifting view of the film is not that his original interpretation was wrong but that all responses to a movie are "partial" and should thus only be seen as "starting points." He is able to see his first "misreading" of *Andre* less as a mistake than as an opportunity to reflect on his own usual ways of seeing and talking about movies.

I would push what Steven says to argue that all strong readings of a text are actually misreadings—interpretations that refuse to accept what a text seems to say about itself, to read it as it seems to ask to be read. This can sometimes mean questioning the sorts of pleasure that a particular film seems to offer its viewers. For instance, Perri, a student in a 1989 section of Writing About Movies, talks about the problems this kind of reading and questioning can cause in a piece on *Working Girl*. Perri begins by saying that at first she identified with the fantasy rise of Tess (Melanie Griffith)—a secretary from Staten Island who fights her way onto Wall Street—and that she applauded Tess's final triumph over her former boss and icy rival, Katherine (Sigourney Weaver). "I didn't feel dazed and amazed as I left the theater, but I felt satisfied. . . . If we judge *Working Girl* on its own terms it is a successful and timely narrative." But for some reason the movie failed to stay simply a bit of implausible fun for her:

There's something beyond the movie itself that in the hours since I saw it has bothered me more and more. . . . After leaving the safe, unquestioning state I was in while watching the movie, certain conflicts have come to mind regarding the relationship between these two women. Katherine's flaws made Tess look as though she deserved success more than Katherine. Tess's flaws made Katherine look like an unfeminine, cold person. Because of Katherine's one-dimensional quality, it was impossible to take her seriously. None of her good qualities as a character were established. For this reason, the relationship between her and Tess is purely competitive. They do not relate to each other in a business like manner; it is catty deception and seeing each other as threatening that characterizes their relationship.

Without getting deeply into a feminist criticism, I want to say that as a woman analyzing this movie, I feel very uncomfortable. While watching the movie I had no complaints, but now I think that Tess's character is more of an exhibit of how a woman should be, as conceptualized by a man. It seems as though Mike Nichols, or whoever originally created these characters, is saying women such as Tess, women "with heads for business and bodies for sin," are preferable, better, and ideal. There is no attractiveness attributed to Tess's compliment, Katherine; she is shown as a domineering bitch, certainly not someone to be emulated in any way. . . .

Working Girl was entertaining. But I don't know if I'm comfortable with the American Dream it subscribes to. Yes, there is a great mass of us dreaming of making it in the corporate world, and this film appeals to those dreams. But whose dream is this movie trying to fulfill? I am uncomfortable with the camera's vantage point on Tess. It was funny when Jack Trainer was in his office with no shirt on, his coworkers jeered and laughed. But it was presented as commonplace when Tess vacuumed in her underwear. This may be some sort of role-reversal but it doesn't seem to indicate any progression toward equality. *Working Girl* was just fine, as long as one doesn't think about it too much.

I remember wondering before we discussed this paper in class if some students might have trouble dealing with such an overtly political reading of a popular movie. This did not turn out to be the case, though, as even those students who ended up arguing against what Perri had to say began by noting their respect for her piece. I think this had to do with how Perri is careful not to deny the pleasure the movie brought her, at least at first. A problem with much recent political criticism is the way it often seems to describe not the response of the critic but of some *other* reader when it talks about the pleasures of pop texts. A consequence, I think, is that readers of such criticism often feel slightly hectored, as though they have just been caught indulging in some illicit pleasure—sitcoms, soaps, skin flicks, smart clothes, slick ads, or magazines—that the critic has somehow resisted. But Perri presents herself as someone who enjoyed *Working*

Girl. And when she moves on to discuss what now troubles her about its fantasy, she phrases this as *her* problem—although by the end of her paper she has also offered a powerful reading of the movie. The effect is not of someone telling other viewers what they missed but of someone puzzling out her own relations to both the movie and the culture at large.

As writers, both Steven and Perri are at times clumsy and repetitious. And I don't claim that their readings of either *Andre* or *Working Girl* are especially original or inventive. But their writings do show a self-reflexiveness that characterizes the kind of critical and intellectual work I admire most. Both pieces offer stories of reading as something other than a simple drawing out of meaning from a text. And, paradoxically, it is through showing how their approaches to *Andre* and *Working Girl* were shaped by many voices and concerns that Steven and Perri can then say their readings of those movies are indeed their own—since it is now clear where those readings come from and how they were selected and composed.

Students spend the last few weeks in Writing About Movies working on a project that asks them to place and read a particular film in relation to another set of texts or interests—to interpret a film or television program, for instance, as it figures in the careers of those involved with it, as it exemplifies or works against the codes of a certain genre, or as it responds to some of the social or political issues of its day. The point of this assignment is not to have students do a "research paper." It is instead to have them read a text as something situated in a network of other texts and concerns, much as the prior series of writings on the process of moviegoing urged them to reflect on how the values and expectations they bring to a film structure the sorts of pleasure and meaning they draw from it.

Finally, at the end of the course, I ask students to look at what has been perhaps the most powerful (and thus often most invisible) shaping force on their work in the past few months—to write, that is, on how being part of this particular class has affected the ways they view and think about movies and television. To do so, I ask them to review their writings for the course in order to locate moments of change or difference between the sorts of things they wrote at the beginning of the term and at its end, or between what they said in their writings and what they would say now, or between the ways they talk about movies outside class and the forms of talk and writing they found themselves taking on within it. My aim is to have them think about the room as a place where certain kinds of talk and writing are privileged over others, to consider how being a student at a university has affected what they now think and say about movies.

Students are thus asked to revise their work at both *textual* and *sequential* levels. I want them to gain practice in taking a particular piece through a series of drafts, rethinking its argument and reworking its phrasings, but I also want them to consider the various writings they've done for the class in relation to each other (and to other texts they've seen and read), to reflect on the trajectory of their work as writers and critics over the course of a term. My hope is that, in doing so, they may begin to imagine the writings they have done as not simply the *results* of a particular composing process but as *contributions* to an ongoing process of inquiry.

4

ERROR

"How Rouse makes his living is none of my business, but I venture that if he manages a decent livelihood it is only because he has somewhere or other submitted to enough socialization to equip him to do something for which somebody is willing to pay him" (852). So thundered Gerald Graff in the pages of *College English* in 1980, as part of a response to an article John Rouse had published in the same journal a year before. Not only was Graff's tone sententious and overbearing, his question was also rhetorical to the point of being disingenuous, since how Rouse made his living should have been clear to anyone who had read his article, which was on the teaching of college writing and included a standard biographical note on its title page identifying him as "a teacher of English and an administrator in public schools" as well as the author of previous pieces in *College English* and of a book called *The Completed Gesture: Myth, Character, and Education* (1979, 1). So Rouse was a teacher and writer, "managing his livelihood" in much the same way as Graff, and probably drawing on much the same sort of skills and "socialization" in order to do so. Except not quite. For what Graff—who was identified by a similar note on the first page of his response as the chair of the English department at Northwestern University, as well as the author of articles in several prestigious literary journals and of a book published by the University of Chicago Press (1980, 851)—was hinting rather broadly at was that he didn't know who this guy was, that Rouse (schoolteacher rather than professor; articles in *College English* rather than *Salmagundi*; book published by trade rather than university press) was not a player in the academic world Graff moved about in. And perhaps this seemed so important because Rouse had presumed to criticize the work of someone who was such a player, someone who by then had in fact become a kind of revered figure in the literary establishment, its sanctioned representative of the good teacher—and that was Mina Shaughnessy.

In many ways, Rouse had seemed to ask for precisely the sort of response he got from Graff and others.[1] His 1979 article "The Politics of Composition" offered what I still see as a trenchant critique of Shaughnessy's 1977 *Errors and Expectations*, a book on the teaching of "basic" or underprepared college writers that had almost immediately gained the status of a classic. Rouse argued that Shaughnessy's relentless focus on the teaching of grammar might in many cases actually hinder the attempts of anxious and inexperienced students to elaborate their thoughts effectively in writing. I agree. But his criticism was couched in language that sometimes seemed deliberately aimed to provoke: Rouse failed to acknowledge, for instance, the crucial political importance and difficulty of the role Shaughnessy took on in the late 1960s when she set up the first basic writing program at City College of New York, and thus found herself in charge of diagnosing and responding to the academic needs of thousands of newly admitted and severely underprepared open-admissions students. He also failed to note the clear sympathy and respect for such students that runs throughout *Errors and Expectations* and that all of her many admirers argue was central to Shaughnessy's work as a teacher and intellectual. And he was either unaware of or did not see the need to mention her tragic and early death from cancer the year before in 1978. Instead, Rouse went ferociously on the attack, arguing that Shaughnessy's "overriding need to socialize these young people in a manner politically acceptable accounts, I think, for her misinterpretations of student work and her disregard of known facts of language learning" (1979, 2). This rabble-rousing tone led right into Graff's magisterial response, and a much-needed argument over teaching aims and strategies became clouded with competing accusations of elitism and pseudoradicalism, as snide guesses about Mina Shaughnessy's psychopolitical needs or John Rouse's means of earning a living were followed by insinuations about who *really* had the best interests of students in mind. "Is this submission with a cheerful smile? 'Mrs. Shaughnessy, we do know our verbs and adverbs,'" sneered Rouse (8). "John Rouse's article . . . illustrates the predicament of the thoughtful composition teacher today," replied Graff, who then went on to explain that it was the very conscientiousness of such teachers that left them "open to attack

---

1. In 1980 *College English* published sharply critical responses to Rouse by Graff, Michael Allen, and William Lawlor, along with a counterstatement by Rouse, "Feeling Our Way Along." That none of Rouse's critics identified themselves with the field of composition studies points to the politically charged quality of the debate about error.

from critics of Rouse's persuasion" (1980, 851). I want to do two things in this chapter: first, to work through what might actually be at stake in this argument over error and socialization, to sort out what competing views of the aims and practices of teaching are being offered in it, and, second, to try to understand why this particular issue in teaching, more than any other I know of, seems to spark such strong feeling. I begin by looking more closely at Mina Shaughnessy, who figures in this debate, I think, less as an advocate of a position that many people now find very compelling than as a kind of icon, a model of what it might mean to be, in Graff's words, a "thoughtful composition teacher."

Shaughnessy was an elegant but evidently also rather slow writer: her entire body of work consists of a few essays and talks along with a single book, *Errors and Expectations*. This text has been enough, though, to secure her place in the history of the field. *Errors and Expectations* showed how students who had often been presumed uneducable, hopelessly unprepared for college work, could in fact be helped to compose reasonably correct academic prose—that their problems with college writing stemmed not from a lack of intelligence but from inexperience. As Shaughnessy put it, "BW students write the way they do, not because they are slow or non-verbal, indifferent to or incapable of academic excellence, but because they are beginners and must, like all beginners, learn by making mistakes" (1977, 5). The students whom Shaughnessy worked with (she calls them "BWs," an abbreviation for "basic writers"), and whose writings fill the pages of her book, were for the most part African Americans and Hispanics who had been given the chance to attend City through its (then) new and controversial program of open admissions for graduates of New York high schools.[2] Shaughnessy's work with these students was thus an intrinsic part of one of the most ambitious democratic reforms of American higher education—as the glowing reviews of her book in popular liberal magazines like *The Nation* and *Atlantic Monthly* attested.

---

2. City College's experiment with open admissions sparked a remarkable number of accounts from its faculty, both advocates and opponents, radicals and conservatives. Both Sidney Hook (1987) and Irving Howe (1982), for instance, have interesting things to say in their memoirs about the struggles of the 1970s at City. And there have also been a number of accounts by people involved in some way with the teaching of English or basic writing, although this did not always mitigate the sententiousness of their prose—as is shown in the titles of Geoffrey Wagner's 1976 *The End of Education* and Theodore Gross's 1980 *Academic Turmoil*. And for a quick overview of the events of the 1970s at City, see James Traub's 1994 *City on a Hill*.

But while politically liberal, the plan of work sketched out in *Errors and Expectations* is in many ways quite intellectually conservative. What people tend to remember and admire about *Errors and Expectations* is Shaughnessy's early defense of the aims of open admissions, her attentiveness throughout to the language of students, and her analysis late in the book of the difficulties students often have in taking on the critical and argumentative stance of much academic writing. What tends to be forgotten or glossed over is that the bulk of *Errors and Expectations* is a primer on teaching for correctness, pure and simple, as the titles of its chapters 2 through 6 show: "Handwriting and Punctuation," "Syntax," "Common Errors," "Spelling," and "Vocabulary." And even the celebrated seventh chapter, "Beyond the Sentence," offers what seems to me a distressingly formulaic view of academic writing and how to teach it. For instance, an extraordinarily detailed "sample lesson" on helping students write about reading (1977, 251–55) offers students an extended list of quotations culled from the book they are reading (*Black Boy*), followed by a set of procedures (Observation, Idea, and Analysis—the three of which are themselves broken into substeps) they are to use in analyzing this list of details, and ends up by instructing them to

> Follow the steps given above. Make observations on parts, repetitions, omissions, and connections. Write down the main idea you get from your observations. Develop that main idea into an essay that makes a general statement, an explanation of the statement, an illustration of the statement, and a concluding statement. (255)

Follow the steps given above. I can't imagine a less compelling representation of the work of a critic or intellectual. Students are not asked in this assignment to say anything about what they thought or felt about their reading, or to connect what the author is writing about with their own experiences, or to take a stand on what he has to say; rather, they are simply told to generate and defend "a main idea" about a list of details that their teacher has given them from the book. What is the point of having students read books (like *Black Boy)* that might speak to their situations and concerns if they are not then encouraged to draw on their life experiences in speaking back to it? The tame parody of critical analysis sketched out in this assignment is "academic" in the worst sense: its form predetermined, its aim less to say something new or interesting than to demonstrate a competence in a certain kind of school writing.

Errors and Expectations thus argues for a new sort of student but not a new sort of intellectual practice. It says basic writers can also do the kind of work that mainstream students have long been expected to do; it doesn't suggest this work be changed in any significant ways. This is a strong part of its appeal. Throughout her writings Shaughnessy offers a consistent image of herself as an *amateur* and a *reformer*. Even as she helped to set up the new field of "basic writing," Shaughnessy identified herself less with composition than with mainstream literary studies. Few of her admirers miss the chance to note how she was the product of a quite traditional education (BA in speech from Northwestern, MA in literature from Columbia) or to mark her love of Milton and drama.[3] Her method in *Errors and Expectations* is essentially that of the literary critic: a close and careful explication of difficult texts—except that in this case the difficulty springs from the inexperience of students rather than from the virtuosity of professionals. And her list of references and suggested readings at the end of her book has an undisciplined and eclectic quality: some literature, some criticism, some linguistics, some psychology, some work on second-language learning and on the writing process—whatever, it seems, that could be found that might help with the task at hand.

This image of the autodidact or amateur was carefully constructed. Shaughnessy often depicts herself and her colleagues as "pioneers" working on a new "frontier," who need to "dive in" and explore previously uncharted waters (the metaphor varies a bit) so they can form a new kind of knowledge and expertise to use in teaching a new kind of college student. In "Mapping Errors and Expectations for Basic Writing" (1994), Bruce Horner points to the troubling (indeed, almost unconsciously racist) implications of describing teachers and students in terms of pioneers and natives. I would add that the "frontier" Shaughnessy claimed to stumble upon was already quite well developed, that even though the field of composition was not disciplined or professionalized

---

3. Shaughnessy's career has perhaps been documented more thoroughly than any other figure in composition studies. Janet Emig briefly traced her work in an obituary appearing in the February 1979 issue of *CCC*, and a series of writers—including E.D. Hirsch, Benjamin DeMott, John Lyons, Richard Hogart, and Sarah D'Eloia—commented on her work in a special issue, "Towards a Literate Democracy," of the *Journal of Basic Writing* in 1980, and then the same journal published still more reminiscences of Shaughnessy in 1994. Robert Lyons has a detailed and affectionate, although not uncritical, biographical essay on Shaughnessy in Brereton's *Traditions of Inquiry* (1985). And, more recently, James Traub writes respectfully of Shaughnessy in a 1994 book, *City on a Hill*, which is more often quite critical of the open admissions experiment at City College.

in the same ways it is now, many teachers and writers had for some time been dealing with much the same sorts of issues.

There is no question that Shaughnessy brought a new sense of urgency to the problem of teaching underprepared writers. But it wasn't a new problem. In 1964, for instance, David Holbrook had written his moving book *English for the Rejected* (still perhaps the bluntest and most accurate name for "basic" writers); in 1967, John Dixon was writing in *Growth through English* about students like Joan, the third grader with an IQ of 76 who wrote her poem about "the yellow bird." (It is this British and school-based tradition that John Rouse identifies himself with in his response to Shaughnessy.) In the United States, in 1977, the same year *Errors and Expectations* came out, Geneva Smitherman published *Talkin and Testifyin*, a book that urged teachers to spend less time correcting the language of African American students and more time responding to what they had to say. And throughout the 1970s, the very time that Shaughnessy was most active in the profession, what remains perhaps the liveliest and most vehement debate in the history of CCCC was going on around the drafting and eventual approval of its 1974 statement on the Students' Right to Their Own Language, a document which militantly asserted the need for teachers to move beyond a simple concern with having students write Standard Written English. None of these texts or authors can be placed in easy agreement with the approach taken by Shaughnessy in *Errors and Expectations*, which remains, again, after everything else is said about it, a book on teaching grammar. What Shaughnessy depicts as a sparse and unpopulated frontier of inquiry, then, looks from another perspective (to make use of a competing cliché) more like a marketplace of ideas, as contending factions hawk their positions and argue against the views of others.

But this contrast also shows the appeal of the metaphor of the frontier, which allowed Shaughnessy to present herself less as criticizing than *extending* the reach of English studies. (Contrast this with critics, like Rouse, who positioned themselves as outsiders arguing *against* the status quo.) Even at her angriest moments (as in her 1980 article "The English Professor's Malady," in which she complains of her colleagues' unwillingness to take on the hard work of teaching students not already familiar with their preferred ways of reading and writing), Shaughnessy's argument was for the profession to live up to its own stated values. Her message was consistently one of *inclusion*—that we can (and should) teach a kind of student, the "basic writer," who has too often slipped beneath the notice of the professoriate. And not only that, but she also showed how this sort of teaching could draw on precisely the sort of skills that people trained in English were likely to have, as well as to offer them much the sort of intellectual rewards they most valued. The pleasures of *Errors and Expectations* are strikingly like that of good literary criticism: passages of student writing that seem almost impossibly convoluted and obscure are patiently untangled and explicated. Shaughnessy thus offered the profession of English studies a useful image of one of its own best selves: the teacher who happily takes on the class of boneheads the rest of us dread encountering and who patiently teaches them the very "basics" that we want to be able to assume they already know.

But *what* Shaughnessy argues can (and should) be taught to these new students is dismaying. Here, for instance, is the plan she offers for a basic writing course near the end of *Errors and Expectations*:

Weeks 1–5	Combined work on syntax and punctuation, following recommendations in Chapters 2 and 3.
Weeks 6–7	Spelling—principles of word formation, diagnostic techniques. (After this, spelling instruction should be individualized.)
Weeks 8–12	Common errors—verb inflections for number, noun inflections for number, verb tenses, agreement.
Weeks 13–15	Vocabulary—prefixes, suffixes, roots, abstract concrete words, precision. (1977, 289)

Fifteen weeks and the focus never moves past correctness. Nowhere here (or anywhere else in her book) do we get a sense that the work of a basic writing course might be not only to train students in the mechanics of writing correct sentences but also to engage them in the life of the mind, to offer them some real experience in testing out and elaborating their views in writing. At no point in *Errors and Expectations* does Shaughnessy talk about how teachers might respond to the gist or argument of student writings, or about how to help students use writing to clarify or revise what they think. Indeed, as Rouse pointed out, Shaughnessy does not even seem to notice how many of the students whose work she cites change what they actually have to say in the process of trying to write more correct sentences.[4] Coupled with this is her nearly complete lack

---

4. In "Politics," Rouse points to how Shaughnessy's first example of a basic writer in action shows "his desperate effort to find *something* to say about the assigned topic" given him

of interest in revision. Almost all of the student writings Shaughnessy analyzes are timed first drafts; her goal in teaching was not to have students go back to edit and revise what they had written but to write new impromptu pieces with fewer mistakes in them. Her measures of good writing, that is to say, centered on fluency and correctness at the almost total expense of meaning. A footnote near the end of her book strikingly shows this mechanistic emphasis. Comparing some pieces written early in the term with those composed later on by the same students, Shaughnessy remarks,

> In all such before-and-after examples, the "after" samples bear many marks of revision (crossed-out words, corrected punctuation, etc.), suggesting that students have acquired the important habit of going back over their sentences with an eye to correctness. (1977, 277)

Revision here is pictured simply as a habit of proofreading. *Errors and Expectations* is thus the sort of book that tells you everything but why—as students and teachers labor together to perfect the form of prose whose actual or possible meanings they never seem to talk about.

Compare this to the sort of work that, at precisely the same time, Geneva Smitherman was arguing ought to go on in writing classes. A sociolinguist active in political and legal debates over the schooling of African American children, Smitherman was also a strong influence in the framing of the 1974 CCCC statement on the Students' Right to Their Own Language. (Shaughnessy was conspicuously absent from this debate.) Her 1977 *Talkin and Testifyin* is an impassioned and lucid defense of the richness and complexity of African American English. In its final chapter, Smitherman turns to language education, which she argues should center (for both African American and white students) on skills in reading and writing that are "intellectual competencies that can be taught in any dialect or language" (228). To teach such a "communicative competence," teachers need to move beyond a fetishizing of correctness and instead focus on the more substantive, difficult, and rhetorical

---

by his teacher, as he changes his position on the prompt no less than four times in an attempt to get his essay started (1979, 2). Similarly, in an article written over ten years later on "Redefining the Legacy of Mina Shaughnessy" (1991), Min-Zhan Lu analyzes the writings of a student whom Shaughnessy singles out for praise, pointing out that while the student does indeed seem to grow stylistically more fluent, the political positions she expresses in her successive writings also seem to shift significantly, although this attracts no comment from Shaughnessy.

aspects of communication such as content and message, style, choice of words, logical development, originality of thought and expression, and so forth. Such are the real components of language power, and they cannot be measured by narrow conceptions of "correct grammar." While teachers frequently correct student language on the basis of such misguided conceptions, saying something correctly, and saying it well, are two entirely different Thangs. (229)

This emphasis on forming something to say and working to say it well could hardly be more different than Shaughnessy's focus on error. Smitherman continues to drive this emphasis home by comparing her responses to two student pieces: one a vacuous (and stylistically bland) comment on Baraka's *Dutchman* by a white student teacher, and the other a poorly developed paragraph on the evils of war by an African American ninth grader. What I find striking is how Smitherman uses much the same strategy in responding to both writers, challenging them to articulate their positions more fully before working to correct their phrasings. To the white student, Smitherman said

as kindly as I could, that his "essay" was weak in content and repetitious, and that it did not demonstrate command of the literary critical tools that teachers of literature are supposed to possess, *plus it didn't really say nothing!* (229)

While in responding to the African American ninth grader writing on war, she asked things like,

"Some say" . . . Who is "some"? . . . Exactly who are the two sides you're talking about here? What category of people? Name them and tell something about them. . . . Give me an example showing when and how such a disagreement leads to war. (230)

While these two responses show some differences in tone (and perhaps appropriately so, given the varying situations of the writers), their aim is quite similar: to get students to think about what they want to say in their writing and about the effects their words have on readers. Smitherman is quick to say that she is not advocating an "off-the-deep-end permissiveness of letting the kids get away with anything," but rather that she is teaching toward a rhetorical and stylistic awareness "deeper and more expansive" than that encouraged by a focus on norms of correctness (233). Her position is much the same as that taken by Rouse in his response to Shaughnessy, and indeed something like it has become in recent years the consensus view of the profession, at least as represented in the pages of *CCC* and *College English* and at the annual meetings of CCCC: students must learn not simply how to avoid mistakes but how to write in ways that engage the attention of educated readers. Teachers need to respond to what students are trying to say, to the effectiveness of their writing as a whole, and not simply to the presence or absence of local errors in spelling, syntax, or usage. Correctness thus becomes not the single and defining issue in learning how to write, but simply one aspect of developing a more general communicative competence.

This shift in focus was given articulate and moving expression by Mike Rose in his 1989 *Lives on the Boundary*, a book which, like *Errors and Expectations*, gained almost immediate acclaim both within and outside the profession. Like Shaughnessy, Rose argues for the intelligence and promise of students too often dismissed as unprepared or even unfit for college work, and like her too, his work and writing speaks to the links between education and politics, since the underprepared students he works with are so often also (and not coincidentally) people of color or from lower socioeconomic classes. And, certainly, even though the students Rose works with in Los Angeles in the 1980s often seem to live in an almost completely different world than those Shaughnessy worked with in New York in the 1970s, what both groups most need to learn is how to find their way into a system of education that seems at many points purposely designed to exclude them. But rather than assuming, like Shaughnessy, that what such students need is yet more training in the "basics," Rose argues that an unremitting focus on the more routine and dull aspects of intellectual work can instead act to dim their ambitions and limit their chances of success. One of the most telling bits of evidence Rose has to offer for this view comes from his own life, since as a boy he was placed in the vocational track of his local schools and so learned of the boredom and condescension of such classrooms first-hand. He was only retracked into college prep when a teacher noticed he was doing suspiciously well in biology. You don't know what you don't know, Rose suggests: "The telling thing is how chancy both my placement into and exit from Voc. Ed. was; neither I nor my parents had anything to do with it" (1989, 30). We can't expect students to grow proficient at kinds of intellectual work that they don't know about, that they've never really been given a chance to try their hands at.

What struggling students need, then, is not more of the basics but a sense of what others find most exciting and useful about books, writing, and ideas. Here's how Rose describes how he began to form his own aims for teaching while working with a group of Vietnam veterans studying to return to college:

> Given the nature of these men's needs and given the limited time I would have with them, could I perhaps orient them to some of the kinds of reading and writing and ways of thinking that seem essential to a liberal course of study, some of the habits of mind that Jack MacFarland and the many [of Rose's own teachers] that followed him helped me develop? . . . I was looking for a methodical way to get my students to think about thinking. Thinking. Not a fussbudget course, but a course about thought. I finally decided to build a writing curriculum on four of the intellectual strategies my education had helped me develop—some of which, I later learned, were as old as Aristotle—strategies that kept emerging as I reflected on the life of the undergraduate: summarizing, classifying, comparing, and analyzing. (1989, 138)

The crucial words here are *habits of mind*, a phrasing even older than Aristotle, at least as it is often used to translate the Greek notion of *areté*, those "virtues" or "excellences" required by the citizens of a democracy.[5] There is an admirable hardheadedness reminiscent of Shaughnessy in this teaching project; like her, Rose wants to demystify the workings of the academy for his students. But a course on habits or strategies of thinking is in practice quite different from one focused on issues of correctness in language. As Rose outlines his course,

> Each quarter, I began by having the students summarize short simple readings, and then moved them slowly through classifying and comparing to

---

5. There is a gendered subtext here as well that I can only begin to hint at: the Greek view of *areté* is closely connected with manliness, valor (the word is etymologically related to *Ares*, the god of war). It is thus peculiarly suggestive (even if also coincidental) that Rose should begin to form his notion of teaching toward "habits of mind" while working with a set of war veterans, and certainly the kind of teaching that he, David Bartholomae, and others have been associated with has strong masculinist overtones. ("Reading involves a fair measure of push and shove" is the first sentence of the introduction to Bartholomae and Petrosky's 1990 *Ways of Reading*.) On the other hand, the sort of "fussbudget" course that Rose wants to avoid, and that Shaughnessy provides with her emphasis on form and correctness, has a stereotypically feminine and nurturing (or perhaps school-marmish) quality. James Catano offers an interesting look into this issue in his 1990 article "The Rhetoric of Masculinity."

analyzing. . . . I explained and modeled, used accessible readings, tried to incorporate what the veterans learned from one assignment to the next, slowly increased difficulty, and provided a lot of time for the men to talk and write. (1989, 143)

Malcolm Kiniry and Rose offer a more elaborate version of such a course in their 1990 *Critical Strategies for Academic Writing*, a text whose aim is to engage students in reading and writing, at a beginning and approximate level, about the kinds of issues and questions that academics in various fields take on. Similarly, in their 1986 *Facts, Artifacts, and Counterfacts*, David Bartholomae and Anthony Petrosky sketch out a plan for a basic writing course that is set up very much like a graduate seminar: students read, write, and talk together about a particular intellectual issue over the course of a term, coming at the same topic from a number of different angles, reading one another's writings, seeing how the individual concerns they bring to their common subject influence what each of them has to say about it. The trick of such teaching is, of course, to find a set of readings underprepared students will find accessible, and not only speak to their concerns but also push their ways of understanding and talking about them. (Some of the classes described in *Facts, Artifacts*, for instance, had students read and write on growth and adolescence, or work, or creativity.) But what's more important is how this sort of teaching signals a shift in focus from *error* to *academic discourse*, from issues of phrasing and correctness to matters of stance and argument.

I support this shift myself, and, again, feel that Shaughnessy's failure to attend in any sustained way to issues beyond the sentence is what now makes her work, less than twenty years after its appearance, seem of mere historical interest rather than of practical use. (There is a dark irony here: the subtitle of *Errors and Expectations* is *A Guide for the Teacher of Basic Writing*, and Shaughnessy is often invoked as a model practitioner whose scholarship was deeply rooted in her day-to-day work with students. And yet I can't now imagine giving *Errors and Expectations* as a guide to a beginning teacher of basic writing, although I still often offer new teachers other writings from the 1960s and 1970s by people like Moffett, Britton, Elbow, and Coles.) Still one can see how this downplaying of error might seem to outsiders simply a way of slipping past the difficulty and drudgery of actually teaching writing. "Students and parents complain that they are being patronized, that the more relaxed, more personalist pedagogy fails to teach anybody how to write" (852), was how Graff (who is no cultural reactionary) put it in 1980. Given his distrust of Rouse and defense of Shaughnessy, it seems clear that for Graff learning "how to write" involves strong attention to issues of correctness, and his complaint about "relaxed" standards has been echoed in countless ways not only by students and parents but also by college faculty and administrators, as well as by writers in the popular press.[6] As one of my colleagues, a biologist, said to me recently after a curriculum meeting in which I argued for a new structuring of introductory writing courses at my college: "The thing is, most of us think that too many students can't write worth a damn, and we wish you'd just do something about it."

It's tempting to dismiss such complaints as misinformed, as in many ways they surely are. But to do so fails to address the problem. For some time now, most compositionists have held that a focus on error can often block the attempts of beginning writers to form their thoughts in prose, and indeed that the explicit teaching of grammatical forms usually has little effect on the abilities of students to write fluently or correctly.[7] But ask anyone *outside* the field (and this includes many writing teachers who are not active in CCCC) what they expect students to learn in a composition course, and you are likely to hear a good bit about issues of proper form and correctness. As even someone like the distinguished liberal philosopher Richard Rorty put it, when asked in an interview about what the aims of a writing course might be:

> I think the idea of freshman English, mostly, is just to get them to write complete sentences, get the commas in the right place, and stuff like that—the stuff we would like to think the high schools do and, in fact, they don't. But

---

6. A poll of parents of public school students, for instance, found them strongly suspicious of "new methods of teaching composition" and desirous for a return to "the basics" (Johnson and Immerwahr 1994); more sustained outsider criticisms of progressive language teaching have also appeared in magazines like *The New Republic* (Traub 1993) and *The Atlantic Monthly* (Levine 1994).

7. The first and still most ringing statement of this professional consensus came from Braddock, Lloyd-Jones, and Schoer in their 1963 *Research on Written Composition*: "In view of the widespread agreement of research studies based upon many types of students and teachers, the conclusion can be stated in strong and unqualified terms: the teaching of grammar has a negligible or, because it usually displaces some instruction and practice in composition, even a harmful effect on improvement in writing" (37–38). Twenty years later, Patrick Hartwell revisited the research on the effectiveness of explicit teaching of rules of correctness and once again concluded (along with virtually everyone he cites) that such teaching has little usefulness and thus that we ought to "move on to more interesting areas of inquiry" (1985, 127).

as long as there's a need for freshman English, it's going to be primarily a matter of the least common denominator of all the jargon. (Olson 1989, 6–7)

Although Rorty's interviewer, Gary Olson, expresses surprise at this response (since Rorty's views on language have influenced many progressive composition theorists), it seems to me both familiar and reasonable enough. What I find more distressing has been the ongoing inability of compositionists (myself among them) to explain ourselves to people like Graff and Rorty. Instead we have too often retreated behind the walls of our professional consensus, admonishing not only our students and university colleagues but the more general public as well when they fail to defer to our views on language learning—answering their concerns about correctness by telling them, in effect, that they should not want what they are asking us for.

This is an unfortunate stance for a field that defines itself through its interest in teaching and the practical workings of language. I am not advocating a return to a Shaughnessy-like focus on error, but I do think we can learn from her responsiveness to the concerns of people outside our field. Rather than either meekly acceding to or simply dismissing what Smitherman called "the national mania for correctness" (1977, 229), we need to argue for a view of literacy that clearly recognizes and includes such concerns but is not wholly defined by them.

A first step might be to reinterpret worries about "grammar" or "correctness" in a more generous and expansive way. Rather than reading them as moves to trivialize the issues involved in learning to write, to turn everything into a simple matter of proofreading, we might see such remarks as somewhat clumsy attempts to voice concerns about how one gains or loses authority in writing. For even if mistakes do not interfere with what a writer has to say, they can still do serious harm to her credibility. Indeed, it is precisely because many mistakes (lapses in spelling or punctuation, for instance) seem so trivial that their appearance in a writer's text can seem to speak of a lack of care or ability. People don't want to be caught out in their writing or to have their students or children caught out. And so many struggling writers speak of their "problems with grammar" as a kind of shorthand for a whole set of difficulties they have with writing that are much harder to name, much as many readers begin to complain about fairly trivial errors in a text they have grown impatient with for other less easily defined reasons. It is one thing to feel that in a particular classroom your language will not be held up for ridicule; it is another to feel confidence in your abilities to write to an indifferent or even hostile reader—to a different sort of teacher or examiner, perhaps, or to an applications committee or potential employer. Something like this concern is, I think, what lies behind many worries about "relaxed" or "permissive" forms of teaching. To gloss over such concerns is to dodge questions about the workings of power in language at their most naked.

Not that responding to them is all that easy either. As I've noted before, simply drilling students in proper forms has been shown to have little effect—and besides, the problem of gaining authority is not merely a matter of getting rid of error; students must also and at the same time acquire a rhetorical ease and power, an ability to write persuasively as well as correctly. And standards of correctness vary from one context to the other, along with the readiness of readers to look for mistakes, as Joseph Williams points out in his stunning 1981 article, "The Phenomenology of Error," in which he shows how the authors of writing handbooks often commit the same errors they decry, and sometimes in the very act of stating them—as when, for instance, while inveighing against the use of negative constructions, one text declares that "the following example . . . is not untypical"; or when in "Politics and the English Language" Orwell casts his famous polemic against the passive voice *in the passive voice*; or when yet another handbook advises that "Emphasis is often achieved . . . by the use of verbs in the active rather than in the passive voice" (158). The reason we don't tend to notice such problems, Williams argues, is that we're not looking for them. And, conversely, the reason we find so many mistakes in student papers is because we expect to, we're on the watch for them. (Williams clinches his case by revealing, at the end of his article, that he has deliberately inserted about a hundred "errors" in his own text. I have never met a reader who claimed to notice more than two or three on a first reading.)

Williams's point is not that we should downplay the significance of error but that we should focus our attention and energies on those mistakes that really count, on those that seriously impugn a writer's authority. (Maxine Hairston added to this line of thinking in a piece that also appeared in 1981, "Not All Errors Are Created Equal: Nonacademic Readers in the Professions Respond to Lapses in Usage.") This makes good sense, but even more important is how Williams locates "error" as something that exists not simply as marks on a page but also as a part of the consciousness of writers, readers, and (in the form of handbooks and such) the culture at large. A mistake is not a mistake unless it's noticed as one, is how the argument goes, and it's a line of thought that sheds light both on why some writers have such difficulty proofreading their work and on the role readers play in creating a mania of correctness. For what is involved in detecting errors seems to be not only an awareness of rules but a shift in attentiveness: one needs to learn how to read for mistakes as well as meaning.[8] This suggests the need for a kind of double approach to the issue of error, one that deals frankly with the practical politics of the situation: what writers need to learn is how to read their work for those lapses that will send many readers into a tailspin; what readers (and the culture) need to learn is to lighten up, to recognize the writing of reasonably correct prose as a fairly complex intellectual achievement and to be a little less quick to damn a writer for a few mistakes.

In practice one often sees this sort of double approach. In the *Facts, Artifacts* course, for instance, students are asked to revise and edit one of their writings for publication in a class book, a process that requires them to carefully proofread and correct their prose. And while his *Lives on the Boundary* is a plea to reform education in America, to make it more forgiving of error and more willing to work with difference, the picture Mike Rose offers of himself *as a teacher* throughout the book is of someone who wants to help students claim whatever power they can in the system as it stands. As one woman tells him,

> You know, Mike, people always hold this shit over you, make you . . . make you feel stupid with their fancy talk. But now *I've* read it, I've read Shakespeare, I can say I, *Olga*, have read it. I won't tell you I like it, 'cause I don't know if I do or I don't. But I like knowing what it's about. (1989, 223)

While in another context, I might want to quibble with the term *fancy talk*, what is crucial to realize here, I think, is that unless you already feel at home in the workings of critical or intellectual discourse, that's all it's likely to seem to you: fancy talk. And I don't see how you could possibly

---

8. Some of the practical difficulties of teaching and learning proofreading are hinted at by the very number of people who have written on its complexities. The first issue of the *Journal of Basic Writing*, founded and edited by Mina Shaughnessy in 1975, was devoted entirely to the topic of error and included pieces by Sarah D'Eloia, Isabella Halstead, and Valerie Krishna. The next decade saw more work on the subject from David Bartholomae (1980), Mary Epes (1985), Glynda Hull (1987), and Elaine Lees (1987). More recently, Bruce Horner (1992) and Min-Zhan Lu (1994) have written on the problematic relations between "error" and "style."

begin to feel at ease in any sort of fancy talk unless you also felt sure both that what you had to say would be listened to seriously and that you weren't likely to commit any egregious nails-on-the-chalkboard kinds of mistakes (*c'est je*, that sort of thing) in trying to speak or write it. So while we can't teach for correctness alone, we also can't *not* teach for it either. I think of the joke in Calvin Trillin's 1977 novel *Runestruck*, when a lawyer goes out "on a drive to relax from the pressures of a civil liberties case he was arguing in a nearby town—the case of an elementary school teacher of progressive views who claimed that she was fired by the local school board solely because she had refused to teach her students to spell" (23). "Better watch my grammar" versus "won't really teach kids how to write." Some choice. (And Trillin probably actually knew something about the debate over error in the 1970s, since he was married to Alice Trillin, who taught basic writing with Shaughnessy at City College.) We need to make sure that in distancing ourselves from poor practice (a focus on error alone) we don't seem to advocate an equally unconvincing stance (no concern with error at all).

In the mid-1980s, a number of teachers and theorists tried to break out of this rhetorical bind by arguing that the job of writing teachers was to initiate students into the workings of the academic discourse community, to learn the specific conventions of college writing. I comment more on this move in the next chapter. For now, I simply want to say that the power of this view has much to do with the elasticity of the term *convention*—which can describe almost anything from a critical habit of mind to a preferred form of citing sources to specific usages and phrasings. Using a term like *convention*, you can argue (and indeed I would) that in learning to write at college, students need to work on everything from spelling and punctuation to active verbs to self-reflexivity—and to do all this at once. Nothing can ruin the credibility of an academic piece more than poor proofreading (I know from hard experience as both a writer and journal editor), but errorless typing doesn't make up for a lack of critical insight either. To gain control over academic discourse, writers need to work on several levels at once—as do their teachers.

There is both a conceptual and rhetorical problem, though, I think, with a stress on specifically academic writing. In her 1991 rereading of *Errors and Expectations*, Min-Zhan Lu criticizes Shaughnessy's tendency to pit the ways with words that students bring with them to college against a seemingly neutral "language of public transactions" (Shaughnessy 1977, 125)—a move which Lu argues allows her to gloss over the fact that academic writing is both characterized by the use of certain linguistic forms and often associated with a particular set of political values. We do not teach a contextless Standard Written English, Lu argues, but a specific kind of writing closely tied to the particular aims and needs of university work. We thus need to recognize there are other Englishes, tied to other contexts or communities, that are not simply underdeveloped or less-public versions of academic discourse, but that work toward different ends and whose use may express a competing or oppositional politics—as when, for instance, Geneva Smitherman draws on the forms and phrasings of African American English throughout *Talkin and Testifyin.* This view of academic discourse as a limited and specific *use* of language, whose characteristic forms and gestures can thus be defined and taught, has proven a powerful tool in sharpening our sense of what might go on in a college writing class. But it can also seem once more to cast its advocates in the role of simply teaching a professional jargon. For instance, when asked by Gary Olson if writing teachers should try to teach students the "normal discourse" of the academic fields they are studying, Richard Rorty replies,

> It strikes me as a terrible idea. . . . I think that America has made itself a bit ridiculous in the international academic world by developing distinctive disciplinary jargon. It's the last thing we want to inculcate in the freshmen. (Olson 1989, 6–7)

Rorty's tone here is sneering, but still the issue he raises is an important one: Is the point of undergraduate study to prepare students to become professional intellectuals? Or to put it another way, even if our aim is to teach students a particular form of writing (and not some neutral "standard"), is that form best described as "academic"? For some time now in composition, *academic* has served as the opposing term to words like *personal* or *expressive*. That is, if one does not ask students to write directly from experience but instead sets them to writing about books and ideas, then, according to common usage, their work is "academic."[9] But I'm not so sure about the usefulness of the term, which at best tends to suggest a stylistic distance or formality and at worst to serve as shorthand

---

9. This standoff between the "academic" and the "personal" gets played out in a 1995 *CCC* interchange between David Bartholomae and Peter Elbow—although, tellingly, when pushed, Bartholomae ends up defending not "academic" writing but something he calls *criticism.* Kurt Spellmeyer offers a powerful reading of this exchange, which began as a series of talks at CCCC, in the last chapter of *Common Ground* (1993).

for pretension and bad writing. And I don't think the sort of writing I usually imagine myself as teaching toward is in any strict sense *academic* (although it is not simply personal either). That is, while I almost always ask undergraduates to write on texts and ideas, I rarely ask them to do the sort of reading through the relevant academic literature I would routinely require of graduate students (who *are* training to become professional intellectuals), and I don't spend much time on issues of citation, documentation, and the like.[10] (I rarely even teach anything like the "research paper.") I'm more interested in having students read the work of others closely and aggressively, and to use their reading in thinking and writing about issues that concern them. I would like my students to begin to think of themselves as critics and intellectuals. But that is not at all the same as preparing them to become academics.

I think this is more than a fussing over terms. In his 1994 "Travels to the Hearts of the Forest: Dilettantes, Professionals, and Knowledge," Kurt Spellmeyer shows how academics routinely lay claim to expertise by denigrating the knowledge of nonspecialists or amateurs (a kind of sinister version of the critical move defined in 1985 by David Bartholomae in "Inventing the University"). By way of example, Spellmeyer shows how university ethnographers and art historians labored to assert the authority of their own systematized and restricted bodies of knowledge over the more idiosyncratic works of "mere" travel writers and connoisseurs. But he might just as easily have chosen to talk about how academic literary scholars have over the years differentiated themselves from mere reviewers or how a newly disciplined generation of composition scholars now seek to distinguish themselves from mere classroom practitioners. With Spellmeyer, I believe we need to be wary of an increasingly narrow professionalization of knowledge—and thus that we should resist equating the "critical" with the "academic."

In making this distinction I also think of books like Peter Medway's 1980 *Finding a Language*, in which he reports on his attempts to do something more than simply pass time as the teacher of a set of working-class British youths near the end of their formal schooling, none of whom were likely to go on to university and all of whom had resisted most other attempts to interest them in their course work. Medway had these students define an issue that mattered to them in their lives outside of school (jobs, politics, sports, and so on), and then had them spend the

---

10. We do sometimes talk, though, about the rhetorical and stylistic uses of footnotes.

rest of the term reading and writing about it. There's little about the course, as thoughtful as it is, that would be likely to startle an informed American teacher of basic writing; in fact, it seems very much like the sort of course described in *Facts, Artifacts*. But that's precisely my point. Medway's aim was not to help his students enter the academy (there was little realistic hope of doing so for all but one or two of them); his goal was to have them reflect critically on the world they were part of right then. Freed from having to prepare his students to write according to the formal standards of an academy they would never enter, Medway was able instead to think about how to engage their intellectual curiosity and urge them toward a self-reflectiveness.

Of course Medway was only freed from such expectations by working in a culture that is more stratified by social class than ours. His students had little prospect of moving out of the circumstances that they were born into, whatever they did in school. But the promise of America is to be able to do just that—and education has long been advertised as one way of doing it. Underneath all the worries about correctness in writing, then, there is hope that getting it right will mean getting ahead (or at least allow the chance of getting ahead). But there is fear, too: What is the point of having a standard that includes everyone, a marker that fails to separate? Language is not only a means of communicating but a form of identification, a badge that seems to define its wearer and yet, paradoxically, can be changed. It is the fear and hope of such change that so powerfully charges the debate on error.

POSTSCRIPT, 2012: DIFFERENCE AS A RESOURCE

Correctness no longer seems as urgent a concern as it once did in the teaching of writing. In part, this is due to advances in technology. We now have machines—spell checks, grammar checks, and other editing tools—to help us with the "mechanics" of writing. And kids these days tend to be faulted for writing too much—or at least texting and messaging too much—rather than too little. Yes, there are still issues of access to technology, and no, a computer can't do everything. But for most of us the practical labor of writing—of putting words on a screen or page—has been transformed. The difficulties of preparing a clean handwritten or typed document have all but been forgotten, as has the tedium of trying to decipher imperfect attempts to do so. If many errors can be imagined as a kind of static that interferes with the reception of a text, then the channels through which we write have become far more reliable and clear. Most college students can now, with minimal effort, produce an easily readable text. We can thus focus our attention where it belongs, which is on what makes a text worth reading.

Andrea Lunsford and Karen Lunsford confirm this decline in "static" in their 2008 analysis of error patterns in student writing. Comparing their study to similar ones published in 1917, 1930, and 1986, they note that students are now writing much longer pieces—an average of 1,038 words per piece in 2006, when almost all students used word processing, as opposed to only 426 in 1986, when most of their texts were handwritten (792). They also point to striking drops in the rate of mistakes in spelling, verb forms, verb endings, and subject-verb agreement (798–99)—all of which are errors flagged by computer spelling and grammar checks.

So the digital era seems to have helped increase fluency and curtail editorial drudgery. But Lunsford and Lunsford also note a higher rate of mistakes involving "wrong words" (2008, 796) and "faulty sentence structure" (798). What's intriguing is that these are mistakes that can stem not only from carelessness or inexperience but ambition. When sentences grow longer, they can also become harder to control, and Lunsford and Lunsford speculate that some errors in sentence structure may have resulted from students "attempting to address complex topics in complex ways" (798). Similarly, problems with word choice can sometimes arise when a writer is trying to say something new (at least for him or her) and quite literally doesn't yet have the words to do so with. In both cases, what may seem at first a simple mistake might actually hint at a meaning that a writer is struggling to articulate.

This is the position taken by Bruce Horner, Min-Zhan Lu, Jacqueline Jones Royster, and John Trimbur in their 2011 manifesto, "Language Difference in Writing: Toward a Translingual Approach." Horner et al. argue that, in a globalized culture, it makes little sense to try to defend a single standard form of academic writing. Instead we should read differences in phrasing and syntax as possible sites of new meaning, marking them as simple mistakes only as "an interpretation of last resort" (304). In its respect for students, this translingual approach builds on two ur-texts in our field: the 1974 CCCC Students' Right to Their Own Language and Shaughnessy's 1977 *Errors and Expectations*. But there is a key difference. Both CCCC and Shaughnessy distinguished sharply between students' "home languages" and academic discourse, suggesting that students must learn to switch, as needed, back and forth from one to the other. Horner et al. argue instead for a hybrid view of academic writing—one that sees difference as a resource, and that, even at the risk of a higher incidence of error, values a mix of discourses, languages, voices, and registers.

Shaughnessy begins *Errors and Expectations* with the memory of

> sitting alone in the worn urban classroom where my students had just written their first essays and where I now began to read them, hoping to be able to assess quickly the sort of task that lay ahead of us that semester. But the writing was so stunningly unskilled that I could not begin to define the task nor even sort out the difficulties. I could only sit there, reading and re-reading the alien papers, wondering what had gone wrong, and trying to understand what I at this eleventh hour of their academic lives could do about it. (1977, vii)

It's a stirring image, the teacher in her classroom, reading the same papers over and over, searching for a place to begin. But it is also an image that poses difference as a problem to be solved. They—students, "aliens"—need to be taught how to write like us.

I don't mean to romanticize the struggles of basic or underprepared writers. But I'm not convinced that what such writers need is to acquire some sort of new discourse—or that we ought to wait until they have done so before we listen to what they have to say. Indeed I suspect that the more we isolate academic writing from other uses of language, the more we define it as a separate genre or code that one must "switch" into, the more we are likely to impoverish it. I am drawn instead to what Suresh Canagarajah calls *codemeshing*—an approach to writing modeled on the strategies of speakers in multilingual environments (2009). In such situations, when no single language is shared by all speakers, everyone must bring all their linguistic resources to the acts of speaking and listening. The result can be a vibrant if unstable meshing of languages, registers, modalities, gestures, and images.

Scott Lyons eloquently demurs from this view in his 2009 essay on "The Fine Art of Fencing." Writing as a Native American scholar and activist, Lyons wants to retain a space for speech and writing in Native languages. That is, he sees the need for fences, for borders between languages. At the same time, though, he insists that "English is indeed an Indian language" (98). Natives don't need to be taught to mesh or switch into English, he suggests, since it is already one of their languages. They just need to learn how to use it more powerfully—since

English offers them access to social power and mobility that Native languages do not. This puts him, Lyons feels, in the position of making "an unsexy argument endorsing the value of teaching Standard English to Natives" (79)— a position remarkably similar to that of Shaughnessy in *Errors and Expectations*. But if Lyons is really convinced of a Shaughnessy-like need to teach what he calls "stodgy old academic prose" (100), then he spectacularly fails to model such writing in his essay—which is a striking blend of Ojibwe history, personal narrative, critical polemic, kidding asides about Native culture and its perception in the white world, and knowing references to the likes of both the critical theorist Homi Bhabha and "Leech Lake rapper Wahwahtay Benais" (100). In short, Lyons brilliantly illustrates the uses of codemeshing in his criticisms of it. If I were his student, I'd follow not his precept but his example.

Canagarajah sometimes refers to codemeshing as *translanguage*, the term used by Horner et al. in "Language Difference in Writing." Whatever term is used, to take a translingual approach is not to deny that all writers sometimes make mistakes that get in the way of what they are trying to do. But it is to suggest that not all moments of difference in a text need to be corrected or erased. To the contrary, such moments may lend depth, complexity, and nuance to a piece of writing. In that sense, calls for codemeshing begin to sound much like recent appeals for alternative forms of academic writing—as students and scholars alike are urged to write in ways that mix voices, styles, and genres.

I find this an immensely appealing view of intellectual writing. It is thus unfortunate that Lunsford and Lunsford saw so little of it in their recent study of student error. In a section of their article on "What We Did Not Find," they write:

> More surprising was the little evidence of what has come to be called—perhaps in homage to Winston Weathers's charming and important *An Alternate Style*—alternate or alternative discourse. With the exception of a handful of funny and often imaginative letters to aliens, all from the same class, as well as some fiction, the papers we examined stuck resolutely to what Weathers dubbed Grammar A: traditional usage, organization, and style. (2008, 799)

This is not just surprising but depressing. Surely as teachers of writing we ought to ask students to do more than produce papers with "traditional usage, organization, and style." We ought to ask for intellectual and stylistic ambition. To talk with students about codemeshing is to tell them not only that we respect their cultures and languages, but also that we value difference and innovation in writing. That's an important message for writers on the margins of the academy to hear, but also an important one for those students who have only been taught how to execute the rules of Grammar A. We need not to restrict but expand the forms in which we invite students to write.

INTERCHAPTER

Another sort of correctness in writing worries people, and that is correctness of a political sort. Many who fear that students are no longer being taught how to write well suspect they are instead being trained how to think correctly, that lessons in politics are supplanting lessons in language. This is a line of thinking that tends to infuriate many teachers of writing, who argue that they want not to indoctrinate but to empower students, to make them more aware of how our uses of language shape how we view and act in the world. But in practice the line between fostering such an awareness and insisting on a kind of correctness often seems to become blurred. Consider, for instance, this letter to the director of composition at a large public university.

Dear ———,

I am extremely disappointed in the composition course here at the University. It fosters an exceedingly stifling environment with respect to creativity and personal opinion. . . .

The only way to get an 'A' in this course is to write what you know the teacher wants to hear. What the teacher wants is always obviously pointed out in the instructions. You will notice that I use the word 'teacher' rather than 'professor' to refer to the instructor. I have never heard of an actual professor teaching a composition class.

One would be unlikely to take extreme exception to pieces written by the masters that have been held up to scrutiny for many years. But, very few of these pieces were included. I was expected not to analyze, but to give the 'popular' views of today's young culture on writings that have not been tested by time and that were written by extremists. These popular answers invariably espouse liberalism, feminism, and the like. . . . I suppose there might not be anything wrong with not using time tested materials. The wrongness lies in the fact that if there haven't been generations of experts that have touted a work as a classic (as in the case of a work by Poe, Shakespeare, Hemingway, or Thoreau) then in my opinion I should not be penalized for criticizing new texts (by the likes of Alice Walker, Richard Rodriguez, and Joyce Carol Oates). One should not be placed at a disadvantage for criticizing even a classic. Independent and creative thought is what universities herald with the highest esteem as the foundations of their educational doctrine. . . .

Please also understand that this is not merely a student grumbling about a bad grade. I received a 'B' in the class. After two years of introspection I believe the grade should have been an 'A.' (As an interesting sidelight (and as evidence that I am no mean student) I will mention that this is the only class in my college career that I have received lower than an 'A' in thus far.)

I can recall a few specific deficiencies in my composition experience. I was criticized for "hiding behind my vocabulary" because I used "big" words. (Whatever that means. The language employed was similar to that used in this letter.) I am not one to throw an essay together in a slapdash fashion. I choose my words carefully so as to convey the specific meanings which I intend.

Whenever I criticized an essay I was repeatedly told that I was "missing the point." This is not true. I understood the point, I merely did not accept the paradigm set forth by the essay. . . . A final petty example occurred when I was criticized for using the accepted practice of using the masculine form of a pronoun (he) when it was expedient to use a pronoun in reference to a group of male and female (or gender neutral or ambiguous) articles. The suggested alternative was a bulky 'he/ she' so as to be politically correct.

Another quarrel that I have with this composition course is that my observations have led me to believe that its goal is not to teach students to be effective writers. It seems to me that it is being used as a vehicle for the University's program of cultural diversity. "Diverse" authors are chosen for the purpose of illustrating literary techniques that might better have been shown by text written by authors that happened to be white, American, and male. This is not to say that only white, American, male authors wrote texts worthy of being in a college classroom. It is merely a fact that throughout much of our relevant history that group has been the primary literary machine. If ninety percent of all excellent and relevant writings for the class happen to have been written by the above mentioned group then I find no reason why somewhere close to the percentages of those types of authors should not be included in the curriculum. To have only one or two readings out of six to come from that group is clearly a ploy at structuring a diversity program. . . .

A fact that has made me even more sure than before of the motives of this program is the content of a recent teacher evaluation given to one of the composition classes. The questionnaire (this part had been devised by the particular teacher rather than as part of the general teacher evaluation form) asked questions like, "Did this class change any of your views or attitudes towards people?" To me this is asking, "Did this class do its job as a diversity program?" I do not dispute the value of diversity, except when it interferes with my education and especially when it is an undisclosed agenda in the classroom (I'd liken that to mind-programming), as in this case. . . .

To conclude, I charge that the University's composition course is wholly inadequate. It's curriculum and goals should be seriously reevaluated. The primary interest of the class should be to instruct students on analyzing and writing about texts in a fashion compatible with a university setting in a way that allows creativity and independent thinking to take place unhampered by nonprofessional teachers with misplaced values.

The reputation of this heretofore fine institution is at stake. I would appreciate any comments or responses that you might have.

Sincerely,

Jeffrey _____

I think the issues Jeffrey raises here will speak to many people who have worked in large composition programs. (I should perhaps note that he was not writing to me.) What is unusual about his letter, though, is that it is *not* a complaint about a grade or a teacher. For while Jeffrey remarks that he now feels he deserved a higher grade in his composition course, he writes some two years after taking it, never asks for his grade to be reviewed, and does not even mention the name of his teacher. His letter is instead something far more cranky and remarkable: an unsolicited political critique of the composition program as a whole. This doesn't mean I fully trust his account of the class he took; his purpose in writing seems less to describe than to indict, and his examples and phrasings are carefully chosen to do just that. And he seems so determined to criticize the course he took that I have to wonder if he has not sometimes misunderstood its aims. (For instance, was the point of bringing readings into the class really to "illustrate literary techniques"? Might not they have been used instead to suggest lines of inquiry into various topics for writing? If so, his convoluted arguments about the racial and gendered makeup of the "classics" have little force.) Still, Jeffrey's comments hint at ways in which teachers can sometimes silence dissent in the name of diversity, and his letter suggests no less than three ways, at some points overlapping and others conflicting, in which one might talk about the politics of teaching writing.

The first has to do with what Wayne Booth called in 1981 "the major scandal in higher education today": the routine practice of staffing composition courses with graduate assistants or part-time instructors who are usually overworked and badly paid, and very often poorly trained and supervised. Jeffrey makes it clear that this is the case at his university and he is right to call its faculty on their bluff. ("I have never heard of an actual professor teaching a composition class...") He also points to a weakness of this book and much other work on teaching: One can't expect people who are exploited by their institutions and undervalued by their colleagues to spend the sort of time and effort required to teach writing well (although an amazing number do anyway). To change how writing actually gets taught day by day in most college classrooms, then, we need not only to draw on the kind of critical work in composition I have looked at in this book but also to agitate for better working conditions for all writing teachers (and not simply tenure-stream compositionists). That sort of practical politics underlies all our work as teachers of writing. It is also by far the most intractable problem we face. It is one thing to change a course, quite another to change how it is staffed, one thing to change a curriculum, another to change a faculty.

And so, in fact, most talk about the politics of teaching has had to do with changing the content of courses or curricula, with teachers "bringing politics into" the classroom in the form of revised reading lists or new critical methodologies. Of course it can be argued that such politics were always already there anyway—that if it is now "political" to read Alice Walker, then so too was it political to read E. B. White or Thoreau; that if it is now "political" to ask students to analyze gender stereotypes in advertisements, then so too was it political to have them compose elegies to summers past and the hometowns they have left behind. The problem with both sides of this argument, though, is the way in which they imagine one can determine the politics of a course simply by consulting its reading list. But what students are asked or allowed to do with their reading, the range of responses to a text or issue that they are permitted to voice—this is not so easily seen from a syllabus. As Jeffrey writes in his letter to the director,

> In my opinion I should not be penalized for criticizing new texts (by the likes of Alice Walker, Richard Rodriguez, and Joyce Carol Oates). One should not be placed at a disadvantage for criticizing even a classic.

But it is no longer clear at this point just what Jeffrey means by "classic." Is it still one of those "pieces written by the masters that have been held up to scrutiny for many years," or is he by now thinking of one those "new" texts advocating "liberalism, feminism, and the like"? Even if unintended, this ambiguity is crucial. For it suggests that the issue goes beyond whether students read Edgar Allan Poe or Joyce Carol Oates or anyone else: It also has to do with the ways in which they are encouraged not just to admire but to criticize the texts they read, not just to apply but to resist or revise the methods of analysis they are shown. And so the cultural politics of the classroom—what views get espoused, what texts get read—begin to merge into questions about the *micropolitics of teaching*, about how teachers set up courses to encourage some kinds of talk and discourage others.

In the course Jeffrey took, the ban on certain phrasings was quite overt:

> A final petty example occurred when I was criticized for using the accepted practice of using the masculine form of a pronoun (he) when it was expedient to use a pronoun in reference to a group of male and female (or gender neutral or ambiguous) articles. The suggested alternative was a bulky 'he/she' so as to be politically correct.

Here political and grammatical correctness come together, as a fairly complex question of style gets resolved (at least according to this student) as a simple matter of law: Don't use the universal *he*. Such teaching somehow manages to be at once coercive and ineffectual. All Jeffrey recalls is a petty assertion of authority. His teacher's insistence on a "politically correct" form two years ago has not led him to rethink his use of pronouns since, but simply to reassert what he (mistakenly) believes is the "accepted practice" of using *he*. Little talk about the reasons for or against either usage seems ever to have taken place. Instead one rule simply replaces another. Even more worrisome is Jeffrey's claim that he was told he had "missed the point" when he offered criticisms of the assigned readings. His linking of this concern to the questionnaire asking if this class had changed "any of your views or attitudes about people" is shrewd, since it supports his hunch that the aim of the course was not only to analyze the workings of language but also to inculcate a certain set of values.

It's important to note that we don't actually know if his teacher dismissed Jeffrey's criticisms of the assigned readings or not. Jeffrey's prose is contentious and assertive, and it's not hard to imagine him interpreting a teacher's attempt to get him to rethink his views as simply an attack on what he believes. And yet his letter is over five pages long in its unedited and double-spaced form, and it is composed in a highly self-reflexive style: he works to draw attention to what might seem small matters of phrasing ("teacher" vs. "professor"), and he is careful to distinguish the words of others from his own, even going to the trouble of signaling two different sorts of quotation (one inverted comma seems to mark a kind of scare quote, as in <the 'popular' views of today's young culture> or <a bulky 'he/she'>; two mark a direct citation: <I was criticized for "hiding behind my vocabulary">. He has enough confidence in his own style to use the letter he is writing to mock his ex-teacher:

> I was criticized . . . because I used "big" words. (Whatever that means. The language employed was similar to that used in this letter.)

And Jeffrey has a fondness for parentheses, for a kind of metacritical commentary on his own language that I have seen in the work of few undergraduates. (In his fourth paragraph, he even embeds one parenthetical comment within another, although he isn't quite able to pull it off stylistically [I'd have used brackets].) He even knows not to push the issue of his grade very much, since to make the argument that he really deserved better he'd need either to show he actually learned something or that he knuckled down and wrote "what the teacher want[ed] to hear"—neither of which he wants to admit. So here is someone who seems highly self-conscious about his uses of language and is still irked enough by or invested enough in what happened in his composition course to write a long letter about it two years later. So I'm inclined to give Jeffrey the benefit of the doubt, to imagine that he and his teacher somehow missed a chance to do some interesting work together.

In *Storm in the Mountains* (1988), James Moffett writes of traveling to West Virginia in the 1970s to talk with people there who had recently voted to remove from their area public schools a set of textbooks he had designed. Moffett tried to assure the people he spoke with that the goal of his textbooks was not to promote any one set of beliefs or attitudes but to present students with a wide range of ways of seeing their world. What he learned was that the people of West Virginia understood his aims well enough, and that in fact the move to allow students a choice among competing values was precisely what they most objected to. Their argument was less against the content of specific readings (although there were of course many they disapproved of) than against the sort of classroom they (correctly) read Moffett's texts as advocating, one whose *form* spoke strongly for the liberal values of tolerance and self-criticism. They understood that the crucial issue is not what sort of politics (if any) a teacher advocates but what sort of politics her classroom enacts.

Jeffrey also works to locate the real politics of a course in the sorts of conversations it tries to set up among students and teachers. While his own cultural politics appear conservative, the plan for a college course in writing he proposes is classically liberal: "to instruct students on analyzing and writing about texts in a fashion compatible with a university setting in a way that allows creativity and independent thinking to take place." The question his letter poses for a liberal teacher of writing, then, is how to set up a space in which students can bring diverse political commitments to their work and still experience having their language and ideas taken seriously. In his 1993 "Eluding Righteous Discourse," James Seitz argues that instead of centering writing courses on "issues of politics" (race, class, gender, and so on), we might better attend to "the political influences at play in any texts examined in class, be they texts by professional writers or those written by the students themselves" (10). How do writers negotiate among and respond to the voices of others? How do they forge a sense of self among the languages available to them? Such an approach shifts attention from politics as a set of issues one writes about to the politics of writing itself—to questions of style, authority, autonomy, stance. It also suggests that one measure of the politics of a teacher might be the range of voices and perspectives that she helps students take on.

5
COMMUNITY

I have structured this chapter somewhat differently than the others in this book. For while *community* becomes a key word fairly late in the narrative of the field I am sketching here, it was in fact through tracing out some of the uses and implications of this term that I began my first work on this project. I got my first full-time college teaching job in 1984, a point when the sort of cognitivist approaches to composition I describe in chapters 3 and 4 were first coming under sustained criticism by a group of teachers and scholars who came to be known, for better or worse, as social constructionists. I was strongly drawn toward this new line of thinking, but I also felt wary of simply replacing one approach with another, and was made particularly uneasy about the ways various ideas of "community" were being invoked at the time, since they so often seemed, perhaps unintentionally, to conjure up precisely the sort of private and chummy club I was least interested in joining. So in the summer of 1987 I began to write what I hoped would seem a sympathetic criticism of the work of some of the people I most admired in composition, a paper that turned two years later into a *CCC* article, "The Idea of Community in the Study of Writing" (1989). This piece seemed at the time to strike a responsive chord for many people in composition; its success was what then prompted me to try to write a book (this one) that traced the competing uses and meanings of other such key words in the teaching of writing. So I have decided to begin this chapter by reproducing that 1989 article (with some small updating of notes and works cited), and to end it not by trying to account for the continued and varied uses of the term *community* since, but simply to suggest how my own thinking around these issues has progressed.

⁜

If you stand, today, in Between Towns Road, you can see either way; west to the spires and towers of the cathedral and colleges; east to the yards and sheds of the motor works. You see different worlds, but there is no frontier between them; there is only the movement and traffic of a single city.

Raymond Williams, *Second Generation*

In *The Country and the City* (1973), Raymond Williams writes of how, after a boyhood in a Welsh village, he came to the city, to Cambridge, only then to hear "from townsmen, academics, an influential version of what country life, country literature, really meant: a prepared and persuasive cultural history" (6). This odd double movement, this irony, in which one only begins to understand the place one has come from through the act of leaving it, proved to be one of the shaping forces of Williams's career—so that, some thirty-five years after having first gone down to Cambridge, he was still to ask himself: "Where do I stand . . . in another country or in this valuing city?" (6).

A similar irony, I think, describes my own relations to the university. I was raised in a working-class home in Philadelphia, but it was only when I went away to college that I heard the term *working class* used or began to think of myself as part of it. Of course by then I no longer was quite part of it, or at least no longer wholly or simply part of it, but I had also been at college long enough to realize that my relations to it were similarly ambiguous—that here too was a community whose values and interests I could in part share but to some degree would always feel separate from.

This sense of difference, of overlap, of tense plurality, of being at once part of several communities and yet never wholly a member of one, has accompanied nearly all the work and study I have done at the university. So when, in the past few years, a number of teachers and theorists of writing began to talk about the idea of *community* as somehow central to our work, I was drawn to what was said. Since my aim here is to argue for a more critical look at a term that, as Williams has pointed out, "never seems to be used unfavourably" (1976, 76), I want to begin by stating my admiration for the theorists—in particular, David Bartholomae and Patricia Bizzell—whose work I will discuss. They have helped us, I think, to ask some needed questions about writing and how we might go about teaching it.

Perhaps the most important work of these theorists has centered on the demystifying of the concept of *intention.* That is, rather than viewing the intentions of a writer as private and ineffable, wholly individual, they have helped us to see that it is only through being part of some ongoing discourse that we can, as individual writers, have things like points to make and purposes to achieve. As Bartholomae argues, "It is the discourse with its projects and agendas that determines what writers can and will do" (1985, 139). We write not as isolated individuals but as members of communities whose beliefs, concerns, and practices both instigate and constrain, at least in part, the sorts of things we can say. Our aims and intentions in writing are thus not merely personal, idiosyncratic, but reflective of the communities to which we belong.

But while this concern with the power of social forces in writing is much needed in a field that has long focused narrowly on the composing processes of individual writers, some problems in how we have imagined those forces are now becoming clear. First, recent theories have tended to invoke the idea of community in ways at once sweeping and vague: positing discursive utopias that direct and determine the writings of their members, yet failing to state the operating rules or boundaries of these communities. One result of this has been a view of "normal discourse" in the university that is oddly lacking in conflict or change. Recent social views of writing have also often presented university discourse as almost wholly foreign to many of our students, raising questions not only about their chances of ever learning to use such an alien tongue, but of why they should want to do so in the first place. And, finally, such views have tended to polarize our talk about writing: one seems asked to defend either the power of the discourse community or the imagination of the individual writer.

In trying to work towards a more useful sense of *community*, I will take both my method and theme from Raymond Williams in his 1976 *Keywords: A Vocabulary of Culture and Society*. Williams's approach in this vocabulary reverses that of the dictionary writer. For rather than trying to define and fix the meanings of the words he discusses, to clear up the many ambiguities involved with them, Williams instead attempts to sketch "a history and complexity of meanings" (15), to show how and why the meanings of certain word—*art, criticism, culture, history, literature,* and the like—are still being contested. Certainly *community*, at once so vague and suggestive, is such a word too, and I will begin, then, with what Williams has to say about it:

> Community can be the warmly persuasive word to describe an existing set of relationships, or the warmly persuasive word to describe an alternative set of relationships. What is most important, perhaps, is that unlike all other terms of social organization (*state, nation, society*, etc.) it seems never to be used unfavourably, and never to be given any positive opposing or distinguishing term. (76)

There seem to me two warnings here. The first is that, since it has no "positive opposing" term, *community* can soon become an empty and sentimental word. And it is easy enough to point to such uses in the study of writing, particularly in the many recent calls to transform the classroom into "a community of interested readers," to recast academic disciplines as "communities of knowledgeable peers," or to translate standards of correctness into "the expectations of the academic community." In such cases, *community* tends to mean little more than a nicer, friendlier, fuzzier version of what came before.

But I think Williams is also hinting at the extraordinary rhetorical power one can gain through speaking of community. It is a concept both seductive and powerful, one that offers us a view of shared purpose and effort and that also makes a claim on us that is hard to resist. For like the pronoun *we, community* can be used in such a way that it invokes what it seems merely to describe. The writer says to his reader, "We are part of a certain community; they are not"—and, if the reader accepts, the statement is true. And, usually, the gambit of community, once offered, is almost impossible to decline—since what is invoked is a community of those in power, of those who know the accepted ways of writing and interpreting texts. Look, for instance, at how David Bartholomae begins his remarkable 1985 essay, "Inventing the University":

> Every time a student sits down to write for us, he has to invent the university for the occasion—invent the university, that is, or a branch of it, like history or anthropology or economics or English. The student has to learn *to speak our language, to speak as we do*, to try on the peculiar ways of knowing, selecting, evaluating, reporting, concluding, and arguing that define *the discourse of our community*. (134; emphases added)

Note here how the view of discourse at the university shifts subtly from the dynamic to the fixed—from something a writer must continually reinvent to something that has already been invented, a language "we" have access to but that many of our students do not. The university becomes "our community," its various and competing discourses become "our language," and the possibility of a kind of discursive free-for-all is quickly rephrased in more familiar terms of us and them, insiders and outsiders.

This tension runs throughout Bartholomae's essay. On one hand, the university is pictured as the site of many discourses, and successful writers are seen as those who are able to work both within and against them, who can find a place for themselves on the margins or borders of a number of discourses. On the other, the university is also seen as a cluster of separate communities, disciplines, in which writers must locate themselves through taking on "the commonplaces, set phrases, rituals and gestures, habits of mind, tricks of persuasion, obligatory conclusions and necessary connections that determine 'what might be said'" (146). Learning to write, then, gets defined both as the forming of an aggressive and critical stance towards a number of discourses, and as a more simple entry into the discourse of a single community.

Community thus becomes for Bartholomae a kind of stabilizing term, used to give a sense of shared purpose and effort to our dealings with the various discourses that make up the university. The question, though, of just who this "we" is that speaks "our language" is never resolved. And so while Bartholomae often refers to the "various branches" of the university, he ends up claiming to speak only of "university discourse in its most generalized form" (1985, 147). Similarly, most of the "communities" to which other current theorists refer exist at a vague remove from actual experience: The University, The Profession, The Discipline, The Academic Discourse Community. They are all quite literally utopias—nowheres, metacommunities—tied to no particular time or place, and thus oddly free of many of the tensions, discontinuities, and conflicts in the sorts of talk and writing that go on every day in the classrooms and departments of an actual university. For all the scrutiny it has drawn, the idea of community thus still remains little more than a notion—hypothetical and suggestive, powerful yet ill defined.[1]

Part of this vagueness stems from the ways that the notion of "discourse community" has come into the study of writing—drawing on one hand from the literary-philosophical idea of "interpretive community," and on the other from the sociolinguistic concept of "speech community," but without fully taking into account the differences between the two. "Interpretive community," as used by Stanley Fish (1980) and others, is a term in a theoretical debate; it refers not so much to specific physical groupings of people as to a kind of loose dispersed network of individuals who share certain habits of mind. "Speech community," however, is usually meant to describe an actual group of speakers living in a particular place and time. Thus while "interpretive community" can

---

1. One might argue that there never really is a "we" for whom the language of the university (or a particular discipline) is fully invented and accessible. Greg Meyers (1985), for instance, has shown how two biologists—presumably well-trained scholars long initiated into the practices of their discipline—had to reshape their writings extensively to make them fit in with "what might be said" in the journals of their own field. Like our students, we too must reinvent the university whenever we sit down to write.

usually be taken to describe something like a world-view, discipline, or profession, "speech community" is generally used to refer more specifically to groupings like neighborhoods, settlements, or classrooms.[2]

What "discourse community" means is far less clear. In the work of some theorists, the sense of community as an active lived experience seems to drop out almost altogether, to be replaced by a shadowy network of citations and references. Linda Brodkey, for instance, argues that

> to the extent that the academic community is a community, it is a literate community, manifested not so much at conferences as in bibliographies and libraries, a community whose members know one another better as writers than speakers. (1987, 12)

And James Porter (1986) takes this notion a step further, identifying "discourse community" with the *intertextuality* of Foucault—an argument that parallels in interesting ways E. D. Hirsch's claim, in *Cultural Literacy* (1987), that a literate community can be defined through the clusters of allusions and references its members share. In such views, *community* becomes little more than a metaphor, a shorthand label for a hermetic weave of texts and citations.

Most theorists who use the term, however, seem to want to keep something of the tangible and specific reference of "speech community"—to suggest, that is, that there really are "academic discourse communities" out there somewhere, real groupings of writers and readers we can help "initiate" our students into. But since these communities are not of speakers, but of writers and readers who are dispersed in time and space, and who rarely, if ever, meet one another in person, they invariably take on something of the ghostly and pervasive quality of "interpretive communities" as well.

There have been some recent attempts to solve this problem. John Swales, for instance, has defined "discourse community" so that the common space shared by its members is replaced by a discursive "forum," and their one-to-one interaction is reduced to a system "providing information and feedback." A forum is not a community, though, and so Swales also stipulates that there must be some common "goal" towards which the group is working (1988, 212–13). A similar stress on a shared

---

2. See, for instance, Dell Hymes in *Foundations in Sociolinguistics*: "For our purposes it appears most useful to reserve the notion of community for a local unit, characterized for its members by common locality and primary interaction, and to admit exceptions cautiously" (1974, 51).

or collaborative project runs through most other attempts to define "discourse community."[3] Thus while *community* loses its rooting in a particular place, it gains a new sense of direction and movement. Abstracted as they are from almost all other kinds of social and material relations, only an affinity of beliefs and purposes, consensus, is left to hold such communities together. The sort of group invoked is a free and voluntary gathering of individuals with shared goals and interests—of persons who have not so much been forced together as have chosen to associate with one another. So while the members of an "academic discourse community" may not meet each other very often, they are presumed to think much like one another (and thus also much *unlike* many of the people they deal with every day: students, neighbors, coworkers in other disciplines, and so on). In the place of physical nearness we are given like-mindedness. We fall back, that is, on precisely the sort of "warmly persuasive" and sentimental view of community that Williams warns against.

One result of this has been, in recent work on the teaching of writing, the pitting of a "common" discourse against a more specialized or "privileged" one. For instance, Bartholomae argues that

> the movement towards a more specialized discourse begins . . . both when a student can define a position of privilege, a position that sets him against a "common" discourse, and when he or she can work self-consciously, critically, against not only the "common" code but his or her own. (1985, 156)

The troubles of many student writers, Bartholomae suggests, begin with their inability to imagine such a position of privilege, to define their views against some "common" way of talking about their subject. Instead, they simply repeat in their writing "what everybody knows" or what their professor has told them in her lectures. The result, of course, is that they are penalized for "having nothing really to say."

The task of the student is thus imagined as one of crossing the border from one community of discourse to another, of taking on a new sort of language. Again, the power of this metaphor seems to me undeniable. First, it offers us a way of talking about why many of our students fail to think and write as we would like them to *without* having to suggest they are somehow slow or inept because they do not. Instead, one can argue that the problem is less one of intelligence than socialization,

---

3. See, for instance, Bizzell on the need for "emphasizing the crucial function of a collective project in unifying the group" (1992, 222), and Bruffee on the notion that "to learn is to work collaboratively . . . among a community of knowledgeable peers" (1984, 646).

that such students are simply unused to the peculiar demands of academic discourse. Second, such a view reminds us (as Patricia Bizzell has often argued) that one's role as a teacher is not merely to inform but to persuade, that we ask our students to acquire not only certain skills and data, but to try on new forms of thinking and talking about the world as well. The problem is, having posited two separate communities with strikingly different ways of making sense of the world, it then becomes difficult to explain how or why one moves from one group to the other. If to enter the academic community a student must "learn to speak our language," become accustomed and reconciled to our ways of doing things with words, then how exactly is she to do this?

Bizzell seems to picture the task as one of assimilation, of conversion almost. One sets aside one's former ways to become a member of the new community. As she writes,

> Mastery of academic discourse must begin with socialization to the community's ways, in the same way that one enters any cultural group. One must first "go native." (1986b, 53)

And one result of this socialization, Bizzell argues, may "mean being completely alienated from some other, socially disenfranchised discourses" (43). The convert must be born again.

Bartholomae uses the language of paradox to describe what must be accomplished:

> To speak with authority [our students] have to speak not only in another's voice but through another's code; and they not only have to do this, they have to speak in the voice and through the codes of those of us with power and wisdom; and they not only have to do this, they have to do it before they know what they are doing, before they have a project to participate in, and before, at least in the terms of our disciplines, they have anything to say. (1985, 156)

And so here, too, the learning of a new discourse seems to rest, at least in part, on a kind of mystical leap of mind. Somehow the student must "invent the university," appropriate a way of speaking and writing belonging to others.

The emphasis of Bartholomae's pedagogy, though, seems to differ in slight but important ways from his theory. In *Facts, Artifacts, and Counterfacts* (1986), a text for a course in basic writing, Bartholomae and Anthony Petrosky describe a class that begins by having students write on what they already think and feel about a certain subject (for example, adolescence or work), and then tries to get them to redefine that thinking through a seminar-like process of reading and dialogue. The course thus appears to build on the overlap between the students' "common" discourses and the "academic" ones of their teachers, as they are asked to work "within and against" both their own languages and those of the texts they are reading (8). The move, then, is not simply from one discourse to another but towards a "hesitant and tenuous relationship" to both (41).

Such a pedagogy helps remind us that the borders of most discourses are hazily marked and often traveled, and that the communities they define are thus often indistinct and overlapping. As Williams again has suggested, one does not step cleanly and wholly from one community to another, but is caught instead in an always-changing mix of dominant, residual, and emerging discourses (1977, 121–27). Rather than framing our work in terms of helping students move from one community of discourse into another, then, it might prove more useful (and accurate) to view our task as adding to or complicating their uses of language.

I am not proposing that such addition creates a neutral or value-free pedagogy. I would instead expect and hope for a kind of useful dissonance as students are confronted with ways of talking about the world with which they are not yet wholly familiar. What I am arguing against, though, is the notion that our students should necessarily be working towards the mastery of some particular, well-defined sort of discourse. It seems to me that they might better be encouraged towards a kind of polyphony—an awareness of and pleasure in the various competing discourses that make up their own.

To illustrate what such an awareness might involve, let me turn briefly to some student writings. The first comes from a paper on *Hunger of Memory*, in which Richard Rodriguez describes how, as a Spanish-speaking child growing up in California, he was confronted in school by the need to master the "public language" of his English-speaking teachers and classmates. In her response, Sylvia, a young African American woman from Philadelphia, explains that her situation is perhaps more complex, since she is aware of having at least two "private languages": a Southern-inflected speech she uses with her parents and older relatives, and the "street talk" she shares with her friends and neighbors. Sylvia concludes her essay as follows:

> My third and last language is one that Rodriguez referred to as "public language." Like Rodriguez, I too am having trouble excepting and using "public

language." Specifically, I am referring to Standard English which is defined in some English texts as:

> "The speaking and writing of cultivated people . . . the variety of spoken and written language which enjoys cultural prestige, and which is the medium of education, journalism, and literature. Competence in its use is necessary for advancement in many occupations."

> Presently, I should say that "public language" is *becoming* my language as I am not yet comfortable in speaking it and even less comfortable in writing it. According to my mother anyone who speaks in "proper English " is "putting on airs."

> In conclusion, I understand the relevance and importance of learning to use "public language," but, like Rodriguez, I am also afraid of losing my "private identity"—that part of me that my parents, my relatives, and my friends know and understand. However, on the other hand, within me, there is an intense desire to grow and become a part of the "public world"—a world that exists outside of the secure and private world of my parents, relatives, and friends. If I want to belong, I must learn the "public language" too.

The second passage is written by Ron, a white factory worker in central Pennsylvania, and a part-time student. It closes an end-of-the-term reflection on his work in the writing course he was taking.

> As I look back over my writings for this course I see a growing acceptance of the freedom to write as I please, which is allowing me to almost enjoy writing (I can't believe it). So I tried this approach in another class I am taking. In that class we need to write summations of articles each week. The first paper that I handed in where I used more feeling in my writing came back with a (✓-) and the comment. "Stick to the material." My view is, if they open the pen I will run as far as I can, but I won't break out because I have this bad habit, it's called eating.

What I admire in both passages is the writer's unwillingness to reduce his or her options to a simple either/or choice. Sylvia freely admits her desire to learn the language of the public world. Her "I understand . . . but" suggests, however, that she is not willing to loosen completely her ties to family and neighborhood in order to do so. And Ron is willing to run with the more free style of writing he has discovered, "if they open the pen." Both seem aware, that is, of being implicated in not one but a number of discourses, a number of communities, whose beliefs and practices conflict as well as align. And it is the tension between those discourses—none repudiated or chosen wholly—that gives their texts such interest.

There has been much debate in recent years over whether we need, above all, to respect our students' "right to their own language," or to teach them the ways and forms of "academic discourse." Both sides of this argument, in the end, rest their cases on the same suspect generalization: that we and our students belong to different and fairly distinct communities of discourse, that we have "our" "academic" discourse and they have "their own" "common" (?!) ones. The choice is one between opposing fictions. The "languages" that our students bring to us cannot but have been shaped, at least in part, by their experiences in school, and thus must, in some ways, already be "academic." Similarly, our teaching will and should always be affected by a host of beliefs and values we hold regardless of our roles as academics. What we see in the classroom, then, are not two coherent and competing discourses but many overlapping and conflicting ones. Our students are no more wholly "outside" the discourse of the university than we are wholly "within" it. We are all at once both insiders and outsiders. The fear (or hope) of either camp that our students will be "converted" from "their" language to "ours" is both overstated and misleading. The task facing our students is not to leave one community in order to enter another, but to *reposition* themselves in relation to several continuous and conflicting discourses. Similarly, our goals as teachers need not be to initiate our students into the values and practices of some new community, but to offer them the chance to reflect critically on those discourses—of home, school, work, the media and the like—to which they already belong.

"Alongside each utterance . . . off-stage voices can be heard," writes Barthes (1974, 21). We do not write simply as individuals, but we do not write simply as members of a community either. The point is, to borrow a turn of argument from Stanley Fish (1980), that one does not *first* decide to act as a member of one community rather than some other, and *then* attempt to conform to its (rather than some other's) set of beliefs and practices. Rather, one is always *simultaneously* a part of several discourses, several communities, is always already committed to a number of conflicting beliefs and practices.[4] As Mary Louise Pratt has pointed out, "People

---

4. Bruce Robbins makes much the same case in "Professionalism and Politics: Toward Productively Divided Loyalties" (1985). Fish too seems to be moving toward this position, arguing that an interpretive community is an "engine of change" fueled by the interaction and conflict of the various beliefs and practices that make it up. As he puts it, "Beliefs are not all held at the same level or operative at the same time. Beliefs, if I may use a metaphor, are nested, and on occasion they may affect and even alter the entire system or network they comprise" (1987, 429).

and groups are constituted not by single unified belief systems, but by competing self-contradicting ones" (1982, 228). One does not necessarily stop being a feminist, for instance, in order to write literary criticism (although one discourse may try to repress or usurp the other). And, as the example of Williams shows, one does not necessarily give up the loyalties of a working-class youth in order to become a university student (although some strain will no doubt be felt).

In *The Country and the City*, Williams notes an "escalator effect" in which each new generation of English writers points to a lost age of harmony and organic community that thrived just before their own, only of course to have the era in which they were living similarly romanticized by the writers who come after them (1973, 9–12). Rather than doing much the same, romanticizing academic discourse as occurring in a kind of single cohesive community, I would urge us instead to think of it as taking place in something more like a city. That is, instead of presenting academic discourse as coherent and well defined, we might be better off viewing it as polyglot, as a sort of space in which competing beliefs and practices intersect with and confront one another. One does not need consensus to have community. Matters of accident, necessity, and convenience hold groups together as well. Social theories of reading and writing have helped deconstruct the myth of the autonomous essential self. There seems little reason now to grant a similar sort of organic unity to the idea of community.

The metaphor of the city would also allow us to view a certain amount of change and struggle within a community not as threats to its coherence but as normal activity. The members of many classrooms and academic departments, not to mention disciplines, often seem to share few enough beliefs or practices with one another. Yet these communities exert a very real influence on the discourses of their members. We need to find a way to talk about their workings without first assuming a consensus that may not be there. As Bizzell has recently come to argue,

> Healthy discourse communities, like healthy human beings, are also masses of contradiction. . . . We should accustom ourselves to dealing with contradictions, instead of seeking a theory that appears to abrogate them. (1992, 235)

I would urge an even more specific and material view of community— one that, like a city, allows for both consensus and conflict, and that holds room for our disciplinary colleagues, our university coworkers, our students, and ourselves. In short, I think we need to look more closely at the discourses of communities that are more than communities of discourse alone. While I don't mean to discount the effects of belonging to a discipline, I think we dangerously abstract and idealize the workings of "academic discourse" by taking the kinds of rarefied talk and writing that go on at conferences and in journals as the norm, and viewing much of the other sorts of talk and writing that occur at the university as deviations from or approximations of that standard. It may prove more useful to center our study, instead, on the everyday struggles and mishaps of the talk in our classrooms and departments, with their mixings of sometimes conflicting and sometimes conjoining beliefs and purposes.

Indeed I would suggest that we reserve our uses of *community* to describe the workings of such specific and local groups. We have other words—*discourse, language, voice, ideology, hegemony*—to chart the perhaps less immediate (though still powerful) effects of broader social forces on our talk and writing. None of them is, surely, without its own echoes of meaning, both suggestive and troublesome. But none, I believe, carries with it the sense of like-mindedness and warmth that makes community at once such an appealing and limiting concept. As teachers and theorists of writing, we need a vocabulary that will allow us to talk about certain forces as social rather than communal, as involving power but not always consent. Such talk could give us a fuller picture of the lived experience of teaching, learning and writing in a university today.

❖

"I don't want no Jesuses in my promised land," is how Lester Bangs put it (1988, 259). The line comes near the end of a piece he wrote on The Clash, and to appreciate what he meant by it, you have to know that Bangs loved The Clash, admired not only their skill and energy as musicians, but also their lack of pretense, the wit and nerve of their lyrics, and, most of all, the open and democratic stance they took toward their fans. In their songs The Clash often railed against the culture and politics of Maggie Thatcher's Britain, but they had little interest in becoming the spokesmen for a cause or the leaders of a movement. But neither did they pose as celebrities or keep a distance from their fans. Instead, at least early in their career, they simply let themselves be part of the crowd, talking and drinking and hanging out with the people who came to listen to their music. Bangs saw in them what rock culture might look like if it wasn't divided into leaders and followers, stars and groupies, backstage insiders and outside nobodies. No Jesus, maybe not even a promised land, but a moment to be part of.

Like Bangs I don't want no Jesuses in my promised land either. Most talk about utopias scares me. What I value instead is a kind of openness, a lack of plan, a chance both to be among others and to choose my own way. It is a kind of life I associate with the city—with the sort of community in which people are brought together more by accident or need than by shared values. A city brings together people who do not so much choose to live together as they are simply thrown together, and who must then make the best they can of their common lot. The core values of this loose form of community, it seems to me, are a tolerance of diversity and a respect for privacy. For instance, I know very few of the people who live on my city block by name, and have at best only a vague idea of what they do for a living, much less of what their politics or beliefs or values are. And yet it is a great block to live on: People take care of their houses, shovel the snow from their walks, keep an eye out for the neighborhood kids, report prowlers, bring lost dogs back to their homes, buy church candy and Girl Scout cookies, and the like. We keep watch but we do not intrude, forming something like what Richard Sennett, also in writing about city life, has called a "community of strangers" (1977, 4).

Although of course such an absence of shared values has more often been viewed as a loss. There is a long tradition of lament among intellectuals about the disappearance of real community, a nostalgia for the closeness of the town or village or parish that, it is argued, has since given way to the anonymous crowds of the city. Such a yearning for community also marks many utopian dreams of reform. I know of very few utopias in film or literature that are set in large industrial cities, although many dystopias are. (Think of *Blade Runner, Robocop, Escape from New York.*) There are no Jesuses in the big city, or actually, there's often a new one on each corner, and their clamor and conflict doesn't much make for a vision of ideal community. But there is also a freedom to be had in the chaos and anonymity of city life. That has always been its allure. In the 1989 essay on community which begins this chapter, I argued that we have tended to talk about "discourse communities" in far too romantic, organic, and pastoral terms, that we have in effect pictured such communities more as small closely-knit villages—where everyone pretty much shares the same set of values and concerns—than as large and heteroglot cities, where everyone doesn't. I want to push that contrast a little further here, to suggest how a more urban and less utopian view of social life might help us rethink the kinds of work that can go on in our classrooms.

In doing so, I want to bring a term back into our conversation that was once a key one in rhetoric but seems somehow recently to have fallen out of use or favor. Back in 1989, I cited Williams's famous remark that, alone among the words used to describe social groups, community seems "never to be used unfavorably, and never to be given any positive opposing or distinguishing term" (1976, 76). Since then no one has come up to me in order to say, why yes there is such a positive opposing term—but in continuing to read and think about the issue, I am growing more convinced that one does exist. The word is *public*, a term that does not even appear in Williams's *Keywords* (1976), but that has been central to the work of many American intellectuals—among them John Dewey, Walter Lippmann, Hannah Arendt, C. Wright Mills, Richard Sennett, and, most recently, Kenneth Cmiel.[5] The particular importance of the term *public* to these thinkers has to do with how they have tried to use it in theorizing a *large-scale* form of democracy, as a key (if troubled) means of bridging the interests of local communities and individuals with those of a state or nation. What I find most interesting and useful about this notion of a *public* is that it refers not to a group of people (like community) but to a kind of space and process, a point of contact that must both be created and continuously maintained.

Richard Sennett draws on a similar distinction in *The Fall of Public Man* (1977). For Sennett, a public space is one where the members of various communities can meet to negotiate their differences. It is a site of conflict rather than consensus, of bartering rather than sharing. The classic example would be a thriving square or market in a cosmopolitan city. It makes little sense to talk of New York, for instance, as a community; it is too sprawling, diverse, heterogeneous. But there is some sense to speaking of it as a kind of public space where the representatives of various boroughs or neighborhoods, the advocates of competing interests or constituencies, can come to argue out their needs and differences. I don't mean here to argue for some idealized version of a public sphere, some free market of viewpoints and ideas. Not all communities or interests are allowed anything near a fair or equal hearing in most public debates, and some are

---

5. In *The Last Intellectuals* (1987), Russell Jacoby calls on American academics to broaden the sphere of their influence. In "Making Journalism More Public" (1991), Jay Rosen both restates this call and provides a useful overview of attempts to theorize a workable notion of the "public."

not allowed access to them at all. I am instead thinking of a public space as a place where differences are made visible, and thus where the threat of conflict or even violence is always present. This means we need to resist moves to romanticize conflict in order to argue for something more like *civility*, a willingness to live with difference. As Jane Jacobs puts it in her classic study of urban life, *The Death and Life of Great American Cities*, "The tolerance, the room for great differences among neighbors . . . are possible and normal only when streets of great cities have built-in equipment allowing strangers to dwell in peace together on civilized but essentially dignified and reserved terms" (1961, 95).[6]

Thinking in terms of public rather than communal life can give us a way of describing the sort of talk that takes place *across* borders and constituencies. It suggests that we speak as public intellectuals when we talk with strangers rather than with the members of our own communities and disciplines (or of our own interdisciplinary cliques). And so what I do want to argue for here is a view of the classroom as a public space rather than as a kind of entry point into some imagined community of academic discourse. Most English classrooms are, I think, set up to move from conflict to consensus, from a diverse and competing set of readings (and maybe misreadings) to a single interpretation that teacher and students forge together as a group. The routine goes something like this: the teacher begins by asking for a reading of a certain line or passage from the text at hand and a student volunteers one. The teacher then points to a difficulty or problem with this reading (or asks another student to do so), and thus prompts an alternative reading of the passage. This second interpretation is also critiqued and then replaced by yet a third reading, and so on, until at some point the class arrives at a (more or less) common understanding of the passage. This problem-solving process is then repeated until the class builds a kind of consensual reading of the text as a whole. (A drawback of this approach is that when students are later asked to write on the text, they often feel there is nothing left for them to say about it.)

Imagine instead a class that worked not to resolve such differences in reading but to highlight them, that tried to show what might be involved

---

6. Readers of her work will recognize the strong influence of Jacobs on my vision here of an urban counterutopia. In revising this chapter for the 1997 edition of this book, I was pleased to discover that Iris Marion Young also invokes this passage from Jacobs in order to make an argument very similar to my own for the city as an alternative model of social life. See her 1990 *Justice and the Politics of Difference* (226–56).

in arguing for the various ways of understanding a text—as well as what might be at stake in the conflicts between them. Such a class would not try to get students to agree on what a certain text means but to see how and why various readers might disagree about what it means. And it would then ask each of them to take a stand, to commit herself to a position on the text and the issues around it. The aim of discussion in such a class would be for most people to leave thinking that just about everybody else has got it wrong, or at best only half right, and that they're going to write a paper over the weekend which shows why.

But I don't think that is likely to occur when the only alternative readings students come across are ones posed by their teacher. Many students are only too well used to coming to class only to find out, in effect, that they've blown it once again, that the poem or story they've just read doesn't mean what they thought it did—or what's probably worse, that the poem or story they couldn't figure out at all last night seems perfectly clear to their teacher. So even when we insist we are only posing an "other" way of looking at the text, many students are likely to take it (and with good reason) as the "right" way of reading it. But something else can happen when they begin to realize that other members of the class disagree with them about what a text means or how good it is. These are real people, after all. To find out that they disagree with you is both less threatening and more troubling than having your reading challenged as a matter of routine by your teacher.

This can become very clear when you have a group of students watch television together in a classroom, for it turns what is usually a private experience into a public one. The freshman who chortles appreciatively at a sitcom line about dumb but sexy blondes, only to realize that the young woman he's been trying to impress for the last few weeks is now sitting in stony silence right next to him, suddenly has some explaining to do. And so does she, if others in the class see her response as being less correct than humorless. Similarly, the student who jokes that Roseanne Arnold is disgusting may soon find himself dealing with several others who think that actually she's pretty funny, much as the one who thinks *My So-Called Life* is moving and realistic will need to answer to those classmates who could care less about a group of whining suburban kids. What happens in such situations is that students start to hold each other to account for their readings. They begin to argue not with their teacher but among themselves about the meaning and value of what they've seen.

Let me try to give you a more detailed sense of what it might mean to set up a classroom as such a public space or zone of contact. In a previous interchapter, I wrote of a beginning undergraduate class that I teach called Writing About Movies. Again, the goal of this course is not so much to introduce students to the academic study of the cinema as it is to get them thinking and writing about the ways they already have of looking at movies and television. As a way of beginning to surface these kinds of viewing strategies, one of the first things I usually ask students to do is to locate a point where their understanding of a film breaks down, to write about a scene or image in a movie that they have trouble making sense of—that confuses or disturbs them, or that they have trouble fitting in with the rest of the film, or that just makes them angry somehow. I then ask them to recreate the scene as well as they can in their writing and to define the problem it poses for them as viewers.

One term we looked at Spike Lee's 1989 *Do the Right Thing.* Lee's movie is set in the Bed-Stuy neighborhood of Brooklyn and offers a picaresque series of glimpses into life on a city block on the hottest day of summer. Lee himself plays Mookie, a young African American man who delivers pizzas for Sal (Danny Aiello), a likable Italian patriarch who owns and runs the neighborhood pizzeria, and who along with his two sons, both of whom work in his shop, are almost the only white characters we see. (City cops, a lost motorist, and a brownstoning yuppie are the only others.) Early on in the movie we see what seems a routine blowup between Sal and one of his customers, Buggin' Out, another young African American man who fancies himself something of a political activist and tries to organize a neighborhood boycott of the pizzeria until Sal replaces some of the pictures of Italians—Rocky Marciano, Frank Sinatra, Al Pacino—on his "Wall of Fame" with photos of African Americans. The only support Buggin' Out is able to raise, though, comes from (even by the standards of this neighborhood) two fringe characters: Radio Raheem, a mean-looking hulk of a man with no visible occupation other than walking up and down the street blaring the rap music of Public Enemy from his giant boom box, and Smiley, a stuttering hawker of photographs of Malcolm X and Martin Luther King (which we see no one but Mookie buy). While tempers flare at a number of other points during the day, none of these exchanges come to much, and the overall mood of the film is comic and quick. So when near the end of the movie Sal decides to reopen his doors to give a few teenagers a late-night slice, it seems as if the boycott and whatever threat it might have posed to the routine peace of the block are over, that the neighbor-hood has managed to get through the hottest day of the year without serious incident. This isn't the case, though, as Buggin' Out, Raheem, and Smiley also take this occasion to renew their threat to close Sal down, and Sal and Raheem find themselves in a fight that erupts quickly and ends tragically. Harsh words lead to a wrestling match that sends the two men crashing into the street. Raheem pins Sal to the sidewalk and seems on the verge of strangling him when a white policeman pulls him away and, as a crowd watches in horror, chokes Raheem to death with his nightstick. Panicked, the police throw Raheem's lifeless body into a squad car and escape, leaving the enraged crowd to loot and burn Sal's pizzeria in revenge.[7]

About a third of the class that spring chose to write on this scene, and it's easy to see why, since it seems so unclear as to who if anyone "does the right thing" in it. So I decided to start our talk about the movie by looking at three of their responses to it. I began by noting that all three pieces had virtually the same concluding paragraph: a plea for greater openness and understanding among all people of all races—be they white, black, yellow, whatever. My sense was that these paragraphs had less to do with the ending of Lee's film than with how these students (and most of the others in the class) felt they were required to end a paper written for school: on a tone of moral uplift, showing that they had indeed learned a valuable lesson from this important work of art, and so on. I didn't push this point much; I simply said I was interested less in what these writers agreed on than in how and why they differed in their views of the film, which meant I wanted us to look more closely at what got said in the body of their pieces than in their official conclu-sions. It's like television sitcoms, I argued—no matter what, they always end happily, with everybody loving and hugging everybody else, but if you pay attention to what goes on *before* they wrap everything up, you often find both a more tense and interesting view of work and family life. (I think most students took my point, since I read far fewer homilies at the end of their second drafts.)

And what most interested me about these three readings, why I chose them to begin our talk in class, was how each writer defines the boundar-ies of the scene differently, so that in each of their accounts a different

---

7. Of course this scene also offers a kind of nightmare counter to my praise of urban life: the city as the site of violence, anarchy. Again, the risk of diversity will always be conflict, as advocates of organic community are usually quick to point out.

action was emphasized, and a different sort of blame or responsibility was assessed. In her paper, "Radio Raheem's Death," Holly described the strangling of Raheem in detail.

> This scene starts out with a racial fight in the street between Radio Raheem, an African American youth who carries around an enormous boom box that symbolizes his power, and Sal, a white, middle-class restaurant owner. People gather around the scuffle as Raheem begins to strangle Sal. This is when the police show up at the scene. Two white policemen pull Raheem off Sal and drag him off into the street. Meanwhile, everyone is screaming in a riotous manner. The police officer, named Gary, with the fair hair and the mustache puts his nightstick around Raheem's neck. Gary then goes through some kind of racial rage and begins to put pressure on Raheem's neck. Every one watches in terror as they see their friend and neighbor get strangled to death.

Before anyone can stop Gary (and perhaps before he fully knows what he is doing), Raheem falls dead to the ground. Then, as Holly recounts the scene,

> [The police] begin to kick him and tell him to get up. When they realized what they had done they picked up Raheem's dead body and put him in the back of a police car. Spike Lee's camera work focuses on Raheem and then out of the back window of the car at people left in the street. . . . They stare into the camera and yell murder and real names of people who were actual fatalities from police brutality cases. That concludes the scene I have chosen.

From this Holly was led to conclude that the "problem . . . in my eyes, is the police brutality and how it is covered up." What bothered Samantha, though, in "Isolating One's Heritage," is the illogic of the riot that follows Raheem's death. She began her account of the scene almost exactly where Holly left off:

> As Sal's pizzeria was burning down the crowd suddenly turned around and altered all there attention toward the Korean family across the street persistently swinging a broom at the people signaling them to stay away from their market. The Korean man was screaming don't touch my store, leave us alone we are the same as you, we are black too. One of the older men in the crowd says he's right there the same as us leave them alone. Instantly the crowd agrees and turns away with aggression yet fatigue.

This turn of events troubles Samantha, since it is made clear throughout the film that Sal treats his customers with an affection and respect that the Korean grocer lacks entirely. In trying to explain the actions of the crowd, Samantha goes on to suggest that while Sal is shown as "open-minded" through most of the film, in the end he proves "not willing to change, or 'go along' with the blacks, but the Koreans were." For her the real issue thus comes down to who gets to claim ownership of the neighborhood. "Whatever the case the blacks were still trying to make the point of saying this is our neighborhood, we have lived here for years and you think you can just come in and take over." Underlying the savagery of the riot, then, is the sort of ethnic pride that warrants the use of "violence to receive . . . social justice"—a phrasing that seems to obliquely criticize Malcolm X's famous claim, quoted at the end of the movie, that oppressed peoples have "the right to do what is necessary" in fighting for their freedom. And so while Holly's horror at the cops' brutality led her to see Lee as arguing against the racism of "the system" or "the man," Samantha read the movie instead as indicting the sort of ethnic or racial pride that can quickly devolve into simple racism and violence.

Jim offered yet a third reading of the scene that focused on the verbal duel between Sal and Raheem that leads up to the fight described by Holly and the riot discussed by Samantha. Looking at how Sal shifts suddenly from the role of friendly *pater familias* to screaming racist led Jim to conclude,

> Here you saw Sal's true, hidden feelings come out. Through the entire film you see how Sal gets along with the blacks, but when confronted, he explodes physically and verbally at the blacks. . . . The film illustrates how deep nested and inevitable racism is. Though Sal accepted the blacks and was thankful for their business, that was the extent of it. As people, he didn't really respect them.

And so while Jim agrees with Samantha and Holly in seeing the movie as an attack on racism, he differs with Samantha in viewing Lee's anger as directed largely against *white* racists, and unlike Holly he refuses to sharply distinguish the actions of Sal from those of the cops. In many ways, Jim gives the bleakest reading of the movie, since he sees its critique as directed at one of the most likable characters in it. If Sal is a racist, he seems to imply, then so are we all, and the inevitable result of this will be violence, either to defend "the power" or to fight it.

In leading our talk about these papers, I insisted that at first our goal would simply be to understand and describe (but not yet to evaluate) the readings of the film they offered. I thus asked the class not to compare these three readings yet, to argue right off for one or the other, but instead to think about how they might go about making the best possible case for each. Where else might you go to in the film, for instance, to support Holly's sense that Lee's anger is directed more against the "system" (as represented by the cops) than against white people in general (as represented by Sal and his sons)? Or how might you strengthen Samantha's claim that the "ethnic pride" of African Americans is also being critiqued in the film? To have them do so, I broke the class into three groups (of about six or seven students), with each assigned the task of coming up with more evidence for one of these ways of reading the film.

Each of the groups proved able to come up with a striking amount of support for the view of the film they had been asked to discuss. The students who talked about Jim's paper noted several other scenes where Sal could be seen less as friendly than as patronizing; they then remarked that it was, after all, the director of the movie, Spike Lee, who plays Mookie, the character who starts the riot, which would seem to suggest that he has at least some sympathy for such actions; and they also pointed to how the last words of the film literally belong to Malcolm X, in a printed passage that speaks of the possible need for violence in a struggle for justice. In response, the group working with Holly's paper pointed out that in the scenes following the riot we see Sal and Mookie come if not to a reconciliation then at least to an uneasy truce. They also noted that, in the closing shot of the film, we hear the voice of a local radio DJ lamenting the violence that has just taken place and exhorting *political* action instead. Similarly, the group dealing with Samantha's paper had a list of scenes that poked fun (sometimes gentle and sometimes not) at the African American residents of the block, and they also noted that the passage by Malcolm X at the end of the movie is preceded by one in which Martin Luther King argues *against* the use of violence. And so by the end of our talk that evening, we had developed not a single collective reading of the film but three distinct and competing views of it. This allowed me to suggest to the class that, in revising their own writings for next week, their task was not to somehow move closer to some ideal or correct understanding of the movie, but to show why, when faced with such an array of competing interpretations, they chose to read it as they did—that our aim was not to reach a consensus about the meaning or value of the text, but to enter into a critical, sustained, and public interchange of views about it.

In *A Rhetoric of Motives* (1969), Kenneth Burke compares the give-and-take of intellectual debate to a "somewhat formless parliamentary wrangle," a "horse-trading" of ideas in which individual critics try to grab support for their own positions through whatever deals, borrowings, and alliances they can strike up with some colleagues, and whatever raids or attacks they can make on the views of others (188). While I prefer this description of intellectual work to Burke's much more often quoted metaphor of an ongoing parlor conversation, I have to admit that there also seems something slightly disreputable about it, and Burke himself points to the temptation, especially among teachers, to give form to such wrangles by placing opposing views in dialectical tension with each other, so their conflicts can then be resolved at some "higher" or "ultimate" level (188–89). The best example of this sort of dialectic can of course be found, as Burke points out, in the dialogues of Plato, which characteristically begin with Socrates facing a diverse set of opinions on a subject (what is piety? what is justice?) and then gradually leading his listeners to a consensus about what can or cannot be known about it. In Book I of *The Republic*, Socrates himself argues for the merit of this approach, saying,

> If we were to oppose him [Thrasymachus, a sophist who is his current foil in the dialogue] . . . with a parallel set speech on the blessings of the just life, then another speech from him in turn, then another from us, then we should have to count and measure the blessings mentioned on each side, and we should need some judges to decide the case. If on the other hand, we investigate the question, as we were doing, *by seeking agreement with each other*, then we ourselves can be both the judges and the advocates. (Plato 1974, 348b; emphasis added)

From opposing speeches to agreement, diversity to consensus, wrangle to dialogue—that is the usual progress of teaching. What I have hoped to suggest here is the value of keeping things at the level of a wrangle, of setting up our classrooms so a variety of views are laid out and the arguments for them made, but then trying *not* to push for consensus, for an ultimate view that resolves or explains the various conflicts that can surface in such talk. A problem with much teaching, it seems to me, is that the teacher often serves only too well as both judge and advocate of what gets said, pointing out the weaknesses of some positions while accenting the strengths of others. I'd like to see instead a classroom where student writings function something more like the "set speeches" that Socrates derides, that serve as positions in an argument whose "blessings" we can count and measure together, but whose final merits we leave students to judge for themselves. That is, I'd rather have a wrangle, even if it is somewhat formless (or perhaps because it is), that gives students a set of chances to come to their own sense of a text or issue than a dialogue whose course has been charted in advance by their teacher. I don't want no Jesus and I don't want no Socrates either. What I do want is a sort of teaching that aims more to keep the conversation going than to lead it toward a certain end, that tries to set up not a community of agreement but a community of strangers, a public space where students can begin to form their own voices as writers and intellectuals.

POSTSCRIPT, 2012: FROM THE SOCIAL TO THE MATERIAL

Chapter 5 traces what has come to be known as the "social turn" in composition—a shift of focus, beginning in the mid-1980s, away from the composing processes of individual writers and toward the social and institutional contexts of writing. In many ways the field has never looked back. We have developed a nuanced awareness of our disciplinary history, of the uses of writing in the academy, and of how discourses of race, gender, class, and sexuality impel and constrain the work that writing teachers and students do together.

And yet the students who populate our books and articles often remain shadowy figures. Sometimes we are offered pocket bios, quick snippets of information about age or race or gender, but often we learn little about student writers other than that they *are* "students"—or "novices," or "unskilled writers," or "BWs." Such a tight focus on the writer as a kind of abstraction sitting at a desk, represented by a set of choices made in producing a text, might have made a certain sense in the heyday of process, when the goal was to define a set of generalized composing behaviors for students to learn and follow. But such a disembodied view of the writer poses a more serious problem after the social turn. When we reduce students to quotations, it becomes tempting to read them (both students and quotations) as products of a totalizing discourse. I think here, for instance, of the passages written by the unnamed freshmen in Bartholomae's 1985 "Inventing the University." As haunting as many of these brief pieces are, in the end they all serve as examples either of writers who are controlled by a discourse, an "available and realizable voice of authority" (136), or of writers who resist such control, who "set themselves in their essays against what they defined as some more naïve way of talking about their subject" (153). A similar criticism might be made of my own uses of student texts in this book. We know little about the writers I cite, about what might drive their work and thinking, except that they happen to have been students in a university writing class. They can thus seem less like actual writers, with aims and projects of their own, than anonymous producers of sample texts.

I have thus grown to feel all the more strongly that our interest in the *social* needs to be deepened by a concern for the *material*. Let me use a scene from Willy Russell's *Educating Rita* (1980) to explain what I mean. The play centers on the ups and downs of the relationship between Rita, a young working-class hairdresser taking an Open University course, and Frank, her Oxbridge-educated tutor. Frank admires Rita's wit and curiosity but feels she needs intellectual discipline. In an early scene, he returns a one-sentence response Rita has written to an exam question with the comment, "I did think you might have let me have a considered essay" (33), only to discover that, since her husband disapproves of her returning to school, Rita needs to complete her work for the course between tending to her customers at the beauty shop. When Frank challenges Rita to write a fuller response, right then and there in his study, she does so (34–38). Her first answer was so brief, we start to realize, not because Rita has access only to some sort of "restricted" code or "common" discourse, but because the material realities of her life, of her marriage and job, didn't allow her enough time and space to do her work.

A similar interest in how the circumstances of students' lives impact their learning characterizes some of the best recent scholarship in our field. For instance, in her landmark 1997 study, *Time to Know Them*, Marilyn Sternglass tracks the progress of several multilingual, working-class, first-generation college students at the City University of New York, demonstrating that they can succeed in the academy, indeed can do very strong intellectual work, *if* they are allowed to pursue their studies beyond the traditional four or five years of college and *if* tests that measure little more than their ability to produce idiomatic and error-free prose are not set up as roadblocks to their continued study. In order to achieve the democratic hopes of American higher education, Sternglass suggests, we need to be willing to work with adult students over extended periods of time and to help them in balancing the demands of school, employment, and family.

Similarly, in his 1999 *Defending Access*, Tom Fox shows how an uncritical embrace of "standards" or "outcomes" can limit access to higher education by minority and working-class students. Fox begins his book with a concise history of how appeals to standards have long served as a gatekeeping mechanism in U. S. colleges—with a particular focus on the uneasy complicity of writing programs with such efforts. He insists that if we are really to understand students' achievements and difficulties as writers, we need to look beyond the walls of the classroom, to situate their work as students in the (often daunting) material circumstances of their lives. When we consider what many nontraditional students go through simply to remain in college, Fox suggests, what might at first seem mediocre performances begin to appear almost heroic. What we can't do, Fox asserts, is judge the work of minority and working-class students according to an abstract set of standards that fails to account for the ways the economic realities of their lives constrain their careers as students.

This has proved a hard case to make in recent years—to both academic and general readers. But if we want to promote a view of writing as more than a mechanical skill, we must argue on behalf of the intelligence of students and for the need to support their work over time. In this regard, the avatar of our field is Mike Rose. Beginning with *Lives on the Boundary* (1989), in which he drew on his experiences in being mistakenly characterized as a "Voc. Ed." student, continuing with his portraits of public-school teachers and reformers in *Possible Lives* (1999), moving to *The Mind at Work* (2005), a study of the intellectual skills required to do "manual" labor, and most recently in his blog, mikerosebooks.com, Rose has consistently and eloquently described the "many manifestations of intelligence in school, work, and everyday life" (2011). It strikes me as crucial that Rose writes here of intelligence *in*—as opposed to the discourses *of*—school, work, and everyday life. His phrasing, that is, roots intellectual work in the local and material realities of students' lives.

In similar ways, what writing teachers are able (or not) to accomplish with students can often be traced to the conditions in which they work. When teachers are overworked or poorly trained, students suffer. This is not a new problem. But I suspect we have begun to feel it more acutely as we've theorized more powerful and nuanced approaches to teaching writing. It turns out to be one thing to develop a thoughtful pedagogy, quite another to scale it up to meet the demands of a large college or university writing program. Teaching writing will always be a difficult and labor-intensive job. You can't exploit teachers and hope to serve students. But neither is it obvious, given the many constraints and contradictions of staffing large writing programs, how to offer faculty the time and support they need to teach writing well.

There have been three main responses to this problem. The first is, in essence, to walk away from it, to abolish first-year composition as a universally required service course. Often called the New Abolitionism, this position was voiced powerfully by Sharon Crowley in her 1998 collection of essays, *Composition in the University*. Without the demand to staff section after section after section of freshman comp, the argument goes, directors of writing programs would no longer need to hire adjunct and graduate student instructors under exploitative conditions. In the place of the required service course, composition could develop a major and electives, staffed by regular-rank faculty, much like the other academic disciplines. But that, of course, is not only the allure but the drawback of this position. It urges us to give up our main source of influence in the curriculum and the lives of students in order to claim academic status for ourselves. Yes, rhetoric and composition could become a bona fide academic discipline—just like classics, or ethnomusicology, or cinema studies. But is that really a trade we want to make?

The second approach also argues for establishing composition as an academic discipline as a response to the problem of poor working conditions, but retains an interest in staffing the required first-year writing course. As put forward in a 2007 *CCC* essay by Douglas Downs and Elizabeth Wardle, the idea is to transform first-year composition into "Intro to Writing Studies"—a course "akin to the introductory courses offered in all other disciplines" (554) and taught by experts in the field. Two practical difficulties immediately become clear: first, such a course would be an introduction to a field of study that doesn't exist at most colleges and universities; second, there will never be enough faculty members trained in graduate programs in writing studies to teach the tens of thousands of first-year writing sections offered each year in the United States. But the real heart of the proposal is that the first-year course should be *about* writing as it is studied in our field—that Intro to Writing Studies should not only be informed by but center on the work of the sorts of scholars I have discussed in this book, and that students in such courses should be asked to conduct some sort of research of their own on topics in writing.

My response is mixed. I think there's no question that you can teach an interesting course in writing on the subject of writing. I've tried to do so a number of times myself. But I also believe there is a nearly inexhaustible range of other subjects you can teach a course in writing on. To imagine the first-year writing course as "akin" to the intro courses in the various majors seems to me to misconstrue its purpose. (Indeed one of the problems with the course in the bad old days was that it was misunderstood as an introduction to the English major.) Downs and Wardle are right to object, along with many others, to the idea of teaching a set of general writing skills divorced from any meaningful context of use. But teaching the content of a particular discipline (in this case, writing studies) is not the only alternative to a general skills course. On the contrary, my experience suggests that teachers from a wide range of fields can design seminars that engage students in reading, writing, and arguing about texts and issues that are not owned by any particular discipline, but that nonetheless offer an exciting introduction to intellectual work. What matters is not the content of the course, but the quality of intellectual engagement it sparks.

In one respect, the new abolitionist and writing-studies approaches are in direct conflict: one wants to eliminate the required first-year course, the other to professionalize it. But they agree in their respect for disciplinarity. In that sense, both responses prove disappointingly conventional, since they both aim, albeit in slightly different ways, to make composition seem more like other fields of academic study.

The third approach does not argue for or against the disciplinary status of composition so much as to propose things we might do to improve working conditions in our programs while we wait for the revolution to come and for all writing teachers to become tenure-track experts in rhetoric. I'd suggest that such proposals share a *programmatic* rather than disciplinary ethos—that they tend to argue for changing local, material conditions rather than overhauling the intellectual superstructure of our field. As such, they tend to be eclectic, a grab bag rather than a coherent philosophy. Two essay collections are perhaps the key texts here: *Moving a Mountain* (2001), edited by Eileen Schell and Patricia Stock, brings together accounts from contingent faculty about steps they've taken to improve working conditions in their programs; *A Field of Dreams* (2002), edited by Peggy O'Neill, Angela Crow, and Larry Burton, collects descriptions of independent programs that, for the most part, offer writing teachers full-time positions outside the tenure stream. The proposals in both books tend to be logistical rather exhortatory—to deal with issues like long-term contracts, caps on enrollments, and the authority of teachers over the design of their own courses. The abolitionist and writing-studies approaches are absorbed with advancing the status of composition as an academic discipline. The programmatic view is not. It is more concerned with the here and now.

As I see it, then, thinking in programmatic terms does not commit you to arguing for or against composition as a discipline, or for or against tenure for all writing teachers. But it does commit you to asking how, at a particular school and a particular time, you can best support the work of writing students and their teachers. The answers to such questions will vary from school to school. For some the English department will still be the best place to teach writing. For others it will be in independent writing programs. Some schools will choose to recruit only people trained in rhetoric and composition. Others will look for interested teachers from a range of disciplines. Terms of contract and the status of faculty positions will vary. The point is to make the best possible use of the resources of a particular institution. So long as good teaching is put first, there is no such thing as a single ideal structure for writing programs.

There are, however, many structures that are clearly bad. I am troubled, for instance, when many programs, by allowing indifferent graduate instructors to teach over the length of their fellowships, prioritize funding graduate students over providing good writing teachers for undergraduates. I am similarly dismayed when many programs try to teacher-proof their curricula by mandating the use of specific textbooks, assignments, or course templates. A writing program should not be an employment service. Writing faculty should be expected to design their own courses, not merely to administer courses prewritten for them. Improving working conditions does not simply mean increasing salaries or decreasing class sizes. It means fostering a workplace culture that encourages teachers to become thoughtful and informed professionals.

I've argued here that we need to pay closer attention to the material contexts of our work as writers and teachers. But I've yet to say much about the actual materials of writing, which have been transformed since this book was published in 1997. In my coda to this book, then, I turn to the question of how the teaching of writing must change in a digital age.

AFTERWORD(S)
Contact and Negotiation

If Stanley Fish was the patron theorist of composition in the 1980s, Mary Louise Pratt is now. With his talk of interpretive conventions and communities, Fish was a key theorist behind what became known as the social constructionist view of teaching writing. And with her strong critique of Fish and other theorists of what she has called "linguistic utopias," Pratt has become a similarly key figure for those arguing for approaches to teaching more open to political conflict and cultural diversity. In particular, rather than speaking of the writing classroom as a kind of "discourse community," with all its overtones of like-mindedness and easy collegiality, many in composition have recently begun to use Pratt's notion of a contact zone to describe the classroom as a contested space where many discourses and cultures may meet and struggle with each other. By now I imagine it is clear that this is a critical move with which I have much sympathy. But I also think there are some real problems with the notion of the contact zone—and, more importantly, with views of teaching that valorize conflict but fail to offer ways of bringing differing positions not simply in contact but also in meaningful interchange with each other. So I want to end here on a note of caution, with some remarks on the limits of the position I have taken up.

In a 1991 article on the "Arts of the Contact Zone," Pratt draws on her work in teaching a large introductory course called Culture, Ideas, Values at Stanford University in order to sketch out what a classroom might look like if thought of as a contact zone rather than as a unified community. In coining the term *contact zone* Pratt borrows from the sociolinguistic notion of a "contact language," a sort of creole or pidgin that speakers of differing languages develop when forced into communication with one another. Pratt defines contact zones as "spaces where cultures meet, clash, and grapple with each other, often in contexts of highly asymmetrical relations of power, such as colonialism, slavery or their aftermaths as they are lived out in the world today" (34). But she also wants to put a positive spin on the term, to use it in theorizing a teaching practice that seeks not to erase linguistic and cultural differences but to examine them—and her ideas have held strong appeal for many working in composition, perhaps since writing class-rooms seem so often a point of contact for various and competing lan-guages and worldviews.

Where Pratt is at her best is in pointing to moments where teachers fail not only to deal with dissent but also even to acknowledge it. For instance, she tells of how when given a homework assignment to write about "a helpful invention" he would like to have and use, her fourth-grade son came up with an idea for a vaccine that would inoculate him with answers for stupid homework assignments (like this one, presum-ably). What did he get in response? "The usual star to indicate the task had been fulfilled in an acceptable way" (1991, 38–39). In a similar vein, Pratt tells of a conversation she had with her son when he switched from a traditional to a more progressive school:

> "Well," he said, "they're a lot nicer, and they have a lot less rules. But know *why* they're nicer?" "Why?" I asked. "So you'll obey all the rules they don't have," he replied. (38)

In both cases dissent is dealt with by not being noticed—much as, Pratt argues, the views, experiences, and writings of minority cultures have been studiously ignored in most American classrooms, even in schools (like her own) where many students are African American, Asian, Hispanic, or working class. This leads Pratt to call for classrooms where such voices do get heard, even if at the cost of some conflict or confu-sion—for pedagogical contact zones rather than communities.

This is an appealing idea. Pratt is vague, however, about how one goes about making sure those voices get their say. What she seems to end up doing is, in effect, importing difference into her classroom through assigning a number of readings from diverse cultures. At no point does she speak of how she tries to get students to articulate or negotiate the differences among themselves. Students are thus brought "in contact" with writings from various cultures, but it remains unclear what sorts of talk about these texts occurs among and across the various groupings of students that make up the class. How, for instance, do white students speak with their African American classmates about a text written by an African author? What forms of evasion, politeness, resistance, hostility, boredom, or incomprehension interfere with their talk? And how might these be lessened or at least acknowledged so that something more like conversation and less like a simple trading of positions can take place? Or what happens when a student finds that—due to the accidents of race or class or gender—he or she has somehow become the "representative" of a text (and by implication, culture) that the class is reading? In what ways is such a student free to criticize or resist as well as to celebrate or identify with the claims that text may be making? Or, conversely, how do students who are not members of the same culture as the author of a text gain the authority to speak critically about it?

Pratt has little to say about such questions. Part of the problem no doubt has to do with the logistics of teaching a large lecture course. But I think her silence about practical issues in teaching also points to a real difficulty with how she has conceptualized the idea of a contact zone. Pratt's phrasings evoke images of war and oppression, of "grappling and clashing" in contexts of "colonialism, slavery or their aftermaths." And yet many students I have asked to read and write about Pratt's article have chosen instead to view the contact zone as a kind of multicultural bazaar, where they are not so much brought into conflict with opposing views as placed in a kind of harmless connection with a series of exotic others. While I think this is a misreading of Pratt, it is one encouraged by her examples, which (in contrast with her language) tend to be either innocuous or esoteric—a clever dodge on a homework assignment, an odd Peruvian text (more on this later). Taken either way, as hinting at conflict or at connection, what is missing from such descriptions of the contact zone is a sense of how competing perspectives can be made to intersect with and inform each other. The very metaphor of *contact* suggests a kind of superficiality: the image is one of cultures banging or sliding or bouncing off each other. Pratt offers little sense of how more tolerant or cosmopolitan cultures might be created out of the collisions of such local groupings, or of how (or why) individuals might decide to change or revise their own positions (rather than simply to defend them) when brought into contact with differing views.

As Pratt describes them, contact languages do not often seem to hold the sort of symbolic or personal value for their users that native languages do; they are rather born out of expediency, as a way of getting by. It is thus a little hard to see who (except perhaps for a teacher) would have much at stake in preserving the classroom as a contact zone, since it is not a space to which anyone owes much allegiance. And, indeed, in her descriptions of her own teaching, Pratt quickly retreats to talk about the importance of what she calls "safe houses," which she describes as places for "healing and mutual recognition . . . in which to construct shared understandings, knowledges, claims on the world" (1991, 40).

Pratt thus fails to do away with the idea of a unified and utopian community; she simply makes it smaller, reduces it to the level of an affinity group. And so while her aim is to offer a view of intellectual life in which difference and controversy figure more strongly than in descriptions of seemingly homogeneous discourse communities, she is left in the end with no real answer to the question of how one constructs a public space in which the members of various "safe houses" or affinity groups are brought into negotiation (not just conflict or contact) with other competing views and factions. Or, to put the question in terms of classroom practice, Pratt never makes it clear how a teacher might help students move between the exhilaration and danger of contact zones and the nurturance of safe houses.

This issue was the subject of an intense debate in the pages of *College English*, sparked by Min-Zhan Lu's 1992 piece "Conflict and Struggle: The Enemies or Preconditions of Basic Writing?" Lu argues that in seeking to make their classrooms more comfortable and less threatening, many basic writing teachers end up disallowing the very expression of conflict and difference that could lend real interest to the writings of their students. Such teachers thus enforce a kind of stylistic and intellectual blandness by in effect making sure students never get to draw on their strengths as writers, since doing so would surface the very sort of conflicts in culture, language, and politics many teachers hope to contain and assuage. Lu's piece attracted a number of vehement responses that appeared in a "Symposium on Basic Writing" (Laurence et al. 1993) the following year in *College English*. Her critics argued variously that Lu romanticized the underclass, didn't work with "real" basic writers, was too hard on her students, and was intent on imposing her own political program upon them. Lu replied that she had been misunderstood, saying it was not she but her respondents who were acting as if they had sure knowledge of what the needs, abilities, and concerns of basic writers were—and thus they and not her who were verging on an intellectual and political dogmatism.

Basically, I agree with Lu on all counts. But I found myself troubled by the form the debate had taken—which reminded me of a couple of difficult and polarizing arguments that had recently occurred in the department where I work over issues in personnel and required course offerings. For while there was plenty of conflict and struggle in these arguments, very little of it seemed to result in a useful negotiation of views or perspectives. Instead, the exchanges quickly devolved into a kind of position taking, as those on both sides of the issue retreated back to the "safe houses" of the very positions they had entered the debate with. As it happens, I was on the losing side of one of those departmental arguments and on the winning side of the other, and I can say I felt equally miserable after both. For neither argument produced anything but a victory or a loss—no refinement of ideas, no negotiation of perspectives, no real surprises (at least of an intellectual sort). And I felt much the same way reading the arguments in *College English*; I knew what side I was on, but that was it: I didn't feel as though I had learned much from the encounter. Such experiences have helped convince me that something is missing from a view of teaching that suggests we simply need to bring people out of their various "safe houses" and into a "contact zone," and that is a sense of how to make such a meeting of differences less like a battle and more like a negotiation. We need, that is, to learn not only how to articulate our differences but how to bring them into useful relation with each other.

Pratt tends to downplay the importance of such negotiation and to romanticize the expression of dissent. "What is the place of unsolicited oppositional discourse?" (1991, 39), she asks—but her few examples of resistance are all suspiciously sympathetic. Her son is clearly a smart and likable kid, and we appreciate his parodies of schooling even if his actual teachers do not. And the only other example Pratt offers of a writer in the contact zone is rather exotic: Guaman Poma, a seventeenth-century Peruvian cleric who wrote a long and slightly mad letter to the king of Spain, explaining and defending his home culture to its new colonial ruler. Pratt praises Poma for his blurring of Western and indigenous discourses, dominant and oppositional ideologies, but his writing could just as readily be seen as a negative example of two cultures brought into contact but not meaningful interaction, since the letter Poma wrote quite literally made nothing happen: the king of Spain never read it and it lay unnoticed in an Amsterdam archive for the next three centuries. Tellingly, much of the current appeal of Poma's text has to do with how it voices the very sort of "opposition" to the status quo that many academics tend to value. His letter, that is, is a hypererudite version of the sort of writing many of us wish we would get from students but rarely do. In particular, Poma says just the right sort of thing for advocates (like both Pratt and myself) of a more culturally diverse reading list for undergraduates in the current debate over the canon. His unsolicited oppositional discourse has made it to *our* mailboxes if not to the king of Spain's. We have read it and we agree.

But what about discourse we don't agree with? What about students or writings that oppose our own views or authority? Pratt herself offers an account of a course she taught at Stanford on Cultures, Ideas, Values that became the focus of a highly publicized debate over "political correctness" (1990). While I don't side with its detractors, I do think we have to see how the inability of Pratt (and many others) to articulate how the competing views of students in their courses are acknowledged, criticized, and negotiated points to a legitimate worry about the micropolitics of teaching—about whose voices get heard in what classrooms and why. This is not a concern that can be answered with new theories or new reading lists; it calls instead for attention to the details of classroom work, to how teachers set up and respond to what students have to say.

This seems to me a point where teachers of writing can not simply apply but also extend and revise the agenda of recent cultural criticism. For instance, in his 1994 "Fault Lines in the Contact Zone," Richard E. Miller contrasts two differing and actual forms of response to what was, in both cases, truly unsolicited and unwanted discourse. In the first instance, the chairman of a large corporation responded to a racist illustration in a company magazine by firing several of the people involved with its production and writing a letter to his employees calling the cartoon a "deplorable mistake" and urging them to "tear that page out and throw it in the trash where it belongs" (389–90). In the second case, an openly gay teacher responded to a homophobic student narrative by treating it as a work of fiction and commenting on its effectiveness as a story—a strategy which, while in some ways dodging the politics of the piece, did not totally avoid or dismiss its troubling content and also kept student and teacher on good working terms. Miller notes that when this teaching situation was discussed at a meeting of CCCC, most of the teachers present argued for a response much closer to that of the corporate chairman's—namely, "that the student be removed from the classroom and turned over either to a professional counselor or to the police" (392); others insisted on ignoring the content of the piece altogether and commenting on its formal surface features alone. Although Miller admits the teacher's decision to treat the essay as fiction was in many ways a problematic one, he argues that

> [the chairman] did not address the roots of the problem that produced the offensive cartoon; he merely tried to make it more difficult for another

"deplorable mistake" of this kind to further tarnish the image of multicultural harmony the company has been at such pains to construct. [The teacher], on the other hand, achieved the kind of partial, imperfect, negotiated, microvictory available to those who work in the contact zone when he found a way to respond to his student's essay that . . . kept the student in his course. (407)

The lesson to be learned here, then, is not that treating troubling student writings as fiction is always or even usually a good idea, but that if we hope to get students to rethink (rather than merely repress) what seem to us disturbing positions—if we wish, that is, to work with students who voice beliefs that are not so much "oppositional" as they are simply opposed to our own—then we need first to find ways of keeping them an active part of the conversation of the class. Miller deepens the idea of the contact zone by imagining it not as a space that one can form simply through bringing differing groups and views together, but as a forum that one can only keep going through a constant series of local negotiations, interventions, and compromises. The contact zone thus becomes something more like a process or event than a physical space—and it thus needs to be theorized, as Miller does, as a local and shifting series of interactions among perspectives and individuals.

A similar interest in how differences get negotiated (or not) in varying situations by particular teachers and students now characterizes some of the best work being done in composition. Tom Fox (1992) has explored how African American students can learn to use writing not only to enter into the university but also (and at the same time) to criticize some of its characteristic values. Similarly, Geoff Chase (1988) and Bruce Herzberg (1994) have described writing courses that have helped students from comfortable backgrounds (white, suburban, upper middle class) take on a much more critical stance toward mainstream American culture than might have been expected; conversely, Cy Knoblauch (1991) and James Berlin (1991) have noted how students can often resist or tune out teachers who seem to push a particular political line too openly or aggressively. And Bruce Horner (1992) and Min-Zhan Lu (1994) have both written on ways of teaching students to edit their writing that problematize easy distinctions between "error" and "style," and thus point to very specific and local ways in which a writer's phrasings can be linked to a set of political choices and affiliations. Such work does more than take the concerns of recent cultural criticism with conflict and diversity and apply them to the classroom. It redefines those concerns by looking for signs of difference not only in the revered texts of a culture (whether these are seen as authored by Guaman Poma or William Shakespeare, Alice Walker or Saul Bellow, Emily Dickinson or Janet Jackson) but also in the views and writings of ordinary people. Rather than representing life in the contact zone through a set of ideal texts or suggestive yet brief classroom anecdotes, such work populates it with the differing and sometimes disturbing writings of actual students. The contact zone thus becomes less of a neo-Marxist utopia and more of a description of what we now often actually confront in our classrooms: a wrangle of competing interests and views. And the goal of pedagogies of the contact zone, of conflict, becomes not the forcing of a certain "multicultural" agenda through an assigned set of readings or lectures but the creating of a forum where students themselves can articulate (and thus perhaps also become more responsive to) differences among themselves.

Still I worry about the view of public intellectual life that the metaphor of the contact zone promotes. The dream of American public education was to create the possibility of a public national culture open to all individuals—regardless of race, gender, or social rank. To invoke this sort of democratic culture is *not* to call for a return to a set of shared and communal values; rather, it is to call for a forum in which issues and concerns that go *beyond* the borders of particular communities or interest groups can be worked through collectively, debated, negotiated. As Richard Sennett has put it in his 1980 "Destructive *Gemeinschaft*," "Powerlessness comes from the very attempt to define a collective identity instead of defining the common interests of a diverse group of people" (312). To return to my earlier metaphor, the citizens of a city need both to be willing to open their streets to strangers and to feel safe in leaving the familiar ground of their neighborhoods. They need, that is, to feel they are indeed citizens of a city and not simply residents of a neighborhood.

Yet talk about contact zones and safe houses can seem to work against such a vision of public life. Look, for instance, at this brief glimpse Pratt offers us of her Stanford course:

> All the students in the class had the experience, for example, of hearing *their culture* discussed and objectified in ways that horrified them; all the students saw *their roots* traced back to legacies of both glory and shame; all the students experienced face-to-face the ignorance and incomprehension, and occasionally the hostility, of others. (1991, 39; emphases added)

"Their culture" and "their roots" subjected to the uncomprehending gaze of "others." There is little to hint here that, despite the differences in their backgrounds, these students might also hold some experiences in common as members of contemporary American culture, or even that they might share a certain set of concerns and issues as U.S. citizens. Instead we are offered an image of a balkanized classroom: a collection of different "cultures" with separate "roots" clustered in their various "safe houses." Who could blame students in such a class if they chose not to venture into the "contact zone" that sprawls dangerously beyond? What reason, beyond the thrill of the exotic, have they been offered for doing so? Why should they care about what goes on in the contact zone if they already have their safe houses to live in?

I don't mean in any way to suggest we should step back from a valuing of difference or a willingness to work through the conflicts that may result from doing so. But I am growing less inclined to valorize notions of conflict or struggle in and of themselves. I want instead to argue for a more expansive view of intellectual life than I now think theories of the contact zone have to offer—one that admits to the ways in which we are positioned by gender, race, and class, but that also holds out the hope of a more fluid and open culture in which we can *choose* the positions we want to speak from and for. To work as teachers toward such a culture, we need to move beyond thinking in terms of fixed affinities or positions and the possible conflicts between them. We instead need to imagine a different sort of social space where people have *reason* to come into contact with each other because they have claims and interests that extend beyond the borders of their own safe houses, neighborhoods, disciplines, or communities. And so I would argue that we need a new rhetoric of courtship or identification—a sense of "common ground," as Kurt Spellmeyer (1993) would have it—to accompany the rhetoric of division or conflict that currently dominates so much of our talk about teaching. We need, that is, to find ways of urging writers not simply to defend the cultures into which they were born but to imagine new public spheres they'd like to have a hand in making.

CODA, 2012
From Dartmouth to New London

Google Maps tells us that New London, NH, lies about twenty miles south of Dartmouth College, straight down Route 89. In 1994, a small group of scholars met in New London to talk about the future of literacy teaching in an age of rapid globalization and technological change. Their meeting has since influenced the teaching of writing more than any other event since the 1966 Dartmouth Seminar.

The New London Group consisted of ten scholars from three countries: Courtney Cazden, James Gee, and Sarah Michaels from the United States; Norman Fairclough and Gunther Kress from Great Britain; and Bill Cope, Mary Kalantzis, Alan Luke, Carmen Luke, and Martin Nakata from Australia. The direct result of their meeting was the 1996 manifesto "A Pedagogy of Multiliteracies" published in the *Harvard Educational Review*. A few years later, they enlisted a number of other scholars and teachers in elaborating on that pedagogy in *Multiliteracies*, a volume of essays edited in 2000 by Cope and Kalantzis.

The concerns driving the work of the New London Group are succinctly captured by Cope and Kalantzis in the opening pages of *Multiliteracies*. Playing on the name of the small and picturesque New England town where the group met, they note that

> now one billion people speak that difficult and messy little language, English, spoken four centuries ago by only about a million or so people in the vicinity of London, old London. The story of the language, and the story of the last few centuries, including its many injustices, is the story of many new Londons. This issue—how the language meets with cultural and linguistic diversity—was one of our main concerns. (2000, 3)

It's a compelling idea—that we now work and study in a world of many new Londons, of constantly emerging and evolving uses of English. It's also an idea that takes you about as far as you can get from a view of English teaching as the transmission of either a single cultural heritage or a standard dialect.

While the New London Group didn't argue for particular uses of the media in teaching, they did urge writing teachers to respond to the accelerating rate of change in the ways we communicate, the kinds of texts we read and compose. They were also acutely aware that studying or teaching English no longer involves, if it ever fully did, identifying with a stable Anglo-American culture. English is now a world language—which means not only that the students we work with will speak and write many different versions of it, but that for many of them English will be only one of several languages they know and use. Where the New London Group was most prescient, though, was in viewing technological change and cultural diversity as aspects of the same phenomenon of globalization. Hence their use of the term *multiliteracies*. Literacies are multiple because of the increasing range of media—print, graphic, aural, digital—writers now have ready access to. But they are also multiple because more and more writers bring the resources of diverse cultures and languages to their work. This led the New London Group to argue for replacing an insistence on teaching the standard written form of the national language with a focus on the expressive possibilities of what they called the new "technologies of meaning" (1996, 64).

Or to put all this another way. *Question*: How do the members of a global and polyglot culture speak with one another? *Answer*: Any way they can. Diverse modes of communication support diverse forms of identity.

The key concept in teaching multiliteracies is *design*. For the New London Group, the task of the writer is to forge new meanings out of existing materials. A writer works not only with the resources of her language but with the artifacts of her culture—print texts, web pages, photos, music, videos, graphic art, and the like. The challenge is not only to respond to these materials but to creatively reuse them. Rather than looking within the self for meaning, the writer looks outward, to the culture around her, reworking and redesigning the texts and materials it has to offer her.

This is by no means a wholly new view of writing. Indeed a focus on design, on manipulating the resources and materials of a culture, synchs readily with the interests of classical rhetoricians in locating the available means of persuasion in a given situation. It also aligns with the aims of those who want to teach students how, as it were, to invent the university, to adopt the established moves and strategies of writers in an academic discipline. Still, there are important differences in emphasis. The concerns of both the theorists of classical rhetoric and academic writing are almost exclusively verbal. They are interested in how writers use and respond to the words of others. The focus of the New London Group spans a wider range of modes and materials. They are interested in how writers work in what Lawrence Lessig calls a remix culture (2008)— an environment in which texts, images, and recordings are constantly recycled and repurposed. It's a difference between learning how to do things with words and how to do things with texts.

After New London, a focus on textuality, design, and access has characterized much of the most interesting work done in composition. The work of the break here was probably Cynthia Selfe's 1999 *Technology and Literacy in the Twenty-First Century*. In this brief and polemical book, Selfe brought what had until then been a kind of subdisciplinary backwater, the study of computers and composition, to the forefront of the field. She did so by shifting the question to be asked from *How do we use computers to teach writing?* to *How can students become critical users of the new technologies of meaning?* A few years later, Stuart Selber outlined a curriculum sponsoring such critical uses of the new media in his 2004 *Multiliteracies for a Digital Age*. Several other books on teaching the emerging technologies of meaning soon joined his—including Wysocki, Johnson-Eloia, Selfe, and Sirc's 2004 *Writing New Media*, and Selfe's 2007 *Teaching Multimodal Composition*.

More important, though, is how the remix culture has spurred many teachers to rethink the forms of academic writing itself. For instance, while Douglas Hesse has exhorted us to continue teaching "extended connective prose" (2009, 605), his own 2005 CCCC chair's address, "Who Owns Writing?", was a remarkable experiment in multimodality in which, drawing on music and images as well as print, he tried to define a place for writing teachers to speak from in a culture that often seems to have left "extended connective prose" far behind. Hesse composed his address in response to yet another virtuoso CCCC chair's address given the previous year by Kathleen Yancey. In her 2004 "Made Not Only in Words," Yancey argued that, if we are not to soon become irrelevant in a digital culture, writing teachers need to grow more interested in the kinds of composing—texting, AIM, YouTube, Facebook— that students do *outside* of school, in large part because these new technologies offer them possibilities of pleasure and meaning that traditional "composition" doesn't. Small wonder, then, that by 2010 Gwendolyn Pough was to center the entire meeting of CCCC on the idea of The Remix, urging participants to rethink their writing and teaching in an age of "mashups to CLUSTERF*%#!s and all the wikis, flashbacks, multimodalities, and mapping in between" (5).

The point is not to turn away from essays and books in favor of tweets, blogs, and videos, but to consider what happens when so much of our work as writers and readers gets done online (or at least onscreen). Katherine Hayles warns against the "hyper attention" she believes is fostered by digital culture—a cognitive style she says is "characterized by switching focus rapidly between different tasks, preferring multiple information streams, seeking a high level of stimulation, and having a low tolerance for boredom" (2007, 187). Hayles contrasts this sort of intellectual restlessness with the "deep attention" she feels is encouraged by print culture. Perhaps. But surely intellectual work is also enriched—and democratized—by the unprecedented range of texts and materials that the web makes available. Students can now quote and analyze images, videos, and sound clips with a precision that a few years ago could only be trained upon print texts. They can also insert video and audio clips they've shot themselves into their writings. In a digital age our task as teachers will increasingly be to help students read and compose such multimodal texts with a deep attention.

In 1997, on what was then the last page of this book, I called on writing teachers and students to begin to "imagine new public spheres they'd like to have a hand in making" (124). It's a grandiose phrase, but the plural *s* of *spheres* may, I hope, save it from meaninglessness. I am encouraged by how the Internet offers us chances to create new sorts of public spaces, *plural*, to allow various groups of writers to make their words and ideas a little more visible to one another. Until very recently, students were routinely asked to produce essays in a format that imitated typewritten texts being submitted for publication in a print journal—double spaced, underlines for italics, MLA works cited, and so forth. Usually, though, these apprentice manuscripts never got sent anywhere at all, but ended up piled in cardboard boxes outside of faculty offices, with a few professorial comments inked on their computer-printed pages. Now students are often asked to compose digital texts that make use of the affordances of the web—layering sounds, images, and writing. Ironically, though, these texts can also end up languishing in the digital dropboxes of their professors, or behind the password-protected firewalls of private, web-based, content-management systems—all of which can seem like little more than a high-tech version of what went on before.

What we need to do, then, is to use the web to change both how student texts circulate and how students interact with each other as readers and writers. When a student posts her work to a public blog, for instance, she enters into what can be a very exciting sort of critical conversation—one in which not only her teacher but all of her classmates, and perhaps even some readers outside the course, can read and respond to what she has to say. This is not a new type of exchange—to the contrary, it is precisely the sort of conversation that many writing teachers have long tried to sponsor—but it is a kind of work that the web makes much easier. More than ever, the writing class can become a small public space, with the possibility of opening onto other such spaces.

Hayles and others worry that digital culture fosters a new sort of intellectual impatience. But while I very well understand the impulse to click on that next link, or to ever-so-quickly check my email or Facebook accounts, I know my own willingness to be distracted has long predated the Internet. Similarly, while I understand that many people now find it hard to sit and read actual print books with close attention, I suspect it has *always* been hard to read books with close attention. That's why we have school, with its deadlines and assignments. I thus remain doubtful that the digital era will lead to broad shifts in cognitive styles.

But the larger context of our work *has* changed—and in ways that for the most part strike me as exciting. Increasing numbers of students bring the resources of several cultures and languages to their work with us. We communicate through more channels and modes than ever before. Writers can create texts that are hybrids of words, images, and sounds—or they can work within the expressive possibilities of a single form (as I decided to do in reissuing this book). Surely intellectual work is augmented by this rich set of choices. It is an extraordinary time to teach writing.

REFERENCES

Abbott, Andrew. 2008. Publication and the future of knowledge. Lecture, American Association of University Presses, Montreal, QC, http://home.uchicago.edu/~aabbott/booksandpapers.html.

Allen, David. 1980. *English teaching since 1965: How much growth?* London: Heinemann.

Allen, Michael. 1980. Writing away from fear: Mina Shaughnessy and the uses of authority. *College English* 41: 857–67.

Anderson, Paul. 1998. Simple gifts: Ethical considerations in the conduct of person-based composition research. *CCC* 49: 63–89.

Anderson, Paul, and Heidi McKee. 2010. Ethics, student writers, and the use of student texts to teach. In Harris, Miles, and Paine, 60–77.

Applebee, Arthur. 1974. *Tradition and reform in the teaching of English: A history.* Urbana, IL: NCTE.

———. 1984. *Contexts for learning to write: Studies of secondary school instruction.* Norwood, NJ: Ablex.

Baird, Theodore. 1952. The freshman English course. *Amherst Alumni News*, May, 194–96.

Bangs, Lester. 1988. The Clash. In *Psychotic reactions and carburetor dung*, edited by Greil Marcus, 224–59. New York: Vintage.

Banks, Adam. 2011. *Digital griots: African American rhetoric in a digital age.* Carbondale: Southern Illinois University Press.

Barker, Pat. 1992. *Regeneration.* New York: Dutton.

Barnes, Douglas, ed. 1968. *Drama in the English classroom.* Champaign, IL: NCTE.

Barthes, Roland. 1974. *S/Z.* Translated by Richard Miller. New York: Hill.

Bartholomae, David. 1980. The study of error. *CCC* 31: 253–69.

———. 1985. Inventing the university. In *When a writer can't write: Studies in writer's block and other composing-process problems*, edited by Mike Rose, 134–65. New York: Guilford.

———. 1990. A reply to Stephen North. *Pre/Text* 11: 122–30.

———. 1995. Writing with teachers: A conversation with Peter Elbow. *CCC* 46: 62–71, 84-87.

Bartholomae, David, and Anthony Petrosky. 1986. *Facts, artifacts, and counterfacts: Theory and method for a reading and writing course.* Upper Montclair, NJ: Boynton/Cook.

———. 1990. *Ways of reading: An anthology for writers.* 2nd ed. Boston: Bedford/St. Martin's.

Basic Issues Conference. 1959. Basic issues in the teaching of English. *PMLA* 74: 1–19.

Bass, Rick. Cats and students, bubbles and abysses. In *Best American short stories 1988*, edited by Mark Helprin, 29–39. Boston: Houghton Mifflin.

Baxter, Charles. 1989. Fenstad's mother. In *Best American short stories 1989*, edited by Margaret Atwood, 1–14. Boston: Houghton Mifflin.

Berkenotter, Carol, and Donald Murray. 1983. Decisions and revisions: The planning strategies of a publishing writer, and response of a laboratory rat—or, being protocoled. *CCC* 34: 156–72.

Berlin, James. 1982. Contemporary composition: The major pedagogical theories. *College English* 44: 765–77.

———. 1984. *Writing instruction in nineteenth-century American colleges.* Carbondale, IL: Southern Illinois University Press.

———. 1987. *Rhetoric and reality: Writing instruction in American colleges, 1900–1985.* Carbondale, IL: Southern Illinois University Press.

———. 1991. Composition and cultural studies. In *Composition and resistance*, edited by C. Mark Hurlbert and Michael Blitz, 47–55. Portsmouth, NH: Boynton/Cook.

Berthoff, Ann. 1971. The problem of problem-solving. *CCC* 22: 237–42.

Bialostosky, Don. 1991. Liberal education, writing, and the dialogic self. In *Contending with words: Composition and rhetoric in a postmodern age*, edited by Patricia Harkin and John Schilb, 11–22. New York: MLA.

Bizzell, Patricia. 1982. Cognition, convention and certainty: What we need to know about writing. *Pre/Text* 3: 213–44.

———. 1986a. Composing processes: An overview. In *The teaching of writing*, edited by Anthony Petrosky and David Bartholomae, 49–70. Chicago: University of Chicago Press.

———. 1986b. Foundationalism and anti-foundationalism in composition studies. *Pre/Text* 7: 37–57.

———. 1992. What is a discourse community? In *Academic discourse and critical consciousness*, 222–37. Pittsburgh: University of Pittsburgh Press.

Booth, Wayne C. 1961. *The rhetoric of fiction.* Chicago: University of Chicago Press.

———. 1981. A cheap, efficient, challenging, sure-fire, and obvious device for combating the major scandal in higher education today. *WPA* 5: 35–39.

———. 1989. Foreword to *The English coalition conference: Democracy through language*, edited by Richard Lloyd-Jones and Andrea Lunsford, vii–xii. Urbana, IL: NCTE.

Braddock, Richard, Richard Lloyd-Jones, and Lowell Schoer. 1963. *Research on written composition.* Urbana, IL: NCTE.

Brannon, Lil, and Cy Knoblauch. 1982. On students' rights to their own texts: A model of teacher response. *CCC* 33: 157–66.

Brick, Allan. 1981. First person singular, first person plural, and exposition. *College English* 43: 508–15.

Britton, James. 1966. Response to working party paper no. 1.—What is English? In *Working papers of the Anglo-American seminar on the teaching of English at Dartmouth College.*

———. 1970. *Language and Learning.* Harrnondsworth: Penguin.

———. 1984. The distinction between participant and spectator role language in research and practice. *Research in the Teaching of English* 18: 320–31.

———. 1989. The spectator as theorist: A reply. *English Education* 21: 53–60.

Britton, James, Tony Burgess, Nancy Martin, Alex McLeod, and Harold Rosen. 1975. *The development of writing abilities (11–18).* London: Macmillan.

Brodkey, Linda. 1987. *Academic writing as social practice.* Philadelphia: Temple University Press.

Brooke, Robert. 1989. Control in writing: Flower, Derrida, and images of the writer. *College English* 51: 405–17.

Brower, Reuben, and Richard Poirer, eds. 1962. *In defense of reading.* New York: Dutton.

Bruffee, Kenneth A. 1984. Collaborative learning and the "conversation of mankind." *College English* 46: 635–52.

Bruner, Jerome. 1960. *The process of education.* Cambridge: Harvard University Press.

———. 1971. The process of education revisited. *Phi Delta Kappan* 53: 18–21.

Burke, Kenneth. 1969. *A rhetoric of motives.* Berkeley: University of California Press.

Canagarajah, Suresh. 2009. Multilingual strategies of negotiating English: From conversation to writing. *JAC* 29: 17–48.

Carr, Stephen. 1990. Educating subjects: Female readers in eighteenth-century Britain. Lecture, MLA Conference on the Responsibilities of Literacy, Pittsburgh, PA.

Catano, James V. 1990. The rhetoric of masculinity: Origins, institutions, and the myth of the self-made man. *College English* 52: 421–36.

CCCC (Conference on College Composition and Communication). 1974. Students' right to their own language. Special issue, *CCC* 25. http://www.ncte.org/cccc/resources/srtol/summary.

————. 2003. Guidelines for the ethical conduct of research in composition studies, http://www.ncte.org/cccc/resources/positions/ethicalconduct.

CEEB (College Entrance Examination Board). 1965. *Freedom and discipline in English.* New York: CEEB.

Chase, Geoffrey. 1988. Accommodation, resistance, and the politics of student writing. *CCC* 39: 13–22.

Coleridge, Samuel Taylor. 1926. *Biographica literaria.* New York: Macmillan. First published in 1834.

Coles, William E., Jr. 1972. An unpetty pace. *CCC* 23: 378–82.

————. 1974a. *Composing: Writing as a self-creating process.* Rochelle Park, NJ: Hayden McNeil.

————. 1974b. *Teaching composing.* Rochelle Park, NJ: Hayden McNeil.

————. 1978. *The plural I: The teaching of writing.* New York: Holt.

————. 1983. Literacy for the eighties: An alternative to losing. In *Literacy for life: The demand for reading and writing,* ed. Richard W. Bailey and Robin Melanie Fosheim, 248-62. New York: MLA.

————. 1988. *Seeing through writing.* New York: Harper McNeil.

Coles, William E., Jr., and James Vopat, eds. 1985. *What makes writing good? A multiperspective.* Lexington, MA: D. C. Heath.

Connors, Robert, and Andrea A. Lunsford. 1988. Frequency of formal errors in current college writing, or Ma and Pa Kettle do research. *CCC* 39: 395–409.

Cope, Bill, and Mary Kalantzis, eds. 2000. *Multiliteracies: Literacy learning and the design of social futures.* New York: Routledge.

Corder, Jim. 1973. *Finding a voice.* Glenview, IL: Scott.

Crowley, Sharon. 1998. *Composition in the university: Historical and polemical essays.* Pittsburgh: University of Pittsburgh Press.

Cushman, Ellen. The rhetorician as an agent of social change. *CCC* 47: 7–28.

DeMott, Benjamin. 1968. Reading, writing, reality, unreality. In Squire, 31–48.

Dixon, John. 1967. *Growth through English: A record based on the Dartmouth seminar 1966.* Reading, England: NATE.

————. 1969. Conference report: The Dartmouth seminar. *Harvard Educational Review* 39: 366–72.

————. 1974. *Growth through English (set in the perspective of the seventies).* 3rd ed. London: NATE.

Do the right thing. 1989. Directed by Spike Lee. Los Angeles: Universal.

Downs, Doug, Heidi Estrem, and Susan Thomas. 2010. Students' texts beyond the classroom: *Young Scholars in Writing*'s challenges to college writing instruction. In Harris, Miles, and Paine, 118–28.

Downs, Douglas, and Elizabeth Wardle. 2007. Teaching about writing, righting misconceptions: (Re)envisioning first-year composition as introduction to writing studies. *CCC* 58: 552–84.

Eastman, Arthur, ed. 1968. *Sequence in continuity.* Champaign, IL: NCTE.

Elbow, Peter. 1973. *Writing without teachers.* New York: Oxford University Press.

————. 1981. *Writing with power: Techniques for mastering the writing process.* New York: Oxford University Press.

————. 1989. The pleasures of voice in the literary essay: Explorations in the prose of Gretel Ehrlich and Richard Selzer. In *Literary nonfiction: Theory, criticism, pedagogy,* edited by Chris Anderson, 211–34. Carbondale, IL: Southern Illinois University Press.

————. 1990. Forward: About personal expressive academic writing. *Pre/Text* 11: 7–20.

————. 1991. Reflections on academic discourse: How it relates to freshman and colleagues. *College English* 53: 135–55.

———. 1995. Being a writer vs. being an academic: A conflict in goals. *CCC* 46: 72–83, 87–92.

Emig, Janet. 1971. *The composing processes of twelfth graders.* Urbana, IL: NCTE.

———. 1979. Mina Pendo Shaughnessy. *CCC* 30: 37–38.

———. 1983. *The web of meaning: Essays on writing, teaching, learning, and thinking,* edited by Dixie Goswami and Maureen Butler. Upper Montclair, NJ: Boynton.

Enos, Theresa, ed. 1987. *Sourcebook for basic writing teachers.* New York: Random House.

Epes, Mary. 1985. Tracing errors to their sources: A study of the encoding processes of adult basic writers. *Journal of Basic Writing* 4 (1): 4–33.

Faigley, Lester. 1986. Competing theories of process: A critique and proposal. *College English* 48: 527–42.

———. 1989. Judging writing, judging selves. *CCC* 40: 395–412.

———. 1992. *Fragments of rationality: Postmodernity and the subject of composition.* Pittsburgh: University of Pittsburgh Press.

Fielding, Sarah. 1987. *The governess, or the female academy.* London: Pandora. First published in 1749.

Fish, Stanley. 1980. *Is there a text in this class?* Cambridge, MA: Harvard University Press.

———. 1987. Change. *South Atlantic Quarterly* 86: 423–44.

Flower, Linda. 1979. Writer-based prose: A cognitive basis for problems in writing. *College English* 41: 19–37.

———. 1981. Revising writer-based prose. *Journal of Basic Writing* 3 (3): 62–74.

———. 1989. Cognition, context, and theory building. *CCC* 40: 282–311.

———. 1993. *Problem-solving strategies for writing.* 4th ed. New York: Harcourt.

———. 1994. *The construction of negotiated meaning: A social cognitive theory of writing.* Carbondale, IL: Southern Illinois University Press.

Flower, Linda, and John Hayes. 1980. Identifying the organization of writing processes. In *Cognitive processes in writing,* edited by Lee W. Gregg and Erwin R. Steinberg, 3–30. Hillsdale, NJ: Erlbaum.

———. 1981. A cognitive process theory of writing. *CCC* 32: 365–87.

Fox, Tom. 1992. Repositioning the profession: Teaching writing to African American students. *JAC* 12: 291–304.

———. 1999. *Defending access: A critique of standards in higher education.* Portsmouth: Boynton/Cook.

Fulwiler, Toby. 1988. *College writing.* Glenview, IL: Scott.

Gibson, Walker. 1966. *Tough, sweet, and stuffy: An essay on modern American prose styles.* Bloomington: Indiana University Press.

———. 1969. *Persona: A style study for readers and writers.* New York: Random House.

———. 1974. *Seeing and writing: Fifteen exercises in composing experience.* 2nd ed. New York: David McKay.

———. 1985. Theodore Baird. In *Traditions of inquiry,* edited by John Brereton, 136–52. New York: Oxford University Press.

Gilyard, Keith. 1991. *Voices of the self: A study of language competence.* Detroit: Wayne State University Press.

Graff, Gerald. 1980. The politics of composition: A reply to John Rouse. *College English* 41: 851–56.

———. 1987. *Professing literature: An institutional history.* Chicago: University of Chicago Press.

Graves, Donald. 1975. An examination of the writing processes of seven-year-old children. *Research in the Teaching of English* 9: 227–41.

Griffith, Peter. 1988. The discourses of English. *English Education* 20: 191–205.

Gross, Theodore. 1980. *Academic turmoil: The reality and promise of open education.* Garden City, NY: Anchor.

Guerard, Albert, Jr., Maclin Guerard, John Hawkes, and Claire Rosenfield. 1964. *The personal voice*. New York: Lippincott.

Guillory, John. 2008. How scholars read. *ADE Bulletin* 146: 8–17.

Habermas, Jurgen. 1975. *Legitimation crisis*. Translated by Thomas McCarthy. Boston: Beacon.

Hairston, Maxine. 1981. Not all errors are created equal: nonacademic readers in the professions respond to lapses in usage. *College English* 43: 794–806.

———. 1982. The winds of change: Thomas Kuhn and the revolution in the teaching of writing. *CCC* 33: 76–88.

———. 1985. Breaking our bonds and reaffirming our connections. *CCC* 36: 272–82.

Hamalian, Leo. 1970. The visible voice: An approach to writing. *English Journal* 59: 227–30.

Hamilton-Wieler, Sharon. 1988. Empty echoes of Dartmouth: Dissonance between the rhetoric and reality. *The Writing Instructor* 8 (2): 29–41.

Harris, Joseph. 1987. The plural text/the plural self: Roland Barthes and William Coles. *College English* 49: 158–70.

———. 1989. The idea of community in the study of writing. *CCC* 40: 11–22.

———. 1994. From the editor: The work of others. *CCC* 45: 439–41.

Harris, Joseph, John D. Miles, and Charles Paine, eds. 2010. *Teaching with student texts: Essays toward an informed practice*. Logan: Utah State University Press.

Hartwell, Patrick. 1985. Grammar, grammars, and the teaching of grammar. *College English* 47: 105–27.

Hashimoto, I. 1986. Toward honesty. *Freshman English News* 15 (1): 15–16.

———. 1987. Voice as "juice": Some reservations about evangelistic composition. *CCC* 38: 70–80.

Haswell, Richard. 1991. *Gaining ground in college writing: Tales of development and appreciation*. Dallas: Southern Methodist University Press.

Hawkes, John. 1967. An experiment in teaching writing to college freshman (voice project). ERIC ED 018 442, http://www.eric.ed.gov/.

Hayles, Katherine N. 2007. Hyper and deep attention: The generational divide in cognitive modes. *Profession 2007*: 187–99.

Herzberg, Bruce. 1994. Community service and critical teaching. *CCC* 45: 307–19.

Hesse, Douglas D. 2005. Who owns writing? *CCC* 57: 335–57.

———. 2009. Response to Cynthia L. Selfe. *CCC* 61: 602–05.

Hirsch, E. D., Jr. 1987. *Cultural literacy: What every American needs to know*. Boston: Houghton Mifflin.

Holbrook, David. 1964. *English for the rejected*. London: Cambridge University Press.

———. 1979. *English for meaning*. New York: Taylor.

Holt, Mara, and John Trimbur. 1990. Subjectivity and sociality: An exchange. *Pre/Text* 11: 47–58.

Hook, Sidney. 1987. *Out of step: An unquiet life in the twentieth century*. New York: Harper.

Horner, Bruce. 1992. Rethinking the sociality of error: Teaching editing as negotiation. *Rhetoric Review* 11: 172–99.

———. 1994. Mapping errors and expectations for basic writing: From frontier field to border country. *English Education* 26: 29–51.

———. 2000. *Terms of work for composition: A materialist critique*. Albany: State University of New York Press.

Horner, Bruce, Min-Zhan Lu, Jacqueline Jones Royster, and John Trimbur. 2011. Language difference in writing: Toward a translingual approach. *College English* 73: 303–21.

Howe, Irving. 1982. *A margin of hope: An intellectual autobiography*. New York: Harcourt.

Hymes, Dell. 1974. *Foundations in sociolinguistics: An ethnographic approach*. Philadelphia: University of Pennsylvania Press.

Hull, Glynda. An attempt to categorize error (or can stray dogs be mermaids?) In Enos, 259–74.

Jacobs, Jane. 1961/1993. *The death and life of great American cities*. New York: Modern Library.

Jacoby, Russell. 1987. *The last intellectuals: American culture in the age of academe*. New York: Basic.

Johnson, Jean, and John Immerwahr. 1994. *First things first: What Americans expect from the public schools*. New York: Public Agenda.

Kameen, Paul. 1980. Rewording the rhetoric of composition. *Pre/Text* 1–2: 73–92.

Kantor, Kenneth. 1979. The revolution a decade later: Confessions of an aging romantic. *English Journal* 68 (6): 28–31.

Kelly, Lou. 1972. *From dialogue to discourse*. Glenview: Scott.

Kiniry, Malcolm, and Mike Rose. 1990. *Critical strategies for academic writing*. Boston: Bedford/St. Martin's.

Kitzhaber, Albert R. 1963. *Themes, theories, and therapy: The teaching of writing in college*. New York: McGraw.

———. 1966. What Is English? Working party paper no. 1. In *Working papers of the Anglo-American seminar on the teaching of English at Dartmouth College*.

———. 1968. *The personal voice: The rhetoric of literature*. ERIC ED 015 914, http://www.eric. ed.gov/.

Knoblauch, C.H. 1991. Critical teaching and dominant culture. *Composition and resistance*, edited by C. Mark Hurlbert and Michael Blitz, 12–21. Portsmouth, NH: Boynton/ Cook.

Laurence, Patricia, Peter Rondinone, Barbara Gleason, Thomas J. Farrell, Paul Hunter, and Min-Zhan Lu. 1993. Symposium on basic writing. *College English* 55: 879–903.

Lawlor, William. 1980. The politics of Rouse. *College English* 42: 195–99.

Leavis, F. R. 1943. *Education and the university: A sketch for an English school*. London: Chatto.

Lees, Elaine O. 1987. Proofreading as reading, errors as embarrassments. In Enos, 216–30.

Lessig, Lawrence. 2008. *Remix: Making art and culture thrive in the hybrid economy*. New York: Penguin.

Levine, Art. 1994. The great debate revisited. *The Atlantic*, December, 38–44.

Lewis, E. Glyn. 1968. Postscript to Dartmouth—or poles apart. *College English* 29: 426–34.

Lu, Min-Zhan. 1991. Redefining the legacy of Mina Shaughnessy: A critique of the politics of linguistic innocence. *Journal of Basic Writing* 10: 26–40.

———. 1992. Conflict and struggle: The enemies or preconditions of basic writing? *College English* 54: 887–913.

———. 1994. Professing multiculturalism: The politics of style in the contact zone. *CCC* 45: 305–21.

Lunsford, Andrea A., and Karen J. Lunsford. 2008. Mistakes are a fact of life: A national comparative study. *CCC* 59: 781–806.

Lyons, Robert. 1985. Mina Shaughnessy. In *Traditions of inquiry*, edited by John Brereton, 171–90. New York: Oxford University Press.

Lyons, Scott. 2009. The fine art of fencing: Nationalism, hybridity, and the search for a Native American writing pedagogy. *JAC* 29: 77–106.

Mackay, David. 1968. Language standards and attitudes: A response. In Marckwardt 1968a, 23–30.

Macrorie, Ken. 1968. *Telling writing*. Rochelle Park, NJ: Hayden.

———. 1970. *Uptaught*. Rochelle Park, NJ: Hayden.

Marckwardt, Albert, ed. 1968a. *Language and language learning*. Champaign, IL: NCTE.

———. 1968b. Language standards and attitudes. In Markwardt 1968a,1–22.

Marsh, Dave. 1985. *Fortunate son*. New York: Random.

Mayher, John. 1990. *Uncommon sense: Theoretical practice in language education*. Portsmouth: Boynton/Cook.

Medway, Peter. 1980. *Finding a language: Autonomy and learning in school.* London: Writers and Readers.

Meyers, Greg. 1985. The social construction of two biologists' proposals. *Written Communication* 2: 219–45.

Miller, James E., Jr. 1971. What happened at Dartmouth? *Use of English* 23 (2): 99–109.

Miller, James E., Jr., and Stephen Judy. 1978. *Writing in reality.* New York: Harper.

Miller, Richard E. 1994. Fault lines in the contact zone. *College English* 56: 389–408.

———. 1998. The nervous system. *College English* 58: 265–86.

Miller, Susan. 1989. *Rescuing the subject: A critical introduction to rhetoric and the writer.* Carbondale: Southern Illinois University Press.

———. 1991. *Textual carnivals: The politics of composition.* Carbondale: Southern Illinois University Press.

Moffet, James. 1968a. *Teaching the universe of discourse.* Boston: Houghton Mifflin.

———. 1968b. *A student-centered language arts curriculum, K–13.* Boston: Houghton Mifflin.

———. 1981. *Coming on center: English education in evolution.* Montclair, NJ: Boynton/Cook.

———. 1985. Liberating inner speech. *CCC* 36: 304–08.

———. 1988. *Storm in the mountains: A case study of censorship, conflict, and consciousness.* Carbondale, IL: Southern Illinois University Press.

Moffett, James, and Kenneth R. McElheny, eds. 1966. *Points of view: An anthology of short stories.* New York: Mentor.

Muller, Herbert J. 1967. *The uses of English.* New York: Holt.

Murray, Donald. 1968. *A writer teaches writing.* Boston: Houghton Mifflin.

———. 1981.Teach writing as a process not product. In *Rhetoric and composition: A sourcebook for teachers and writers,* edited by Richard L. Graves, 79–82. Upper Montclair, NJ: Boynton/Cook. First published in 1972.

NCTE. 1961. *The national interest and the teaching of English.* Champaign, IL: NCTE.

New London Group. 1996. A pedagogy of multiliteracies: Designing social futures. *Harvard Educational Review* 66: 6–92.

North, Stephen. 1987. *The making of knowledge in composition: A portrait of an emerging field.* Upper Montclair, NJ: Boynton/Cook.

———. 1990. Personal writing, professional ethos, and the voice of "common sense." *Pre/Text* 11: 105–20.

Nystrand, Martin. 1990. Sharing words: The effect of readers on developing writers. *Written Communication* 7: 3–24.

Olson, Gary A. 1989. Social construction and composition theory: A conversation with Richard Rorty. *JAC* 9: 1–9.

Olson, Paul, ed. 1968. *The uses of myth.* Champaign, IL: NCTE.

O'Neil, Wayne. 1969. Conference report: The Dartmouth seminar. *Harvard Educational Review* 39: 359–65.

O'Neill, Peggy, Angela Crow, and Larry W. Burton, eds. 2002. *A field of dreams: Independent writing programs and the field of composition studies.* Logan: Utah State University Press.

Ong, Walter. 1962. *The barbarian within.* New York: Macmillan.

Owen, Wilfred. 1984. *Wilfred Owen: The complete poems and fragments.* New York: Norton.

Parker, Robert P., Jr. 1979. From Sputnik to Dartmouth: Trends in the teaching of composition. *English Journal* 68 (6): 32–37.

Peck, Wayne Campbell, Lorraine Higgins, and Linda Flower. 1995. Community literacy. *CCC* 46: 189–212.

Perl, Sondra. 1979. The composing processes of unskilled college writers. *Research in the Teaching of English* 13: 317–36.

Phelps, Louise Wetherbee. 1988. *Composition as a human science: Contributions to the self-understanding of a discipline.* New York: Oxford University Press.

———. 1989. Images of student writing: The deep structure of teacher response. In *Writing and response: Theory, practice, and research*, edited by Chris M. Anderson, 37–67. Urbana, IL: NCTE.

Phillips, Donna Burns, Ruth Greenberg, and Sharon Gibson. 1993. *College Composition and Communication*: Chronicling a discipline's genesis. *CCC* 44: 443–65.

Pianko, Sharon. 1979. Reflection: A critical component of the composing process. *CCC* 30: 275–78.

Plato. 1974. *The Republic*. Translated by G. M. A. Grube. Indianapolis: Hackett.

Poirer, Richard. 1971. *The performing self: Compositions and decompositions in the languages of contemporary life*. New York: Oxford University Press.

———. 1990. Hum 6, or reading before theory. *Raritan* 9 (4): 14–31.

Porter, James. 1986. Intertextuality and the discourse community. *Rhetoric Review* 5: 34–37.

Postman, Neil, and Charles Weingartner. 1967. *Teaching as a subversive activity*. New York: Delacorte.

Pough, Gwendolyn. 2010. Greetings from the 2010 CCCC program chair. Urbana, IL: NCTE, http://www.ncte.org/cccc/review/2010program.

Powell, Arthur G., Eleanor Farrar, and David K. Cohen. 1985. *The shopping mall high school*. Boston: Houghton Mifflin.

Pradl, Gordon. 1987. The hidden agenda of English 1. *Amherst* 39 (3): 29–30.

Pratt, Mary Louise. 1982. Interpretive strategies/strategic interpretations: On Anglo-American reader response criticism. *Boundary 2* 11: 201–31

———. 1990. Humanities for the future: Reflections on the western culture debate at Stanford. *South Atlantic Quarterly* 89: 7–26.

———. 1991. Arts of the contact zone. *Profession* 91: 33–40.

Raising Arizona. 1987. Directed by Joel Coen. Los Angeles: Universal.

Ransom, John Crowe. 1935. *Topics for freshman writing*. New York: Holt.

Robbins, Bruce. 1985. Professionalism and politics: Toward productively divided loyalties. *Profession* 85: 1–9.

Robillard, Amy E. 2006. *Young Scholars* affecting composition: A challenge to disciplinary citation practices. *College English* 68: 253–70.

Rodriguez, Richard. 1981. *Hunger of memory: The education of Richard Rodriguez*. Boston: Godine.

Rose, Mike. 1989. *Lives on the boundary: A moving account of the struggles and achievements of America's educationally underprepared*. New York: Penguin.

———. 1999. *Possible lives: The promise of public education in America*. New York: Penguin.

———. 2005. *The mind at work: Valuing the intelligence of the American worker*. New York: Penguin.

———. 2011. mikerosebooks.com.

Rosen, Jay. 1991. Making journalism more public. *Communication* 12: 267–84.

Rouse, John. 1979. The politics of composition. *College English* 41: 1–12.

———. 1980. Feeling our way along. *College English* 41: 868–75.

Russell, Willy. 2001. *Educating Rita*. London: Methuen. First published in 1980.

Sale, Roger. 1970. *On writing*. New York: Random.

Salvatori, Mariolina, and Patricia Donahue. 2010. The figure of the student in composition textbooks. In Harris, Miles, and Paine, 129–41.

Schell, Eileen E., and Patricia Lambert Stock, eds. 2001. *Moving a mountain: Transforming the role of contingent faculty in composition studies and higher education*. Urbana, IL: NCTE.

Schultz, John. 1977. The story workshop method: Writing from start to finish. *College English* 39: 411–36.

———. 1982. *Writing from start to finish: The story workshop basic forms rhetoric reader*. Upper Montclair, NJ: Boynton/Cook.

Schwartz, J. Brian. 2007. Fear of narrative: Revisiting the Bartholomae-Elbow debate through the figure of the writing teacher in contemporary American fiction. *Rhetoric Review* 26: 425–39.

Sedlak, Michael W., Christopher W. Wheeler, Diana C. Pullin, and Philip A Cusick. 1986. *Selling students short: Classroom bargains and academic reform in the American high school.* New York: Teachers College Press.

Seitz, James. 1993. Eluding righteous discourse: A discreet politics for new writing curricula. *WPA* 16 (3): 7–14.

Selber, Stuart. 2004. *Multiliteracies for a digital age.* Carbondale: Southern Illinois University Press.

Selfe, Cynthia L. 1999. *Technology and literacy in the twenty-first century: The importance of paying attention.* Carbondale: Southern Illinois University Press.

———, ed. 2007. *Teaching multimodal composition: Resources for teaching composition.* Cresskill, NY: Hampton.

Sennett, Richard. 1977. *The fall of public man.* New York: Knopf.

———. 1980. Destructive *gemeinschaft.* In *The philosophy of sex and love,* edited by A. Soble, 291–321. Totowa: Rowman.

Shaughnessy, Mina. 1977. *Errors and expectations: A guide for the teacher of basic writing.* New York: Oxford University Press.

———. 1980. The English professor's malady. *Journal of Basic Writing* 3 (1): 91–97.

Shugrue, Michael F. 1968. *English in a decade of change.* New York: Pegasus.

Slevin, James. 2006. Academic literacy and the discipline of English. *ADE Bulletin* 140: 11–16.

Smith, Summer. 1997. The genre of the end comment: Conventions in teacher response to student writing. *CCC* 48: 249–68.

Smitherman, Geneva. 1977. *Talkin and Testifyin: The Language of Black America.* Detroit: Wayne State University Press.

Sommers, Jeffrey. 1989. *Model voices: Finding a writing voice.* New York: McGraw.

Sommers, Nancy. 1980. Revision strategies of student writers and experienced adult writers. *CCC* 31: 378–88.

———. 1982. Responding to student writing. *CCC* 33: 148–56.

Sommers, Nancy, and Donald McQuade. 1986. *Student writers at work and in the company of other writers.* 2nd series. New York: St. Martin's.

Spellmeyer, Kurt. 1989. Foucault and the freshman writer: Considering the self in discourse. *College English* 51: 715–29.

———. 1993. *Common ground: Dialogue, understanding, and the teaching of composition.* New York: Prentice Hall.

———. 1994. Travels to the hearts of the forest: Dilettantes, professionals, and knowledge. *College English* 56: 788–809.

Spooner, Michael, and Kathleen Yancey. 1996. Postings on a genre of email. *CCC* 47: 252–78.

Squire, James, ed. 1968. *Response to literature.* Champaign, IL: NCTE.

Squire, James, and James Britton. 1974. Foreword to *Growth through English,* 3rd ed., by John Dixon, vii–xviii. London: NATE.

Sternglass, Marilyn S. 1997. *Time to know them: A longitudinal study of writing and learning at the college level.* Mahwah: Erlbaum.

Stewart, Donald. 1972. *The authentic voice: A pre-writing approach to student writing.* Dubuque: Brown.

Straub, Richard, and Ronald E. Lunsford. 1995. *Twelve readers reading: Responding to college student writing.* Cresskill, NJ: Hampton.

Summerfield, Geoffrey, ed. 1968. *Creativity in English.* Champaign, IL: NCTE.

Swales, John. 1988. Discourse communities, genres, and English as an international language. *World Englishes* 7: 211–20.

Thompson, Denys. 1966. Knowledge and proficiency in English. In *Working papers of the Anglo-American seminar on the teaching of English at Dartmouth College.*

Torbe, Mike, and Peter Medway. 1981. *The climate for learning.* Montclair, NJ: Boynton.

Traub, James. 1993. P.C. vs. English: Back to the basics. *The New Republic*, February 8, 18–19.

———. 1994. *City on a hill: Testing the American dream at City College.* Reading, MA: Addison-Wesley.

Trillin, Calvin. 1977. *Runestruck.* Boston: Little, Brown.

Trimbur, John. 2007. The Dartmouth conference and the geohistory of the native speaker. *College English* 71: 142–69.

Tuman, Myron. 1986. From Astor Place to Kenyon Road: The NCTE and the origins of English studies. *College English* 48: 339–49.

Villanueva, Victor. 1993. *Bootstraps: From an American academic of color.* Urbana, IL: NCTE.

Wagner, Geoffrey. 1976. *The End of education.* South Brunswick, NJ: Barnes.

Whitehead, Frank.1964. *The disappearing dais.* London: Chatto.

———. 1975. Continuity in English. *Use of English* 22 (1): 164–79.

———. 1976. Stunting the growth. *Use of English* 28 (1): 164–79.

Williams, Joseph. 1981. The phenomenology of error. *CCC* 32: 152–68.

Williams, Raymond. 1964. *Second generation.* New York: Horizon.

———. 1973. *The country and the city.* New York: Oxford University Press.

———. 1976. *Keywords: A vocabulary of culture and society.* New York: Oxford University Press.

———. 1977. *Marxism and literature.* New York: Oxford University Press.

Wollen, Peter. 1969. *Signs and meaning in the cinema.* Bloomington: Indiana University Press.

Working papers of the Anglo-American seminar on the teaching of English at Dartmouth College (Dartmouth seminar). 1966. ERIC ED 082 200 to 082 216, http://www.eric.ed.gov/.

WPA (Council of Writing Program Administrators). 2000/2008. WPA outcomes statement for first-year composition. http://www.wpacouncil.org/positions/outcomes.html.

Wysocki, Anne Frances, Johndan Johnson-Eloia, Cynthia L. Selfe, and Geoff Sirc. 2004. *Writing new media: Theory and applications for expanding the teaching of composition.* Logan: Utah State University Press.

Yancey, Kathleen. 2004. Made not only in words: Composition in a new key. *CCC* 56: 297–328.

Young, Iris Marion. 1990. *Justice and the politics of difference.* Princeton: Princeton University Press.

INDEX

ABOUT THE AUTHOR

JOSEPH HARRIS is an associate professor of English at Duke University, where he teaches courses in academic writing, critical reading, creative nonfiction, and digital writing. From 1999-2009, he was the founding director of the Thompson Writing Program at Duke—an independent, multidisciplinary program noted for its approach to teaching writing as a form of critical inquiry. Harris is the author of *Rewriting: How to Do Things with Texts* (Utah State University Press, 2006) and coeditor of *Teaching with Student Texts* (Utah State University Press, 2011). He served as editor of the CCC journal from 1994-99 and of the SWR book series from 2007-12. He is currently working on a book about how the teaching of writing has been depicted in film and fiction.

To learn more, please visit http://josephdharris57.wordpress.com/.

UTAH STATE UNIVERSITY
HELEN COLL LIBRARY